INDIA

TOP SIGHTS, AUTHENTIC EXPERIENCES

John Noble,
Michael Benanav, Abigail Blasi, Lindsay Brown,
Paul Harding, Bradley Mayhew,
Kevin Raub, Sarina Singh, Iain Stewart

Contents

Plan Your Trip

India's Top 12 4
Need to Know 16
Hot Spots For 18

Local Life 20
Month by Month 22
Get Inspired 25

Itineraries 26
Family Travel 32

Delhi 34
...at a glance 36

Red Fort 38
Old Delhi's
Bazaars 42
Qutb Minar 44
Sights 46
Tours 50
Shopping 51
Eating 52
Drinking & Nightlife 56
Where to Stay 63

Agra &
Taj Mahal 64
...at a glance 66

Taj Mahal 68
Fatehpur Sikri 76
Agra Fort 80
Sights 84
Eating 84

Jaisalmer 86
...at a glance 88

Jaisalmer Fort 90
Camel Safaris 92
Sights 96
Activities 96
Shopping 97

Eating 98
Drinking &
Nightlife 99

Jaipur 100
...at a glance 102

Amber Fort 104
City Palace 106
Walking Tour:
Pink City 108
Sights 110
Activities 110
Shopping 111
Eating 113
Drinking &
Nightlife 114

Ranthambhore
National Park 116

Mumbai 118
...at a glance 120

Bazaar District 122
Dining in Mumbai ... 124
Bollywood 126
Walking Tour:
Architectural
Mumbai 128
Sights 130

Shopping 132
Eating 132
Drinking &
Nightlife 136

Ajanta & Ellora 140
...at a glance 142

Ajanta Caves 144
Ellora Caves 148
Aurangabad 154

Goa 158
...at a glance 160

A Day in Old Goa 162
Best Goan
Beaches 164
Yoga in its
Homeland 168
Panaji 170
Palolem 172
Anjuna 174

Kerala 176
...at a glance 178

Backwater
Boat Trips 180
Ayurvedic Resorts ... 182

**Best Keralan
Beaches**.....................**184**
Kathakali...................**186**
Trivandrum 188
Kovalam 189
Alleppey......................190
Kochi 192

Karnataka   196
...at a glance   198

Mysuru.....................**200**
Hampi **204**
Bengaluru 206
Mysuru......................209

Darjeeling   210
...at a glance   212

**Singalila
Ridge Trek** **214**

Tea Experience.........**218**
Sights........................ 220
Shopping 223
Eating.........................223
Drinking &
Nightlife 224

Varanasi   226
...at a glance   228

The Ghats................**230**
Sights.........................234
Tours 235
Shopping 236
Eating........................ 236
Drinking &
Entertainment...........239

**Himachal
Pradesh   242**
...at a glance   244

**Tibetan Culture in
McLeod Ganj** **246**
**Manali Adventure
Activities** **250**
McLeod Ganj 254
Manali 257

In Focus   260
India Today 262
History 264
The Way of Life...........275
Hindu India 278
Delicious India...........280
Architecture &
the Arts 283
Landscape
& Wildlife....................286

Survival Guide 289
Directory A–Z 290
Transport 305
Language.................... 312
Index 315
Symbols & Map Key...322

Diwan-i-Am, Amber Fort (p104), Jaipur
MARK DAFFEY/GETTY IMAGES ©

Plan Your Trip
India's Top 12

OLENA TUR/SHUTTERSTOCK ©

Agra & Taj Mahal
A timeless monument to love

The exquisite tomb of an emperor's beloved wife, the Taj Mahal (p68) is arguably the world's most beautiful building, and has been enshrined in the writings of Tagore and Kipling. Built by Emperor Shah Jahan in adoration of his third wife, Mumtaz Mahal, this white marble mausoleum is inlaid with calligraphy, precious stones and intricate floral designs representing paradise, and represents the pinnacle of Mughal architecture as well as romance.

1

Kerala

Drifting dreamily on the backwaters

It's like heading into a dream, lazily navigating the tropical back-waters of Kerala (p180): 900km of interconnected rivers, lakes, canals and lagoons lined by coconut groves and picturesque villages. Cruise the waterways on a teak-and-thatch houseboat (pictured above) as the sun sinks behind the trees, while snacking on succulent Keralan seafood (pictured top) – and forget all about life on land for a while.

2

FRANCO RICCI/ALAMY ©

Jaipur

An enthralling, quintessentially Indian city

Jaipur (p101) encapsulates the chaotic, colourful magic of the
state that it's capital of, Rajasthan. It's a city of seething bazaars
selling everything from saris to jewellery to local meenakari enamel
work, honking traffic, wonderful palaces, mighty fortresses and an
extraordinary old observatory. And in between seeing the sights
there's wonderful shopping, fine dining and even balloon flights
over the majestic Amber Fort (pictured; p104).

3

4

Varanasi
City of life and death

Welcome to one of India's most revered sacred cities (p227). Pilgrims flock here to worship, take a holy dip in the Ganges River, or cremate loved ones. Hindus believe the Ganges' waters cleanse away sins, and dying here is deemed particularly propitious as it offers liberation from the life-and-death cycle. Varanasi will sweep you into its dizzying spiritual whirlwind – just take a deep breath and immerse yourself in pondering the meaning of life, death...and beyond. Ritual bathing in the Ganges (p230)

5

Goa
Palm-fringed tropical beach paradise

With palms nodding on one side of the sugar-white sands and powder-blue waves lapping on the other, Goa's (p159) coastline is lined by beautiful beaches and has an easy-going hedonistic atmosphere like nowhere else in India. It's not an undiscovered paradise: this cool coastal strip bustles with fellow travellers, vendors and beach-shack eateries. Goa appeals to social creatures and fans of creature comforts who like their seafood fresh and their holidays easy. Palolem (p172)

Delhi

Fallen empires, fine food, fabulous shopping

India's throbbing capital (p35) bears the mighty remnants of former empires, from great Mughal tombs to grandiose British-era mansions. There's so much to see here, from the crumbling splendour of Old Delhi to the wonders of the Qutb Minar (p44; pictured above) and Mehrauli. Add the many fine eateries, superb museums and amazing shopping, and it's easy to see why Delhi mesmerises many.

6

Darjeeling

Time for tea at a classic hill station

One of those British-founded mountain retreats known as hill stations, Darjeeling (p211) spreads over a steep Himalayan ridge staring at the world's third-highest mountain, Khangchendzonga. It's a cool escape where you can visit estates growing the tea that has spread Darjeeling's name around the world – and if you're the energetic type, trek some spectacular routes in the mighty Himalayas. Makaibari tea estate (p219)

Mumbai

India's eclectic film star city

Mumbai (p119) absorbs influences into her midst and inventively makes them her own. Architecturally, the art deco and modern towers lend the city its cool, but it's the dramatic flourishes of its Victorian-era structures that are the essence of Mumbai's visual magic. Today, the city is gathering culinary threads from around the world and leads India in the inventiveness of its restaurants. It's the country's capital of cinema, fashion and nightlife too. Chhatrapati Shivaji Terminus (p130)

NEMOTO SHINGO/SHUTTERSTOCK ©

Jaisalmer

Castles and camels in the desert

A gigantic, golden sandcastle rising like a mirage from the deserts of Rajasthan, Jaisalmer's 12th-century citadel (p90; pictured left) is a fantastical structure and a small town in itself, elegantly blending with the toffee-gold hues of its desert environs. It rises above a city (p87) whose narrow lanes conceal magnificent *havelis* (traditional, ornately decorated residences) carved from the same golden-honey sandstone. Take a camel safari (p92; pictured far left) outside town to experience the full desert magic.

Himachal Pradesh

Himalayan experiences for all comers

The green valleys and snowy peaks of this wonderfully scenic Himalayan state (p243), north of Delhi, are a canvas on which many kinds of traveller can paint. Trek, ski, raft, mountain bike, paraglide or just chill out at the hippie hangout-cum-adventure centre of Manali; or soak up the Buddhist and Tibetan vibes at McLeod Ganj, home of the Dalai Lama. Top: Snow sports near Manali (p252); Above left: Tibetan monastery, Manali; Above right: Rafting on Beas River (p252)

10

Ajanta & Ellora

Stunning millennia-old works of sacred art

Renunciation of the worldly life was never so serenely sophisticated. The temples, monasteries and prayer halls carved out of remote rock faces by Buddhist, Hindu and Jain monks at Ajanta (p144; pictured above) and Ellora (p148), between one and more than two millennia ago, were not just places of worship and retreat but supreme artistic homages to the divine. Few works of ancient match the conception and execution of Ajanta's murals and Ellora's sculptures.

Karnataka

India future and past

This southern state (p197) encompasses many faces of India. The booming IT capital of Bengaluru (Bangalore) is arguably India's most progressive city. Not far away, Mysuru (Mysore) is home to one of the most glittering of all India's princely palaces. A bewitchingly different vibe envelops Hampi, the vast ruined capital of a medieval Hindu empire set among rice paddies, red earth and giant boulders. Mysuru Palace (p200)

Plan Your Trip
Need to Know

When to Go

Leh
GO Jul–Sep

Delhi
GO Nov–Mar

Kolkata (Calcutta)
GO Nov–Mar

Mumbai (Bombay)
GO Nov–Feb

Bengaluru (Bangalore)
GO Nov–Mar

Alpine desert (including snow)
Desert, dry climate
Mild to hot summers, cold winters
Tropical climate, rain year-round
Tropical climate, wet & dry seasons
Warm to hot summers, mild winters

High Season (Dec–Mar)

○ Pleasant weather – warm days, cool nights. Peak tourists. Peak prices.

○ December and January bring chilly nights in the north.

Shoulder Season (Jul–Nov)

○ Passes to Ladakh and the high Himalaya open from July to September.

○ Monsoon rain showers persist through to September.

Low Season (Apr–Jun)

○ April is hot; May and June are scorching. Competitive hotel prices.

○ From June, the monsoon sweeps from south to north, bringing draining humidity.

○ Beat the heat (but not the crowds) in the cool hills.

Currency

Indian rupee (₹)

Languages

Hindi, English (official languages)

Visas

Apart from citizens of Nepal, Bhutan and Maldives, everyone needs to apply for a visa before arriving in India. More than 100 nationalities can obtain a 30-day e-Tourist visa/Visa on Arrival, applying online prior to arrival; this is valid from the day you arrive. For longer trips, you'll need to obtain a six-month tourist visa.

Money

There are ATMs in most towns; carry cash as back up. MasterCard and Visa are the most accepted credit cards.

Mobile Phones

Roaming connections are excellent in urban areas, poor in the countryside and Himalayas. Local prepaid SIMs are widely available; they involve straightforward paperwork and a possible wait of up to 24 hours for activation.

Time

India Standard Time (GMT/UTC plus 5½ hours)

Daily Costs

Budget: Less than ₹3000

o Dorm bed: ₹400–600

o Double room in a budget hotel: ₹400–700

o All-you-can-eat thalis (plate meals): ₹120–300

o Bus or train tickets: ₹300–500

Midrange: ₹3000–9000

o Double hotel room: ₹1500–5000

o Meals in midrange restaurants: ₹600–1500

o Admission to historic sights and museums: ₹500–1000

o Local taxis/autorickshaws: ₹500–2000

Top End: More than ₹9000

o Deluxe hotel room: ₹5000–22,000

o Meals at superior restaurants: ₹2000–5000

o 1st-class train travel: ₹1000–8000

o Renting a car and driver: ₹1800 upwards per day

Useful Websites

Lonely Planet (www.lonelyplanet.com/india) Destination information, the Thorn Tree Travel Forum and more.

Incredible India (www.incredibleindia.org) Official India tourism site.

Templenet (www.templenet.com) Temple talk.

Rediff News (www.rediff.com/news) Portal for India-wide news.

World Newspapers (www.world-newspapers.com) Links to India's English-language publications.

Arriving in India

Indira Gandhi International Airport, Delhi (p305)

Prepaid taxis From ₹450 to the centre, radio cars around ₹100 to ₹200 more.
Express buses Every 20 minutes (₹100).
Airport express metro trains Link up with the metro system (₹60/100 Sunday/Monday to Saturday).

Chhatrapati Shivaji International Airport, Mumbai (p305)

Prepaid taxis ₹680/820 (non-AC/AC) to Colaba and Fort and ₹400/480 to Bandra.
Train Take an autorickshaw (₹18 per km) to Andheri train station and then the Churchgate or CST train (₹10, 45 minutes). From Colaba, an UberGo is around ₹385 off-peak. Avoid the train during the 6am to 11am rush hour.

Kempegowda International Airport, Bengaluru (p305)

Metered AC taxis ₹750 to ₹1000 to the centre, including the airport toll of ₹120. Air-conditioned Vayu Vajra buses run regularly to and from the airport to the city; fares start at ₹180.

Cochin International Airport, Kerala (p194)

AC Volvo buses Between the airport and Fort Cochin (₹80, one hour, 22 daily) via Ernakulam. **Taxis** To/from Ernakulam around ₹850; to/from Fort Cochin around ₹1200.

Getting Around

Transport in India is frequent and inexpensive, though not always fast. Consider domestic flights or sleeper trains as an alternative to long, uncomfortable bus rides.

Air Flights to most major centres and state capitals; cheap flights with budget airlines.

Train Frequent services to most destinations; inexpensive tickets available, even on sleeper trains.

Bus Buses go everywhere; some destinations are served 24 hours but longer routes may have just one or two buses a day.

For more on **getting around**, see p305 ➡

Plan Your Trip
Hot Spots for...

BHASKAR DUTTA/GETTY IMAGES ©

Architecture

Towering temples, opulent palaces, massive forts, mesmerising mosques – India's parade of empires and cultures has created some of the world's most stunning buildings.

Agra (p65)
Home to the Taj Mahal, Agra also has one of India's greatest forts and the superb Fatehpur Sikri is nearby.

Taj Mahal
Simply the most beautiful building in the world (p68).

Delhi (p35)
The eight historical cities of Delhi have bequeathed a treasure trove of forts, mosques, temples and more.

Red Fort
A superb Mughal palace inside a compound (p398).

Ellora (p148)
Architecture that wasn't built but excavated, Ellora's temples were carved by Buddhist, Hindu and Jain monks.

Kailasa Temple
The world's largest monolithic sculpture (p151).

ANAND PUROHIT/GETTY IMAGES ©

Outdoors

Hiking in the Himalaya, searching for tigers in lowland jungles, swimming and water sports in the waters of the Arabian Sea – opportunities for getting out into nature are endless.

Manali (p250)
The adventure-sports capital of the north: trekking, paragliding, skiing, rafting, climbing – it's all here.

Chandrakani Pass Trek
A beautiful two-day hike from Naggar to Malana (p250).

Ranthambhore National Park (p116)
These wild jungles offer some of the best prospects of tiger sightings. There's plenty of other wildlife too.

4WD Safaris
Views are best from 4WD; organise well in advance (p116).

Goa (p159)
Legendary for beach-based hedonism, Goa's sunset-facing strands also offer plenty of water sports.

Palolem
Goa's safest swimming beach; good kayaking too (p172).

Indian Food

From tandoori kebabs to fish curries and vegetarian thalis, India is a spicy riot of flavours, whether you're eating at a street stall or an elegant contemporary restaurant.

SANTHOSH VARGHESE/SHUTTERSTOCK ©

Mumbai (p119)
Cuisines from all over India meet up with international trends.

Masala Library
Cutting-edge Indian cuisine (p125).

Delhi (p35)
The capital proffers an increasingly fine and diverse choice of regional Indian and international food.

Bukhara
Meaty Northwest Frontier cuisine (p56).

Kerala (p177)
With coconuts and spices in abundance and rich seafood pickings, this state has a flavourful cuisine.

Villa Maya
Superbly crafted seafood and veg dishes (p189).

Spirituality

The devotion on display in sacred places and the spectacle of colourful religious festivals demonstrate the deep spiritual current running through most Indians, of whatever religion.

PACIFIC PRESS/ALAMY ©

Varanasi (p227)
Hindus flock here to wash away their sins, achieve moksha (liberation from rebirth) and cremate loved ones.

The Ghats
Throngs washing, worshipping and cremating (p230).

McLeod Ganj (p246)
Home to the Dalai Lama and a large Tibetan exile community; has a strong Buddhist and international vibe.

Tsuglagkhang Complex
Two temples and a monastery (p247).

Delhi (p35)
Delhi is adorned with many architecturally superb and atmospherically unforgettable places of worship.

Hazrat Nizam-ud-din Dargah
Mystical-feeling shrine of a Muslim Sufi saint (p47).

Plan Your Trip
Local Life

ELENA DIJOUR/SHUTTERSTOCK ©

Activities

With snowy mountain ranges, humid rain-forests, warm seas and sun-baked deserts, India presents endless options for outdoor activities. In the mountainous north, you can go trekking, paragliding, skiing and mountaineering. In India's many protected areas, you can take jungle safaris seeking tigers, elephants, leopards, birds and other wildlife. Along the southern beaches you can go diving, surfing, kayaking, swimming or dolphin-spotting, and in Kerala you can cruise inland waterways on houseboats. And in this birthplace of yoga and ayurveda, there are thousands of opportunities to practise different forms of yoga, meditation and healing.

Shopping

India's exuberant bazaars and tantalising shops offer a treasure trove of goodies, in-cluding fabulously patterned textiles, finely crafted woodwork, chunky silver bangles,

delicate gemstone jewellery and a tremen-dous mix of village creations. The array of arts and handicrafts is vast, with every region, sometimes every village, having its own unique traditions.

Government-run emporiums, fair-trade cooperatives, department stores and mod-ern shopping centres charge fixed prices. Anywhere else you may need to bargain, as initial asking prices can be highly inflated.

The first 'rule' to haggling is don't show too much interest in an item. Second, resist purchasing the first thing that takes your fancy. Wander around several shops and check their prices. Decide how much you would be happy paying, and then express a casual interest. If you have no idea of the going rate, try slashing the asking price by half. From there, you and the vendor can work up and down in small increments until you reach a deal. You'll find that many shopkeepers lower their so-called 'final price' if you head out of the store saying you'll 'think about it'.

SANTHOSH VARGHESE/SHUTTERSTOCK ©

Entertainment

Cultural performances, including Indian music and dance, and more contemporary live-music gigs, mostly take place in larger cities, while entertainment in smaller places centres on the year-round whirl of festivals, with music, costumes, parades and dance. Annual arts festivals featuring Indian classical dance and music happen in many places and are good opportunities to see the best of Indian traditional culture.

Eating

India has it all: from sizzling street-food stands, where crowds wait impatiently for the next batch of taste-sensation snacks, to fantastic fine-dining restaurants where desserts are brought out on a bed of dry ice. In between is a mass of regular eateries churning out honed-for-generations specialities. Restaurants in main cities and tourism hubs usually embrace a range of international as well as Indian cuisines. This is the world's best country for vegetarian

★ Best Indian Meals

Bukhara (p56)

Indian Accent (p56)

Peshawri (p124)

Esphahan (p84)

Villa Maya (p189)

travel, with tasty, nourishing, meat-free food available everywhere.

Drinking & Nightlife

There's a wide choice of bars and some nightclubs in India's large cities, catering to a glamorous mix of local men and women. However, in many smaller towns the only nightlife you're likely to find is the possibility of drinking alcohol at a restaurant, if that, and any bars will be patronised only by men.

From left: Shawls for sale in a street bazaar; Dussehra festival (p24), Mysuru

Plan Your Trip
Month by Month

January

Post-monsoon cool lingers, with downright cold in the mountains. Pleasant weather and several festivals make it a popular time to travel (book ahead!).

♣ Free India

Republic Day commemorates the founding of the Republic of India on 26 January 1950; the biggest celebrations are in Delhi, which holds a huge military parade along Rajpath, and the Beating of the Retreat ceremony three days later.

February

A good time to be in India, with balmy weather in most non-mountainous areas.

♣ Carnival in Goa

The four-day party preceding Lent is particularly big in Goa. Sabado Gordo, Fat Saturday, starts it off with elaborate parades, and the revelry continues with street parties, concerts and general merrymaking. Can also fall in March.

♣ Taj Mahotsav

This 10-day carnival of culture, cuisine and crafts is Agra's biggest party. Held at Shilpgram, the festival features more than 400 craft makers from all over India, a potpourri of folk and classical music and dance, and enough regional food to induce a curry coma.

March

The last month of the travel season, March is full-on hot in most of the country, with rains starting in the Northeast.

♣ Holi

One of North India's most ecstatic festivals; Hindus celebrate the beginning of spring according to the lunar calendar by throwing coloured water and *gulal* (powder) at anyone within range. (2 March 2018, 21 March 2019, 10 March 2020)

Above: Holi festival

23

DIPAK SHELARE/SHUTTERSTOCK ©

⚡ Wildlife Watching

With water sources drying out, animals venture into the open to find refreshment: your chance to spot elephants, deer and, if you're lucky, tigers and leopards. Visit www.sanctuaryasia.com for detailed info.

April

The heat has officially arrived in most places, which means you can get deals and avoid tourist crowds. It's peak time for visiting upland West Bengal.

⚛ Rama's Birthday

During Rama Navami, which lasts anywhere from one to nine days, Hindus celebrate Rama's birth with processions, music, fasting and feasting, and enactments of scenes from the Ramayana. (26 March 2018, 14 April 2019, 2 April 2020)

May

It's hot almost everywhere. Hill stations are hopping, though, and in the mountains it's pre-monsoon trekking season.

★ Best Festivals

Holi, February or March

Ganesh Chaturthi, August or September

Onam, August or September

Navratri & Dussehra, September or October

Diwali, October or November

⚛ Ramadan (Ramazan)

Thirty days of dawn-to-dusk fasting mark the ninth month of the Islamic calendar. Muslims traditionally turn their attention to God, with a focus on prayer and purification. Ramadan begins around 16 May 2018, 6 May 2019 and 24 April 2020.

June

The rainy season, or pre-monsoon extreme heat, is on just about everywhere.

From left: Holi festival; Ganesh Chaturthi (p24)

✤ Eid al-Fitr

Muslims celebrate the end of Ramadan with three days of festivities. Prayers, shopping, gift-giving and, for women and girls, *mehndi* (henna designs) may all be part of the celebrations. (15 June 2018, 5 June 2019, 24 May 2020)

August

Monsoon is going strong.

✤ Independence Day

This public holiday on 15 August celebrates India's independence from Britain in 1947. The biggest celebrations are in Delhi, where the Prime Minister addresses the nation from the Red Fort.

✤ Krishna's Birthday

Janmastami celebrations range from fasting to *puja* (prayers), and offering sweets to drawing elaborate *rangoli* (rice-paste designs) outside the home. (15 August 2018, 3 September 2019, 23 August 2020)

✤ Eid al-Adha

Muslims commemorate Ibrahim's readiness to sacrifice his son to God by slaughtering a goat or sheep and sharing it with family, the community and the poor. (22 August 2018, 12 August 2019, 31 July 2020)

✤ Onam

Onam is Kerala's biggest cultural celebration, when the entire state celebrates the golden age of mythical King Mahabali for 10 days. (24 August 2018, 10 September 2019, 30 August 2020)

September

The rain is now petering out (with temperatures still relatively high). The second trekking season begins mid-month in the Himalaya.

✤ Ganesh's Birthday

Hindus celebrate the 10-day Ganesh Chaturthi, commemorating the birth of the much-loved elephant-headed god, with verve, particularly in Mumbai. Clay idols of Ganesh are ceremonially immersed in rivers, tanks (reservoirs) or the sea. (13 September 2018, 2 September 2019, 22 August 2020)

October

The travel season starts to kick off in earnest. October brings festivals and mostly good weather.

✤ Navratri

The exuberant Hindu 'Festival of Nine Nights' leading up to Dussehra celebrates the goddess Durga in all her incarnations. Festivities are vibrant in West Bengal and Maharashtra. (9 October 2018, 29 September 2019, 17 October 2020)

✤ Dussehra

Colourful Dussehra celebrates the victory of the Hindu god Rama over the demon-king Ravana and the triumph of good over evil. (19 October 2018, 8 October 2019, 25 October 2020)

November

The climate is blissful in most places, hot but not uncomfortably so, but the southern monsoon is sweeping Kerala.

✤ Diwali

In the lunar month of Kartika, Hindus celebrate The Festival of Lights for five days. There's a massive build up, and on the day people exchange gifts, light fireworks, and light lamps to lead Lord Rama home from exile. (7 November 2018, 27 October 2019, 14 November 2020)

✤ The Prophet Mohammed's Birthday

The Islamic festival of Eid-Milad-un-Nabi celebrates the birth of the Prophet Mohammed with prayers and processions. It falls around 21 November 2018, 10 November 2019 and 29 October 2020.

December

December is peak tourist season for a reason: you're guaranteed glorious weather (except for the chilly mountains), the humidity's low, the mood is festive and the beach rocks.

Plan Your Trip
Get Inspired

Read

Midnight's Children (1981) Salman Rushdie's allegory about Independence and Partition.

A Fine Balance (1995) Rohinton Mistry's beautifully written, tragic tale set in Mumbai.

White Tiger (2008) Aravind Adiga's Booker-winning novel about class struggle in globalised India.

A Suitable Boy (1993) Vikram Seth's 1300-plus pages of romance, heartbreak, family secrets and political intrigue.

Shantaram (2003) Gregory David Roberts' vivid experiences of his life in India. A traveller favourite!

The God of Small Things (1997) Magically written novel of passion and caste in Kerala, by Arundhati Roy.

Watch

Fire (1996), **Earth** (1998) and **Water** (2005) Trilogy directed by Deepa Mehta.

Pather Panchali (1955) Haunting masterpiece from Satyajit Ray.

Pyaasa (Thirst; 1957) and **Kaagaz Ke Phool** (Paper Flowers; 1959) For a taste of nostalgia.

Gandhi (1982) The classic.

Sairat (2016) Low-budget success confronting caste and gender issues generally ignored by Bollywood; directed by a Dalit, Nagraj Manjule.

Dhobi Ghat (2011) Understated, absorbing tale touching on many levels of Mumbai, and Indian, life; directed by Kiran Rao.

Listen

Taal Original Motion Picture Soundtrack (AR Rahman; 1999)

Sajda (Jagjit Singh and Lata Mangeshkar; 1987)

Kashmir (Led Zeppelin; 1975)

Live at the Monterey Pop Festival 1967 (Ravi Shankar; 1967)

Call of the Valley (Shivkumar Sharma; 1967)

Music Baba (Goa Gil; 2014)

Afternoon Ragas (Nikhil Banerjee; 1970)

Above: High Court, Mumbai

SAIKO3P/SHUTTERSTOCK ©

Plan Your Trip
Five-Day Itineraries

Northern Magic

This action-packed three-city trip combines India's enormous and historic capital, Delhi, with Agra, home of the glorious Taj Mahal, and the holy city of Varanasi – India at its most intense.

Delhi (p35) Delhi mixes the evocative relics of fallen empires with teeming bazaars, mystical places of worship and some very fine dining.
🚌 2hr to Agra

Agra (p65) Agra isn't just home to the Taj Mahal, also here you'll find one of India's mightiest fortresses and other beautiful monuments.
✈ 2½hr to Varanasi

Varanasi (p227) This holy city on the Ganges River brings you into intimate contact with India's rituals of life and death.

Rajasthan Ramble

Head out west to the colourful state of Rajasthan, realm of maharajahs, palaces, tiger-prowled jungles and massive desert forts, where history can never quite be disentangled from legend.

Jaipur (p101) Jaipur's city palace and magnificent Amber Fort preside over a city that offers some of India's best shopping.
🚊 3hr to Sawai Madhopur

Jaisalmer (p87) The fabled Jaisalmer Fort rises like a mirage out of deserts whose mystique is best explored on a camel safari.

Ranthambhore National Park (p116) Jungle safaris with serious chances of sighting wild tigers.
🚊 3hr to Jaipur, then 🚊 12hr to Jaisalmer

Plan Your Trip

10-Day Itinerary

Southern Odyssey

Soak up Mumbai's city vibes, take a trip to the ancient rock-cut architecture of Ellora, then head south for beach bliss in Goa, before moving on down to Kerala for a backwaters cruise from Alappuzha (Alleppey).

Ellora (p141) Stunning rock-cut temples, monasteries and chapels, carved out by three religions more than 1000 years ago.
🚍 1hr to Aurangabad, then ✈ 6hr to Goa, then 🚗 1½hr to Palolem

Mumbai (p119) India's energetic second-largest city has some of the world's grandest colonial-era architecture and the country's premier restaurant and nightlife scene.
✈ 1hr to Aurangabad, then 🚍 1hr to Ellora

Palolem (p172) One of Goa's most beautiful beaches, Palolem has accommodation and activities (and inactivities) for all kinds of traveller.
🚍 1½hr to Goa, then ✈ 5hr to Kochi, then 🚎 1hr to Fort Cochin

Kochi (p192) A quaintly charming blend of old Portugal, Holland and England on the tropical Malabar coast.
🚎 1½hr to Alleppey

Alleppey (p190) Relax on a houseboat cruising between coconut plantations along Kerala's lazy canals, rivers and lakes.

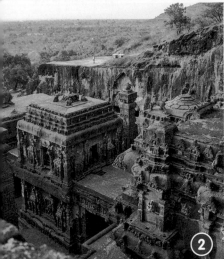

Plan Your Trip
Two-Week Itinerary

Mountains, Cities & Beaches

Internal flights can get you quickly around the subcontinent and maximise your time in its most special destinations, from the Himalaya to the southern beaches via the cities of the Ganges plain.

Varanasi (p227) Sunrise over the ghats from a boat on the holy Ganges is likely to be one of your most memorable images of all.
✈ 6hr to Bagdogra, then
🚗 2½hr to Darjeeling

Agra (p65) As well as the Taj Mahal and Agra Fort, try to get to the abandoned Mughal capital of Fatehpur Sikri.
✈ 2½hr to Varanasi

Darjeeling (p211) Stare at mighty Khangchendzonga (8598m), tour a tea plantation, ride the colonial-era toy train and maybe take a short Himalayan trek.
🚗 2½hr to Bagdogra, then
✈ 8hr to Goa, then 🚗
1½hr to Palolem or Anjuna

Hampi (p204) From Goa take a side trip to the ruined capital of the old Hindu Vijayanagar empire, with an otherworldly setting and a unique atmosphere.

Goa (p159) Wind up with some R&R on Goa's gorgeous beaches – try broadly appealing Palolem and/or hippie-chic Anjuna.
🚗 1½hr to Margao, then
🚆 or 🚌 8hr to Hosapete, then
🚌 30min to Hampi

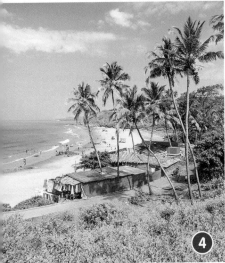

Plan Your Trip
Family Travel

Fascinating and thrilling; India will be even more astounding for children than for their wide-eyed parents. Its scents, sights and sounds make for an unforgettable adventure and one that most kids will take in their stride.

You (and your kids) may have to get used to being the centre of attention. Locals will thrill at taking a photograph beside your bouncing baby. If this becomes tiring or disconcerting, you can always politely decline.

On the Road

○ Indian travel can be arduous at times – so plan easy, fun days to follow longer journeys.

○ Pack plenty of diversions (iPads or laptops with downloaded movies, audiobooks, old-fashioned story books, local toys).

○ If you're hiring a car and driver – a sensible, flexible option – and you require safety capsules, child restraints or booster seats, bring these with you or make this absolutely clear to the hiring company as

early as possible. If necessary, don't be afraid to tell your driver to slow down and drive responsibly.

Fun Forms of Transport

Autorickshaw Bump thrillingly along in these child-scale vehicles (p307).

Toy Train to Darjeeling Ride the cute little steam train past colourful mountain villages and rushing waterfalls (p223).

Houseboat, Alappuzha (Alleppey) Boat along Kerala's beautiful backwaters (p190), with interesting stops en route.

Eating

○ In regions such as Rajasthan, Himachal Pradesh, Goa or Kerala, or the big cities, you'll find it easy to feed your brood. Major cities and more touristy towns always offer a range of international cuisines.

○ Easy portable snacks such as bananas, samosas, *puri* (puffy dough pockets), white-bread sandwiches and packaged biscuits are available.

LONELY PLANET/GETTY IMAGES ©

Many children will delight in paneer (unfermented cheese) dishes, simple dhals (mild lentil curries), buttered naans (tandoori breads) and pilaus (rice dishes) – and few can resist the finger food fun of a vast South Indian dosa (paper-thin lentil-flour pancake).

Health

○ Access to healthcare is better in traveller-frequented parts of the country where it's almost always easy to track down a doctor at short notice.

○ Diarrhoea can be very serious in young children. Seek medical help if it is persistent or accompanied by fever; rehydration is essential.

What to Take

You can get these items in many parts of India too:

○ Nappies, nappy cream, extra bottles, wet wipes, infant formula and canned, bottled or rehydratable food.

★ Best for Kids

Camel Safaris (p92)

Ranthambhore National Park (p116)

Palolem (p172)

Taj Mahal (p68)

Kerala houseboats (p180)

○ A fold-up baby bed or the lightest possible travel cot you can find (hotel cots may prove precarious).

○ A backpack is a better option than a stroller/pushchair, as pavements are often scarce.

○ Insect repellent, mosquito nets, hats, sun lotion.

From left: Camel safari (p92), Thar desert; Palolem beach (p172)

Chandni Chowk (p42)

DELHI

Jama Masjid
(p46)

Paharganj
Hectic backpacker central, packed with cheap and midrange accommodation, restaurants and shops, handy for New Delhi station.

Connaught Place
Colonial-era colonnade with midrange shops, eateries and bars, wrapped around a chaotic-feeling central hub.

New Delhi
Tree-lined boulevards, expensive real estate, parks, upscale hotels and grand, Raj-era buildings.

Safdarjung Enclave
An upmarket neighbourhood with some appealing bar-restaurants.

Indira Gandhi
International Airport

Hauz Khas
Hauz Khas village is home to boutiques, bars and eateries, and next to a lovely park.

QUTB MINAR

Tomb of Bara Gumbad, Lodi Gardens (p49)

Arriving in Delhi

Indira Gandhi International Airport
Terminal 1: Indian low-cost airlines.
Terminal 3: other flights. Fixed-price
taxis, the metro and AC buses all run
into the city.

New Delhi train station Near
Paharganj.

Delhi train station (Delhi Junction) in
Old Delhi.

Nizamuddin train station South of
Sunder Nagar, southeast of the centre.

Sleeping

Delhi hotels range from wallet-friendly
dives to lavish five-stars; wherever you
are on the scale, it's wise to book ahead
and tell the hotel your expected arrival
time. Most places offer airport pick-up,
if arranged in advance. See Where to
Stay (p63) for more information on
accommodation areas.

TUKARAM KARVE/SHUTTERSTOCK ©

Red Fort

The defining monument of Mughal Delhi, the massive Red Fort still conjures up vivid pictures of Mughal splendour at its peak, despite the depredations of time and the British army.

Great For...

☑ **Don't Miss**

The incongruous Orpheus (thought to be Florentine) behind the throne in the Diwan-i-Am.

Founded by Mughal emperor Shah Jahan, the Red Fort was constructed between 1638 and 1648, just a few decades before the Palace of Versailles in France. Surrounded by an 18m-high wall, it had decapitated prisoners' bodies built into its foundations for luck. The *nahr-i-bihisht* (river of paradise), a tree-lined waterway fed from the Yamuna River, ran through the fort and out along Chandni Chowk.

After the First War of Independence (Indian Uprising), the British destroyed buildings and gardens inside the fortress and replaced them with ugly barrack blocks.

The fort is the setting for an evening **sound and light show** (www.theashokgroup.com; Tue-Fri ₹60, Sat & Sun ₹80; ⊘in Hindi/English 7/8.30pm Feb-Apr, Sep & Oct, 7.30/9pm May-Aug, 6/7.30pm Nov-Jan), narrated by film star Amitabh Bachchan.

Diwan-i-Am, Red Fort

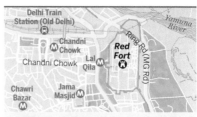

ℹ Need to Know

Map p48; Indian/foreigner ₹30/500, with museum ticket ₹35/500, audio guide in Hindi/English or Korean ₹69/115; ⊘dawn–dusk Tue–Sun, museums 10am–5pm; ⓂChandni Chowk)

✕ Take a Break

Head to the lane **Gali Paratha Wali** (Map p48; parathas ₹15-35; ⊘7am–11pm; ⓂJama Masjid) for delectable fresh *parathas*.

★ Top Tip

The audio-guide tour, by acclaimed company Narrowcasters, is worthwhile as it brings the site to life.

Entering through the Lahore Gate, you pass through **Chatta Chowk** (Covered Bazaar), formerly an imperial bazaar glittering with silk and jewels for royal women. Today's wares are rather more mundane souvenirs. Just north of here, the **Museum on India's Struggle for Freedom** (⊘10am-5pm Tue-Sun) covers the struggle for independence from Britain. Eastward, the arched **Naubat Khana** (Drum House) once accommodated royal musicians and served as parking for royal horses and elephants. Beyond is the Diwan-i-Am, the arcaded hall of public audience, where the emperor greeted guests from a throne on the marble platform, which is backed by fine pietradura (inlaid stone) work.

On the east side of the fort you reach the private royal quarters. The emperor lived and slept in the **Khas Mahal** (Special Palace), shielded from prying eyes by lacelike carved marble screens. The cooling *nahr-i-behisht* flowed through here to an elegant lotus-shaped fountain in the **Rang Mahal** (Palace of Colour), home to the emperor's chief wife. The Mumtaz Mahal is thought to have been built for Arjumand Banu Begum (also known as Mumtaz Mahal), the wife for whom Shah Jahan built the Taj Mahal.

The wonderfully decorated Diwan-i-Khas, or Hall of Private Audience, was used for bowing and scraping to the emperor. Bahadur Shah Zafar became the last Mughal emperor here in May 1857, but was tried (here, again) by the British seven months following the First War of Independence, and exiled.

Further north, the Shahi Burj, a three-storey octagonal tower, was Shah Jahan's favoured workplace, where he planned the running of his empire. In front are remains of an elegant formal garden.

Red Fort

HIGHLIGHTS

The main entrance to the Red Fort is through ❶ **Lahore Gate** – the bastion in front of it was built by Aurangzeb for increased security. You can still see bullet marks on the gate, dating from 1857, the First War of Independence, when the Indian army rose up against the British.

Walk through the Chatta Chowk (Covered Bazaar), which once sold silks and jewellery to the nobility; beyond it lies ❷ **Naubat Khana**, a russet-red building, which houses Hathi Pol (Elephant Gate), so called because visitors used to dismount from their elephants or horses here as a sign of respect. From here it's straight on to the ❸ **Diwan-i-Am**, the Hall of Public Audiences. Behind this are the private palaces, the ❹ **Khas Mahal** and the ❺ **Diwan-i-Khas**. Entry to this Hall of Private Audiences, the fort's most expensive building, was only permitted to the officials of state. The artificial stream the Nahr-i-Behisht ('stream of paradise') used to run a cooling channel of water through all these buildings. Nearby is the ❻ **Moti Masjid (Pearl Mosque)** and south is the ❼ **Mumtaz Mahal**, housing the Museum of Archaeology, or you can head north, where the Red Fort gardens are dotted by palatial pavilions and old British barracks. Here you'll find the ❽ **baoli**, a spookily deserted water tank. Another five minutes' walk – across a road, then a railway bridge – brings you to the island fortress of ❾ **Salimgarh**.

Salimgarh
Salimgarh is the 16th-century fort built by Salim Shah Sur. It was constructed on an island of the Yamuna River and only recently opened to the public. It is still partly used by the Indian army.

Museum on India's Struggle for Freedom

Chatta Chowk

Lahore Gate
Lahore Gate is particularly significant, as it was here that Jawaharlal Nehru raised the first tricolour flag of independent India in 1947.

Naubat Khana
The Naubat Khana (Drum House) is carved in floral designs and once featured musicians playing in the upper gallery. It housed Hathi Pol (Elephant Gate), where visitors dismounted from their horse or elephant.

Baoli

The Red Fort step well is seldom visited and is a hauntingly deserted place, even more so when you consider its chambers were used as cells by the British from August 1942.

CARLOS NETO / SHUTTERSTOCK ©

KIMBERLEY COOLE/GETTY IMAGES ©

Moti Masjid

The Moti Masjid (Pearl Mosque) was built by Aurangzeb in 1662 for his personal use. The domes were originally covered in copper, but the copper was removed and sold by the British.

Diwan-i-Khas

This was the most expensive building in the fort, consisting of white marble decorated with inlay work of cornelian and other stones. The screens overlooking what was once the river (now the ring road) were filled with coloured glass.

Baidon Pavilion

Zafar Mahal

Hammam

6

5

Rang Mahal

4

Mumtaz Mahal

7

3

2

PIT STOP

To refuel, head to Gali Paratha Wali, a foodstall-lined lane off Chandni Chowk noted for its many varieties of freshly made paratha (traditional flat bread).

←NORTH

Delhi Gate

Diwan-i-Am

These red sandstone columns were once covered in shell plaster, as polished and smooth as ivory, and in hot weather heavy red curtains were hung around the columns to block out the sun. It's believed the panels behind the marble throne were created by Florentine jeweller Austin de Bordeaux.

POWEROFFOREVER / GETTY IMAGES ©

Khas Mahal

Most spectacular in the Emperor's private apartments is a beautiful marble screen at the northern end of the rooms; the 'Scales of Justice' are carved above it, suspended over a crescent, surrounded by stars and clouds.

ABIGAIL HOLE ©

EDWIN REMSBERG/ALAMY ©

Old Delhi's Bazaars

Old Delhi's bazaars are a bamboozling, sensual whirlwind, combining incense, spices strong enough to make you sneeze, rickshaw fumes, brilliant colours, and hole-in-the-wall shops packed with goods that shimmer and glitter.

Great For...

☑ Don't Miss

The sight of the giant jars of pickles and chutneys in the spice market.

The bazaar district is less retail therapy, more heightened reality. Whole streets and areas are devoted to specific items.

Chandni Chowk

Old Delhi's backbone is this iconic **shopping strip** (Map p48; ☉10am-7pm Mon-Sat; Ⓜ Chandni Chowk), dotted by temples, snarled by traffic and crammed with stores selling everything from street food to clothing, electronics and break-as-soon-as-you-buy-them novelties.

Tiny bazaars lead off the main drag, so you can dive off and explore these small lanes, which glitter with jewellery, decorations, paper goods and more. For silver jewellery, head for **Dariba Kalan** (Map p48; ☉approx 10am-8pm; Ⓜ Chawri Bazaar), the alley near the Sisganj Gurdwara. Off this lane, the **Kinari Bazaar** (☉11am-8pm; Ⓜ Jama Masjid), literally

Spice Market

ℹ️ Need to Know

Most of the market areas operate from about 10am to 8pm. Some shops close on Sunday.

✗ Take a Break

Stop into clean, bright **Haldiram's** (Map p48; 1454/2 Chandni Chowk; mains ₹70-180; ⊙10am-10.30pm; Ⓜ Chandni Chowk) for top-notch dosas (paper-thin lentil-flour pancake).

★ Top Tip

The best time to visit is midmorning or late afternoon, when the streets are less busy.

'trimmings market', is a blaze of colour famous for *zardozi* (gold embroidery), temple trim and wedding turbans.

Running south from the old Town Hall, **Nai Sarak** (⊙approx 10am-8pm; Ⓜ Jama Masjid) is lined with stalls selling saris, shawls, chiffon and *lehanga* (long skirt with a waist cord), while nearby **Ballimaran** (⊙10am-8pm; Ⓜ Chandni Chowk) has sequinned slippers and curly-toed jootis (traditional slip-on shoes).

Spice Market

Khari Baoli means 'salty step-well', but there's no well here any more, just Delhi's nose-numbing wholesale **Spice Market** (Gadodia Market; Map p48; Khari Baoli; Ⓜ Chandni Chowk), ablaze with piles of scarlet-red chillis, ginger and turmeric roots, peppercorns, cumin, coriander seeds, cardamom, dried fruit and nuts. It seems little has changed here for centuries, as labourers hustle through the narrow lanes with huge sacks of herbs and spices on their heads. Deeper inside the market, it's so spicy that everyone can't help coughing and sneezing.

You can buy small packets of items, despite it being a wholesale market.

Chawri Bazaar

For gorgeous wrapping paper and wedding cards, head to **Chawri Bazaar** (Map p48; ⊙10am-7pm), leading west from the Jama Masjid.

Daryaganj Sunday Book Market

Come Sunday, books spread across the pavements for around 2km from Delhi Gate northwards to the Red Fort, and west along Jawaharlal Nehru Marg. This is **Daryaganj Kitab Bazaar** (Book Market; Map p48; ⊙8am-6pm Sun). Rummage for everything from Mills & Boon to vintage children's books. It's best to arrive early, as it gets busy.

Qutb Minar

If you only have time for one of Delhi's ancient ruins sites, make it the complex centred on the soaring Qutb Minar, erected by Delhi's first Muslim sultan, Qutb-ud-din Aibak.

The Afghan Qutb-ud-din Aibak raised the Qutb Minar in 1193 to proclaim his triumph over the Hindu city of Qila Rai Pithora (Lal Kot), which he razed to the ground to build the Qutb Minar and his nearby capital Mehrauli. Subsequent Muslim rulers expanded on this beginning, and the complex is studded with ruined tombs and monuments. Qutub-ud-din's successor Altamish is entombed in a magnificent sandstone and marble mausoleum covered in Islamic calligraphy, while Ala-ud-din Khilji's sprawling madrasa (Islamic college) and tomb (early 14th century) stand in ruins at the rear of the complex.

The complex is a 1km autorickshaw ride from Qutab Minar metro station. For the most atmosphere, try to visit at dawn, before the crowds arrive.

Great For...

☑ **Don't Miss**

The recycled pre-Islamic stonework on the walls of the Quwwat-ul-Islam Masjid.

Qutb Minar

Qutb Minar

The Qutb Minar itself is an unmissable, soaring Afghan-style victory tower and minaret, ringed by intricately carved sandstone bands bearing verses from the Quran. It stands nearly 73m high and tapers from a 15m-diameter base to a mere 2.5m at the top. Qutb-ud-din only completed the first of its five storeys before his unlucky death (impaled on his saddle while playing polo). His successors completed the job. The tower was struck by lightning in the 14th century, after which Feroz Shah had it repaired in marble.

Quwwat-ul-Islam Masjid

At the foot of the Qutb Minar stands the **Quwwat-ul-Islam Masjid** (Might of Islam Mosque), the first mosque built in India. An inscription over its east gate states that it was constructed with materials obtained from

demolishing '27 idolatrous temples'. Its walls are studded with sun disks, *shikharas* and other pieces of Hindu and Jain masonry.

In the courtyard stands a 6.7m-high **iron pillar** (Ⓜ Qutab Minar) that is much more ancient than any of the surrounding monuments. It hasn't rusted in 1600 years, due to both the dry atmosphere and its incredible purity. A Sanskrit inscription indicates that it was initially erected outside a Vishnu temple, possibly in Bihar, in memory of Chandragupta II (r AD 375–413).

Ala-ud-din Khilji added the exquisite marble and sandstone Alai Darwaza gatehouse in 1310.

Alai Minar

Sultan Ala-ud-din Khilji wanted to build a second tower of victory, twice as high as Qutb Minar. Construction only reached the first level before the sultan died, and the project with him. The 27m-high plinth can be seen just north of the Qutb Minar.

◎ SIGHTS

Most sights in Delhi are easily accessible via the metro. Note that many places are closed on Mondays.

◎ Old Delhi

'Old Delhi' is roughly equivalent to the Mughal city of Shahjahanabad. The main drag is Chandni Chowk (p42), a tumult of noise, colour and traffic stretching from Red Fort (p39) to the Fatehpur Masjid. The easiest way to get around is by cycle-rickshaw (costing around ₹10 per kilo-metre) or on foot.

Jama Masjid   Mosque
(Friday Mosque; Map p48; camera & video each ₹300, tower ₹100; ☺non-Muslims 8am-1hr before sunset, minaret 9am-5.30pm; ℳChawri Bazaar) A beautiful pocket of calm at the heart of Old Delhi's mayhem, India's largest mosque is built on a 10m elevation, towering above the surrounding hubbub. It can hold a mind-blowing 25,000 people. The marble and red-sandstone 'Friday Mosque' was Shah Jahan's final architectural triumph,

built between 1644 and 1658. The four watchtowers were used for security. There are two minarets standing 40m high, one of which can be climbed for amazing views. All of the three gates allow access to the mosque.

◎ New Delhi & Around

Humayun's Tomb   Historic Building
(Mathura Rd; Indian/foreigner/under 15 ₹30/500/free, video ₹25; ☺dawn-dusk; ℳJLN Stadium) Humayun's tomb is sublimely well proportioned, seeming to float above its symmetrical gardens. It's thought to have inspired the Taj Mahal, which it predates by 60 years. Constructed for the Mughal emperor in the mid-16th century by Haji Begum, his Persian-born wife, the tomb marries Persian and Mughal elements, with restrained decoration enhancing the ar-chitecture. The arched facade is inlaid with bands of white marble and red sandstone, and the building follows strict rules of Islamic geometry, with an emphasis on the number eight.

Jama Masjid

Hazrat Nizam-ud-din Dargah
Shrine

(off Lodi Rd; ☉24hr; Ⓜ JLN Stadium) Visiting the marble shrine of Muslim Sufi saint Nizam-ud-din Auliya is Delhi's most mystical, magical experience. The dargah is hidden away in a tangle of bazaars selling rose petals, attars (perfumes) and offerings, and on Thursday evenings from sunset you can hear Sufis singing *qawwali* (Islamic devotional singing), amid crowds of devotees. The ascetic Nizam-ud-din died in 1325 at the ripe old age of 92. His doctrine of tolerance made him popular not only with Muslims, but with Hindus, Sikhs and Buddhists as well.

Crafts Museum
Museum

(☎011-23371641; Bhairon Marg; ☉10am-5pm Tue-Sun; Ⓜ Pragati Maidan) **FREE** Much of this lovely museum is outside, including tree-shaded carvings and buildings. Displays celebrate the traditional crafts of India, with some beautiful textiles on display indoors, such as embroidery from Kashmir and cross-stitch from Punjab. Highlights include an exquisite reconstructed Gujarati *haveli* (traditional house). Artisans sell their products in the rear courtyard. The museum includes the excellent Cafe Lota (p55) and a very good shop.

Rajpath
Area

(Map p53; Ⓜ Central Secretariat) Rajpath (Kingsway) is a vast parade linking India Gate to the offices of the Indian government. Built on an imperial scale between 1914 and 1931, this complex was designed by Edwin Lutyens and Herbert Baker, and underlined the ascendance of the British rulers. Yet just 16 years later, the Brits were out on their ear and Indian politicians were pacing the corridors of power.

At the western end of Rajpath, the official residence of the president of India, **Rashtrapati Bhavan** (President's House; ☎011-23015321; www.presidentofindia.nic.in/visit-to-rashtrapati-bhavan.htm; ₹50, online reservation required; ☉9am-4pm Fri-Sun; Ⓜ Central Secretariat), now partially open

Gandhi's Last Days

Gandhi Smriti (Map p53; ☎011-23012843; 5 Tees Jan Marg; ☉10am-5pm Tue-Sun, closed 2nd Sat of every month; Ⓜ Racecourse), the poignant memorial to Mahatma Gandhi, is in Birla House, where he was shot dead on the grounds by a Hindu zealot on 30 January 1948, after campaigning against intercommunal violence.

The house itself is where Gandhi spent his last 144 days. The exhibits include rooms preserved just as Gandhi left them, a detailed account of his life and last 24 hours, and vivid miniature dioramas depicting scenes from his life.

SAIKO3P/SHUTTERSTOCK ©

to the public via guided tour, is flanked by the mirror-image, dome-crowned **North Secretariat** (Map p53) and **South Secretariat** (Map p53), housing government ministries. The Indian parliament also meets nearby at the **Sansad Bhavan** (Parliament House; Sansard Marg), a circular, colonnaded edifice at the end of Sansad Marg.

At Rajpath's eastern end is mighty **India Gate** (Map p53; Rajpath; ☉24hr; Ⓜ Central Secretariat). This 42m-high stone memorial arch, designed by Lutyens, pays tribute to around 90,000 Indian army soldiers who died in WWI, the Northwest Frontier operations and the 1919 Anglo-Afghan War.

Old Delhi

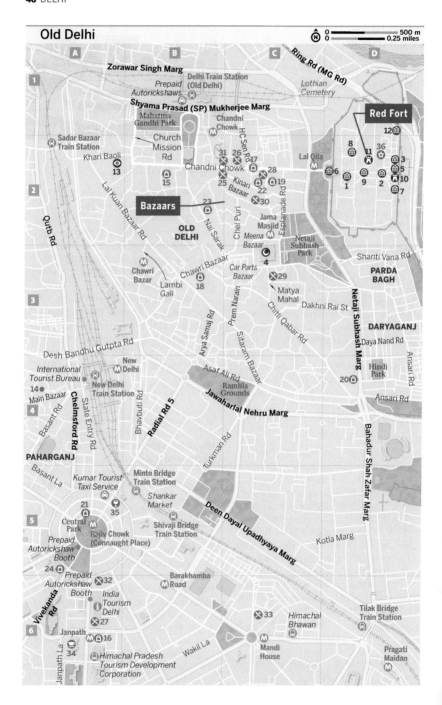

0 — 500 m
0 — 0.25 miles

Zorawar Singh Marg

Prepaid Autorickshaws

Delhi Train Station (Old Delhi)

Ring Rd (MG Rd)

Lothian Cemetery

Shyama Prasad (SP) Mukherjee Marg

Mahatma Gandhi Park

Chandni Chowk

Church Mission Rd

HC Sen Rd

Red Fort

Sadar Bazaar Train Station

Khari Baoli

13

Lal Qila

Lal Kuan Bazaar Rd

Bazaars

Chandni Chowk

31 26 17
15 28
25 Kinari Bazaar 22 19
23 30

OLD DELHI

Nai Sarak

Chel Puri

Jama Masjid

Meena Bazaar

4

Netaji Subhash Park

Shanti Vana Rd

PARDA BAGH

Qutb Rd

Chawri Bazar

Lambi Gali

Chawri Bazaar

18

Car Parts Bazaar

29

Matya Mahal

Dakhni Rai St

Chitli Qabar Rd

DARYAGANJ

Daya Nand Rd

Desh Bandhu Gutpta Rd

Arya Samaj Rd

Prem Narain

Sitaram Bazaar

International Tourist Bureau

14

Main Bazaar

Basant Rd

New Delhi

New Delhi Train Station

Chelmsford Rd

State Entry Rd

Bhavbuti Rd

Radial Rd 5

Asaf Ali Rd

Ramlila Grounds

Jawaharlal Nehru Marg

Turkman Rd

Netaji Subhash Marg

Hindi Park

20

Ansari Rd

Ansari Rd

Bahadur Shah Zafar Marg

PAHARGANJ

Basant La

Kumar Tourist Taxi Service

21 35

Central Park

Prepaid Autorickshaw Booth

24

Prepaid Autorickshaw Booth

32

India Tourism Delhi

27

Vivekanand Rd

Janpath

34

16

Janpath La

Minto Bridge Train Station

Shankar Market

Shivaji Bridge Train Station

Rajiv Chowk (Connaught Place)

Barakhamba Road

Deen Dayal Upadhyaya Marg

Kotla Marg

33

Himachal Bhawan

Wakil La

Mandi House

Himachal Pradesh Tourism Development Corporation

Tilak Bridge Train Station

Pragati Maidan

Old Delhi

⊚ **Sights**
1 Chatta Chowk.. D2
2 Diwan-i-Am.. D2
3 Diwan-i-Khas D2
4 Jama Masjid... C3
5 Khas Mahal.. D2
6 Lahore Gate... D2
7 Mumtaz Mahal D2
8 Museum on India's Struggle for
    Freedom... D2
9 Naubat Khana D2
10 Rang Mahal.. D2
11 Red Fort... D2
12 Shahi Burj D1
13 Spice Market A2

◐ **Activities, Courses & Tours**
14 Salaam Baalak Trust A4

🛍 **Shopping**
15 Ballimaran... B2
16 Central Cottage Industries
    Emporium... A6
17 Chandni Chowk... C2
18 Chawri Bazaar... B3

19 Dariba Kalan... C2
20 Daryaganj Kitab Bazaar............................ D4
21 Fabindia... A5
22 Kinari Bazaar C2
23 Nai Sarak... B2
24 People Tree... A5

✕ **Eating**
25 Gali Paratha Wali...................................... B2
26 Haldiram's... C2
27 Hotel Saravana Bhavan............................. A6
28 Jalebiwala.. C2
29 Karim's.. C3
30 Lakhori.. C2
31 Natraj Dahi Balle Wala.............................. B2
32 Rajdhani.. A6
33 Triveni Terrace Cafe C6

◑ **Drinking & Nightlife**
    1911... (see 34)
34 Atrium, Imperial A6
35 Unplugged... A5

✦ **Entertainment**
36 Sound & Light Show D2

National Museum
Museum

(Map p53; ☎011-23019272; www.national
museumindia.gov.in; Janpath; Indian/foreigner
₹20/650, camera Indian/foreigner ₹20/300;
◷10am-5pm Tue-Sun, free guided tour 10.30am
& 2.30pm Tue-Fri, 10.30am, 11.30am & 2.30pm
Sat & Sun; Ⓜ Central Secretariat) This glorious
if dusty museum is full of treasures.
Mind-bogglingly ancient, sophisticated
figurines from the Harappan civilisation, almost 5000 years old, include the
remarkable Dancing Girl, and there are
also some fine ceramics from the even
older Nal civilisation. Other items include
Buddha relics, exquisite jewellery, miniature
paintings, medieval woodcarvings, textiles
and musical instruments.

Allow at least two hours. Bring identification to obtain an audio guide (included
in the foreigner ticket price; ₹150 extra for
Indian tourists). There's also a cafe.

Lodi Gardens
Park

(Lodi Rd; ◷6am-8pm Oct-Mar, 5am-8pm Apr-Sep;
Ⓜ Khan Market or Jor Bagh) Delhi's loveliest
escape was originally named after the wife
of the British Resident, Lady Willingdon,
who had two villages cleared in 1936 in
order to landscape a park to remind her
of home. Today named after their Lodi-era
tombs, the gardens, favoured getaway for
Delhi's elite and courting couples, contain
the 15th-century Bara Gumbad tomb and
mosque, the strikingly different tombs of
Mohammed Shah (Ⓜ Khan Market) and
Sikander Lodi (Map p53; Ⓜ JLN Stadium), and
the Athpula (eight-piered) bridge across
the lake, which dates from Emperor Akbar's
reign.

Gurdwara
Bangla Sahib
Sikh Temple

(Ashoka Rd; ◷4am-9pm; Ⓜ Patel Chowk) This
magnificent, huge, white-marble gurdwara
(Sikh temple), topped by glinting golden onion domes, was constructed at the site where
the eighth Sikh guru, Harkrishan Dev, stayed
before his death in 1664. Despite his tender
years, the six-year-old guru tended to victims
of Delhi's cholera and smallpox epidemic, and
the waters of the large tank are said to have
healing powers. It's full of colour and life, yet
tranquil, and live devotional songs waft over
the compound.

Pocket of Calm

Designed for tranquil worship, Delhi's beautiful **Bahai House of Worship** (Lotus Temple; ☑011-26444029; www.bahaihouseofworship.in; Kalkaji; ☻9am-7pm Tue-Sun Apr-Sep, to 5.30pm Oct-Mar; ⓂKalkaji Mandir) offers a rare pocket of calm in the hectic city. This architectural masterpiece was designed by Iranian-Canadian architect Fariburz Sahba in 1986. It is shaped like a lotus flower, with 27 delicate-looking white-marble petals. The temple was created to bring faiths together; visitors are invited to pray or meditate silently according to their own beliefs. The attached visitor centre tells the story of the Bahai faith.

National Rail Museum
Museum

(☑011-26881816; Service Rd, Chanakyapuri; adult/child ₹20/10, video ₹100; ☻10am-5pm Tue-Sun; ⓂSafdarjung) A contender for one of Delhi's best (and best-value) museums, the National Rail Museum has steam locos and carriages spread across 11 acres. Among the venerable bogies are the former Viceregal Dining Car, and the Maharaja of Mysore's rolling saloon. The new indoor gallery includes some hands-on exhibits, a miniature railway, and three simulators (weekends only). A toy train (adult/child ₹20/10) chuffs around the grounds.

◉ South Delhi

Mehrauli Archaeological Park
Park

(☻dawn-dusk; ⓂQutab Minar) FREE There are extraordinary riches scattered around Mehrauli, with more than 440 monuments – from the 10th century to the British era – dotting a forest and the village itself. In the forest, most impressive are the time-ravaged tombs of Balban and Quli Khan, his son, and the Jamali Khamali mosque, attached to the tomb of the Sufi poet Jamali. To the west is the 16th-century Rajon ki Baoli, Delhi's finest step-well, with a monumental flight of steps.

At the northern end of Mehrauli village is Adham Khan's Mausoleum, which was once used as a British residence, then later as a police station and post office. Leading northwards from the tomb are the pre-Islamic walls of Lal Kot.

To the south of the village are the remains of the Mughal palace, the Zafar Mahal, once in the heart of the jungle. Next door to it is the Sufi shrine, the Dargah of Qutb Sahib. There is a small burial ground with one empty space that was intended for the last king of Delhi, Bahadur Shah Zafar, who died in exile in Burma (Myanmar) in 1862. South of here is a Lodi-era burial ground for *hijras* (eunuchs), **Hijron ka Khanqah** (Kalka das Marg; ☻dawn-dusk; ⓂQutab Minar). The identity of those buried here is unknown, but it's a well-kept, peaceful place, revered by Delhi's *hijra* community. A little further south are Jahaz Mahal ('ship palace', also built by the Mughals) and the **Haus i Shamsi tank** (off Mehrauli-Gurgaon Rd).

You can reach the forested part of the park by turning right from the metro station onto Anuvrat Marg and walking 500m. A good way to explore the ruins is by guided walking tour.

☉ TOURS

DelhiByCycle
Cycling

(☑9811723720; www.delhibycycle.com; per person ₹1850; ☻6.30-10am) Founded by a Dutch journalist, these cycle tours are the original and the best, and a thrilling way to explore Delhi. Tours focus on specific neighbour-hoods – Old Delhi, New Delhi, Nizamuddin, and the banks of the Yamuna – and start early to miss the worst of the traffic. The price includes chai and a Mughal breakfast. Child seats are available.

Delhi Metro Walks Walking
(www.delhimetrowalks.com; half- to full-day group walks per person ₹300-600) Delhi-wallah Surekha Nurain shares her extensive learn-ing about architecture, history and culture on recommended group or private tours, visiting both mainstream sights and off-the-beaten-track locations. She has several specially themed walks for families.

Salaam Baalak Trust Walking
(SBT; Map p48; ☎011-23584164; www.salaam-baalaktrust.com; Gali Chandiwali, Paharganj; suggested donation ₹200; Ⓜ Ramakrishna Ashram Marg) ✔ Founded on the proceeds of Mira Nair's 1988 film about the life of street children, *Salaam Bombay!,* this charitable organisation offers two-hour 'street walks'

guided by former street children, who will show you first hand what life is like for Delhi's homeless youngsters. The fees help the Trust assist street children.

🔒 SHOPPING

Wares from all over India glitter in Delhi's back-in-time bazaars, emporiums and markets. The city is also increasingly a centre of contemporary design (especially fashion), with independent boutiques and big shiny malls.

Away from government-run emporiums and fixed-price shops, haggle with good hu-mour. Many taxi/autorickshaw drivers earn commissions (via your inflated purchase price) by taking travellers to overpriced places – don't fall for it.

🔒 Connaught Place Area

Central Cottage Industries Emporium Arts & Crafts
(Map p48; ☎011-23326790; Janpath; ⊙10am-7pm; Ⓜ Janpath) This government-run multilevel store is a wonderful treasure

Tombs in Lodi Gardens (p49)

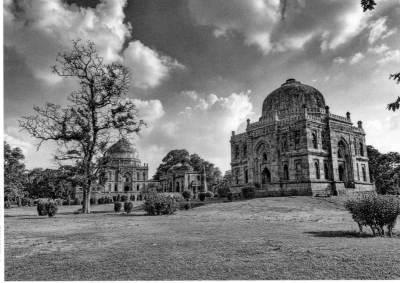

MUKUL BANERJEE/SHUTTERSTOCK ©

trove of fixed-price, India-wide handicrafts. Prices are higher than in the state empoﬁriums, but the selection of woodcarvings, jewellery, pottery, papier mâché, stationery, brassware, textiles (including shawls), toys, rugs, beauty products and miniature paintings makes it a glorious one-stop shop for beautiful crafts. Downstairs there's the Smoothie Factory cafe.

State
Emporiums   Handicrafts, Clothing
(Baba Kharak Singh Marg; ⊙11am-1.30pm & 2-6.30pm Mon-Sat; Ⓜ Shivaji Stadium) Handily in a row are these regional treasure-filled emporiums. They may have the air of torpor that often afflicts governmental enterprises, but shopping here is like travelling around India – top stops include Kashmir, for papier mâché and carpets; Rajasthan, for miniature paintings and puppets; Uttar Pradesh, for marble inlay work; Karnataka, for sandalwood sculptures; Tamil Nadu, for metal statues; and Odisha, for stone carvings.

Fabindia   Clothing, Homewares
(Map p48; www.fabindia.com; 28 B-Block, Connaught Place; ⊙10am-8.30pm; Ⓜ Rajiv Chowk) Reasonably priced ready-made clothes in funky Indian fabrics, from elegant kurtas (long shirts with either short collar or no collar) and dupattas (long scarves) to Western-style shirts, plus stylish homewares.

Kamala   Arts & Crafts
(Baba Kharak Singh Marg; ⊙10am-7pm Mon-Sat; Ⓜ Rajiv Chowk) Crafts, curios, textiles and homewares from the Crafts Council of India, designed with flair and using traditional techniques but offering some contemporary, out-of-the-ordinary designs.

🅐 New Delhi & Around
Khan Market   Market
(Map p53; ⊙approx 10.30am-8pm Mon-Sat; Ⓜ Khan Market) 🖉 Khan Market is Delhi's most upmarket shopping enclave, the most expensive place to rent a shop in India, and is favoured by the elite and expats. Its boutiques focus on fashion, books and homewares, and it's also a good place to eat and drink.

🅐 South Delhi
Dilli Haat   Arts & Crafts
(Aurobindo Marg; foreigner/Indian ₹100/20; ⊙10.30am-10pm; Ⓜ INA) This open-air food-and-crafts market is a cavalcade of colour and sells regional handicrafts from all over India; bargain hard. With lots of food stands it's also a good place to sample cheap, delicious regional specialities – try food from Nagaland or Tamil Nadu (dishes are around ₹70 to ₹100).

People Tree   Handicrafts, Clothing
(Map p48; Regal Bldg, Sansad Marg; ⊙11am-7pm; Ⓜ Rajiv Chowk) 🖉 This hole-in-the-wall shop sells fixed-price, fair-trade, ubercool T-shirts with funky Indian designs and urban attitude, as well as bags, jewellery and Indian-god cushions.

✖ EATING

While Delhi-ites graze all day on the city's masterful, taste-tingling *Dilli-ka-Chaat* (street-food snacks), the city's dining scene is also becoming increasingly diverse, with creative cuisine at Delhi's modern Indian restaurants alongside all the traditional favourites and purveyors of meaty Mughal cuisine and delicate dhals.

Reservations are recommended for high-end restaurants.

🅧 Old Delhi
Natraj Dahi Balle
Wala   Street Food $
(Map p48; 1396 Chandni Chowk; plates ₹50; ⊙10.30am-11pm; Ⓜ Chandni Chowk) This tiny place with the big red sign and the big crowds is famous for its *dahi bhalle* (fried lentil balls served with yoghurt and garnished with chutney) and deliciously crispy *aloo tikki* (spiced potato patties).

Jalebiwala   Sweets $
(Map p48; Dariba Corner, Chandni Chowk; jalebis per 100g ₹50; ⊙8am-10pm; Ⓜ Lal Qila) Century-old Jalebiwala does Delhi's – if not India's – finest *jalebis* (deep-fried, syrupy

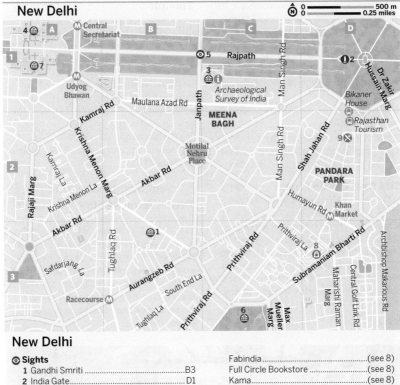

New Delhi

◎ **Sights**
1	Gandhi Smriti	B3
2	India Gate	D1
3	National Museum	C1
4	North Secretariat	A1
5	Rajpath	B1
6	Sikander Lodi's Tomb	C3
7	South Secretariat	A1

◎ **Shopping**
	Anand Stationers	(see 8)
	Anokhi	(see 8)
	Bahrisons	(see 8)

	Fabindia	(see 8)
	Full Circle Bookstore	(see 8)
	Kama	(see 8)
8	Khan Market	D3
	Mehra Bros	(see 8)

⊗ **Eating**
	Chicken Inn	(see 9)
	Gulati	(see 9)
	Havemore	(see 9)
9	Pandara Market	D2
	Pindi	(see 9)
	Sodabottleopenerwala	(see 8)

dough), so pig out and worry about the calories tomorrow.

Karim's
Mughlai $$

(Map p48; Gali Kababyan; mains ₹120-400; ⊙9am-12.30am; Ⓜ Jama Masjid) Just off the lane leading south from Jama Masjid, Karim's has been delighting carnivores since 1913. Expect meaty Mughlai treats such as mutton *burrah* (marinated chops), delicious mutton *mughlai*, and

the breakfast mutton and bread combo *nahari*. There are branches all over town, including at **Nizamuddin West** (168/2 Jha House Basti; dishes ₹120-400; ⊙8am-10pm Tue-Sat; Ⓜ JLN Stadium), but this location is the oldest and best.

Lakhori
Indian $$$

(Map p48; Haveli Dharampura, 2293 Gali Guliyan; tasting menus veg/non-veg ₹1800/2200, other dishes around ₹400-600; ⊙10am-10.30pm; 🛜;

 Jama Masjid) A different experience in the old city, this restored *haveli* is a labour of love by politician Vijay Goel, and it's good to see one of Old Delhi's grand *havelis* finally get some TLC. The restaurant is especially atmospheric in the evening, with tables in the courtyard and Mughal and local recipes on the menu.

Paharganj

Paharganj's restaurants proffer a wide-ranging mishmash of global cuisine ranging from pizza to banana pancakes.

Sita Ram Dewan Chand   Indian $

(2243 Chuna Mandi; half-/full plate ₹30/55; 8am-5pm; M Ramakrishna Ashram Marg) A family-run hole-in-the-wall serving inexpensive portions of just one dish – *chole bhature* (spicy chickpeas), accompanied by delicious, freshly made, puffy, fried bread. It's a traditional breakfast but many people are partial to some at any time of day.

Shimtur   Korean $$

(3rd fl, Navrang Guesthouse, Tooti Galli; meals ₹240-500; 10am-11pm; M Ramakrishna Ashram Marg) It takes determination to find this place: take the turning for the Hotel Rak International, opposite which is the grotty, unsigned Navrang Guesthouse. Follow the stairs to its rooftop and you'll find a small, bamboo-lined, softly lit terrace. The Korean food is fresh and delicious here. Try the *bibimbap* (rice bowl with a mix of vegetables, egg and pickles; ₹240). Beer is available (₹170).

Connaught Place Area

Triveni Terrace Cafe   Cafe $

(Map p48; 205 Tansen Marg, Mandi House; dishes ₹55-220; 10am-7.30pm; M Mandi House) Run by the same folks in charge of the Craft Museum's Cafe Lota, this is a focus for Delhi's arty set, with good-value tasty Indian meals and snacks, such as chilli toast, and nice seating on a leafy terrace overlooking a grassy amphitheatre or inside in a fan-cooled room.

Karim's (p53)

Hotel Saravana Bhavan
South Indian $$

(Map p48; 46 Janpath; dishes ₹95-210, thali ₹210; ⊘8am-11pm; MJanpath) Fabulous dosas, *idlis* (spongy, round, fermented rice cake) and other South Indian delights. This is the biggest and the best of Delhi's Saravana Bhavan branches, and you can see dosas being made in the back. Also offers great South Indian coffee.

Rajdhani
Indian $$$

(Map p48; ☎011-43501200; 1/90 P-Block, Connaught Place; thalis ₹475; ⊘noon-3.30pm & 7-11pm; MRajiv Chowk) Thalis (traditional 'all-you-can-eat' plate meal) fit for a king. Treat yourself with food-of-the-gods vegetarian thalis that encompass a fantastic array of Gujarati and Rajasthani dishes.

New Delhi & Around

New Delhi, with its opulent five-star hotels, malls and upmarket enclaves around Khan Market, Lodi Rd and Mathura Rd, is where to head if you feel like a swanky meal, with a fabulously wide mix of cuisines.

Andhra Pradesh Bhawan Canteen
South Indian $

(1 Ashoka Rd; dishes ₹130-160, thalis ₹110; ⊘8-10.30am, noon-3pm & 7.30-10pm; MPatel Chowk) A hallowed bargain, the canteen at the Andhra Pradesh state house serves cheap and delicious unlimited South Indian thalis to a seemingly unlimited stream of patrons. Come on Sunday for the fabled Hyderabadi biryani (₹200).

Cafe Lota
Modern Indian $$

(Crafts Museum; dishes ₹215-415; ⊘8am-10pm; MPragati Maidan) Bamboo slices the sunlight into flattering stripes at this outdoor restaurant offering delicious cooking with a twist. Sample their take on fish and (sweet potato) chips, or *palak patta chaat* (crispy spinach, potatoes and chickpeas with spiced yoghurt and chutneys), as well as amazing desserts and breakfasts. It's great for kids.

Hauz Khas Village

It's not quite as hip as it was a few years ago, but **Hauz Khas Village** (⊘11am-7pm Mon-Sat; MGreen Park) is still well worth a browse. This arty little enclave has narrow lanes crammed with boutiques selling designer Indian clothing, handicrafts, contemporary ceramics, handmade furniture and old Bollywood movie posters. Shops to seek out include **Claymen** (24 Hauz Khas Village; ⊘hours vary), Maarti, Ogaan and Bodice.

The area gets its name from the **Hauz Khas reservoir** (⊘dawn-dusk) built by Sultan Ala-ud-din Khilji in the 13th century. This 'noble tank' once covered 28 hectares and collected enough monsoon water to last the nearby Siri Fort throughout the dry season. Today it's much smaller, but still a beautiful place to be, thronged by birds and surrounded by parkland. Alongside it are the ruins of 14th-century sultan Feroz Shah's madrasa (Islamic college) and tomb.

Sodabottleopenerwala
Parsi $$

(Map p53; Khan Market; dishes ₹85-900; ⊘noon-11pm; MKhan Market) The name is like a typical trade-based Parsi surname, the place emulates the Iranian cafes of Mumbai, and the food is authentic Persian, including vegetable berry *pulav*, mixed-berry trifle and *lagan nu custer* (Parsi wedding custard).

Bukhara
Indian $$$

(☎011-26112233; ITC Maurya, Sardar Patel Marg; mains ₹800-2600; ⊘12.30-2.45pm & 7-11.45pm)

Tea at the Imperial

Is there anything more genteel than high tea at **the Atrium** (Map p48; Imperial; Janpath; ⊙8am-11.30pm; Ⓜ Janpath)? Sip tea from bone-china cups and pluck dainty sandwiches and cakes from tiered stands, while discussing the latest goings-on in Shimla and Dalhousie. High tea is served in the Atrium from 3pm to 6pm daily (weekday/weekend ₹1200/1500 plus tax).

ARCO IMAGES GMBH/ALAMY ©

One of Delhi's best restaurants, this hotel eatery with low seating and crazy-paving walls serves wow-factor Northwest Frontier–style cuisine, with silken kebabs and its famous Bukhara dhal. Reservations are essential.

Pandara Market   Indian $$$

(Map p53; Pandara Rd; mains ₹400-800; ⊙noon-1am; Ⓜ Khan Market) This is the enduring go-to place for excellent Mughlai and Punjabi food. Prices, standards and atmosphere are high along the strip. For quality food, try **Gulati** (mains ₹385-685; ⊙noon-midnight), **Havemore** (mains ₹375-725; ⊙noon-2am), **Pindi** (mains ₹330-570; ⊙noon-midnight) or **Chicken Inn** (mains ₹380-700; ⊙noon-midnight).

🗙 South Delhi

There are some fantastic independent restaurants tucked into the southern suburbs.

Greenr   Indian $$

(☎7042575339; mains ₹250-375; ⊙11am-7.30pm; 🛜; Ⓜ Hauz Khas) A hip 1st-floor cafe that's spacious and serene, Greenr offers lots of interesting vegan options, such as vegan seitan with ginger coleslaw and teriyaki sauce, plus delicious salads and pasta, and serves up some of Delhi's best coffee, by local roasters Blue Tokai.

Indian Accent   Indian $$$

(☎011-26925151; Manor, 77 Friends Colony (West); dishes ₹725-1425, tasting menu nonveg/veg ₹2995/3095) In the boutique hotel Manor, chef Manish Mehrotra creates inspired modern Indian cuisine, where seasonal ingredients are married in surprising and beautifully creative combinations. The tasting menu is astoundingly good, with wow-factor combinations such as tandoori bacon prawns or paper dosa filled with wild mushroom and water chestnuts. Book well ahead.

Swagath   South Indian $$$

(14 Defence Colony Market; dishes ₹365-1300; ⊙11.30am-11.30pm; Ⓜ Lajpat Nagar) Famous for its top-notch Mangalorean seafood, such as pomfret, prawns or lobster, this busy multilevel restaurant is always heaving and also has regular South and North Indian dishes.

🍷 DRINKING & NIGHTLIFE

Delhi's ever-growing cafe scene has given rise to some cafes with artisanal coffee beans, coffee menus and Turkish pastries. The city's bar and live-music choices are also burgeoning, though licences rarely extend later than 12.30am. For the latest places to go at night, check the hip and informative Little Black Book (littleblackbookdelhi.com) or Brown Paper Bag (bpbweekend.com/delhi). For gigs, check Wild City (thewildcity.com).

🚇 Connaught Place Area

Unplugged   Bar

(Map p48; ☎011-33107701; 23 L-Block, Connaught Place; ⊗noon-midnight; Ⓜ Rajiv Chowk) There's nowhere else like this in Connaught Place. You could forget you were in CP, in fact, with the big garden, wrought-iron chairs and tables, and swing seats, all under the shade of a mother of a banyan tree hung with basket-weave lanterns. In the evenings there are regular live gigs, anything from alt-rock to electro-fusion. A Kingfisher costs ₹100.

1911   Bar

(Map p48; Imperial Hotel, Janpath; ⊗11am-12.45am; Ⓜ Janpath) The Imperial, built in the 1930s, resonates with bygone splendour. This bar is a more recent addition, but still riffs on the Raj. Here you can sip the perfect cocktail (around ₹900) amid designer-clad clientele, against a backdrop of faded photos and murals of maharajas.

🚇 South Delhi

Blue Tokai   Cafe

(Khasra 258, Lane 3 West End Marg, Saidulajab; ⊗9am-8.30pm; Ⓜ Saket) In an unlikely, tiny lane behind the fake Dilli Haat shopping centre ('Delhi Haat'), Blue Tokai produces and grinds its own amazing coffee; you can get serious caffeine hits such as nitrogen-infused cold brew – there's even a tasting menu. Snacks include 'no leaf salad with pumpkin'.

Ek Bar   Bar

(D17, 1st fl, Defence Colony; ⊗noon-3.30pm & 6pm-12.30am; Ⓜ Lajpat Nagar) On the upper floors of a building in the exclusive area of the Defence Colony, this place has stylish, kooky decor in deep, earth-jewel colours, serious mixology (drinks ₹250 to ₹800) showcasing Indian flavours (how about a gin and tonic with turmeric?), modern Indian bar snacks, nightly DJs, and a see-and-be-seen crowd.

INDIAPICTURE/ALAMY ©

Bukhara

Piano Man Jazz Club   Club

(http://thepianoman.in; B 6 Commercial Complex, Safdarjung Enclave; ⊘noon-3pm & 7.30pm-12.30am) The real thing, this popular, proper-muso, atmospheric place is a dimly lit speakeasy with some excellent live jazz performances.

Bandstand   Bar

(Aurobindo Market; ⊘noon-1am; ; Ⓜ Green Park) This popular place is near Hauz Khas and has a great glass-covered terrace with views over the tombs of Green Park. It's also one of Delhi's live-music venues, with gigs from 9pm on Thursday and Sunday.

ℹ INFORMATION

DANGERS & ANNOYANCES

Delhi has, unfortunately, a deserved repu- tation as being unsafe for women. However, you can take some precautions. See Women Travellers (p302).

TOUTS

Taxi-wallahs at the airport and around tourist areas frequently act as touts for hotels, claiming that the hotel you want to go to is full, poor value, dangerous or closed, or that there are riots in Delhi. Any such story is a ruse to steer you to a hotel where they will get a commission. Insist on being taken to where you want to go – it may help to make a show of writing down the registration plate number and/or phoning the autorickshaw/taxi helpline. Men who approach you at Connaught Place run similar scams to direct you to shops and tourist agents.

TRAIN STATION HASSLE

Touts at New Delhi station try to steer travellers away from the legitimate International Tourist Bureau (ticket office) and into private travel agencies where they earn a commission. They often tell people that their tickets are invalid, there's a problem with the trains, or say you're not allowed on the platform. They then 'assist' in booking expensive taxis or 3rd-class tickets passed off as something else. You're particularly vulnerable when arriving tired at night. As a rule of thumb: don't believe anyone who approach- es you trying to tell you anything at the train station, even if they're wearing a uniform or have an official-looking pass.

A bar in Connaught Place

FAKE TOURIST OFFICES

Many Delhi travel agencies claim to be tourist offices, even branding themselves with official-looking logos. There is only one India Tourism Delhi office; ask here for a list of recommended travel agents, if you need one. Be wary of booking a multistop trip out of Delhi: travellers are often hit for extra charges, or find out they've paid over the odds.

TOURIST INFORMATION

India Tourism Delhi (Government of India; Map p48; ☑011-23320005, 011-23320008; www. incredibleindia.org; 88 Janpath; ☺9am-6pm Mon-Fri, to 2pm Sat; ⓂJanpath) This is the only official India Tourism office, apart from the booth at the airport. Ignore touts who (falsely) claim to be associated with this. It's a useful source of advice on Delhi, getting out of Delhi, and visiting surrounding states. Come here to report tourism-related complaints.

 GETTING THERE & AWAY

AIR

Indira Gandhi International Airport

(☑01243376000; www.newdelhiairport.in) is about 14km southwest of the centre. International and domestic flights use gleaming Terminal 3. Terminal 1 is reserved for low-cost carriers. Free shuttle buses (present your boarding pass and onward ticket) run between the two terminals every 20 minutes. To be safe, allow at least three hours for transfers (and from November to January, when fog often disrupts flight schedules, it's wise to allow a day between connecting flights).

The arrivals hall at Terminal 3 has 24-hour foreign exchange, ATMs and tourist information.

You'll need to show your boarding pass to enter the terminal. At check-in, be sure to collect tags for all your carry-on bags and ensure these are stamped as you go through security.

BUS

Buses are a useful option to some destinations and if the trains are booked up.

 Shopping in Shahpur Jat

A 1km rickshaw ride northeast from Hauz Khas metro, the urban village of Shahpur Jat is one of the best places in Delhi to buy upmarket independent designer threads. Stores to seek out include **Nimai** (☑011-64300113; 416 Shahpur Jat Village; ☺11am-7.30pm; ⓂHauz Khas) for one-of-a-kind costume jewellery and **NeedleDust** (www.needledust.com; 40B, ground fl, Shahpur Jat; ☺10.30am-7.30pm Mon-Sat, 11am-6.30pm Sun; ⓂHauz Khas) for embroidered leather shoes, and there are some choice independent restaurants, such as artsy Bihari **Potbelly** (116C Shahpur Jat Village; mains ₹250-420, thalis ₹250; ☺12.30-11pm; ⓂHauz Khas), and vegan organic Greenr (p56). For superb fine tea tastings head to **Anandini Tea Room** (12A, DDA Flats; ☺11am-7pm; ⓂHauz Khas).

Most state-run services leave from **Kashmere Gate Inter State Bus Terminal** (ISBT; ☑011-23860290; ⓂKashmere Gate) in Old Delhi. Destinations include Dharamsala (₹1250, 20 hours, four buses daily), Jaipur (₹196 to ₹655, five hours, hourly), Manali (₹651 to ₹1285, 15 hours, 6.40am, 7.45am, 11.30am, about hourly 3.45pm to 10pm) and Shimla (₹415 to ₹915, 10 hours, about hourly 5am to 11.40pm). Some buses to destinations in Uttar Pradesh and Rajasthan leave from the **Sarai Kale Khan Inter State Bus Terminal** (ISBT) near Nizamuddin train station.

You can avoid hassles by paying a little more for private deluxe buses that leave from locations in central Delhi – enquire at travel agencies or your hotel for details. You can also book tickets or check information on **Cleartrip** (www.cleartrip.com) or **Make My Trip** (www. makemytrip.com).

Himachal Pradesh Tourism Development Corporation (HPTDC; Map p48; http://hptdc. gov.in; Chanderlok Building, 36 Janpath;

Ⓜ Janpath) runs comfortable Volvo AC buses from **Himachal Bhawan** (Map p48; ☏ 011-23716689; Sikandra Rd; Ⓜ Mandi House) to Manali (₹1300, nine hours) and Shimla (₹900, 10 hours) at 6.30pm.

Rajasthan Tourism (Map p53; ☏ 011-23381884; www.rtdc.com; Bikaner House, Pandara Rd; Ⓜ Khan Market) runs deluxe buses to Jaipur (non-AC/super deluxe/Volvo ₹400/625/900, six hours) from **Bikaner House** (Map p53; ☏ 011-23383469; Pandara Rd; Ⓜ Khan Market), near India Gate, every one to two hours. Women receive a discount of 30%.

TRAIN

There are three main stations in Delhi – (Old) Delhi train station (aka Delhi Junction) in Old Delhi, New Delhi train station near Paharganj, and Nizamuddin train station, south of Sunder Nagar. Make sure you know which station your train is leaving from.

The best ticketing option for foreign travellers is the helpful **International Tourist Bureau** (ITB; Map p48; ☏ 011-23405156; 1st fl, New Delhi Train Station; ⏰ 24hr) at New Delhi station. Its entrance is before you go onto platform 1 (on the Paharganj side of the station), via a staircase just to the right of the entrance to the platform. Do not believe *anyone* who tells you it has shifted, closed or burnt down – this is a scam to divert you elsewhere. The ITB is a large room with about 10 or more computer terminals – don't be fooled by other 'official' offices.

When making reservations here, you can pay in cash (rupees) only. Bring your passport. When you arrive, take a ticket from the machine that gives you a place in the queue. Then complete a reservation form – ask at the information counter to check availability. You can then wait to complete and pay for your booking at the relevant counter. This is the best place to get last-minute bookings for quota seats to popular destinations, but come prepared to queue.

Major Trains from Delhi

Destination	Train No & Name	Fare (₹)	Duration (hr)	Departures
Agra	12280 Taj Exp	100/370 (A)	3	7am NZM
	12002 Bhopal Shatabdi	515/1010 (B)	2	6am NDLS
Goa (Madgaon)	12780 Goa Express	170/540/740 (D)	27	3pm NZM
Jaipur	12916 Ashram Exp	235/590/825 (D)	5	3.20pm DLI
	12015 Ajmer Shatabdi	355/740 (B)	4½	6.05am NDLS
Kalka (for Shimla)	12011 Kalka Shatabdi	640/1295 (B)	4	7.40am NDLS
Mumbai	12952 Mumbai Rajdhani	2085/2870/4755 (C)	16	4.45pm NDLS
Varanasi	12560 Shivganga Exp	415/1100/1565 (D)	12½	6.55pm NDLS

Train stations: NDLS – New Delhi; DLI – Old Delhi; NZM – Hazrat Nizamuddin

Fares: (A) 2nd class/chair car; (B) chair car/1st-class AC; (C) 3AC/2AC/1st-class AC; (D) sleeper/3AC/2AC

All trains listed above depart daily.

SILENTGUNMAN/SHUTTERSTOCK ©

Cycle-Rickshaws

GETTING AROUND

TO/FROM THE AIRPORT

Organised city transport runs to/from Terminal 3; a free shuttle bus runs every 20 minutes between Terminal 3 and Terminal 1.

Pre-arranged pick-ups Hotels offer airport pick-ups, but these are usually more expensive than just getting a taxi – however, it may be worth it to ease your arrival.

Metro The Airport Express line (www.delhi metrorail.com) runs every 10 to 15 minutes from 5.15am to 11.40pm, taking around 20 minutes from Terminal 3 to New Delhi train station (₹60/50 from the international/domestic terminal). It's usually empty because it's a separate line from the rest of the metro.

Bus Air-conditioned buses run from outside Terminal 3 to Kashmere Gate ISBT every 10 minutes, via the Red Fort, New Delhi Station Gate 2, Connaught Place, Parliament St and Ashoka Rd.

Taxi In front of the arrivals buildings at Terminal 3 and Terminal 1, **Delhi Traffic Police Prepaid**

Taxi counters (⌨complaints 56767, women's helpline 1091; www.delhitrafficpolice.nic.in) offer fixed-price taxi services. You'll pay about ₹350 to New or Old Delhi, and ₹450 to the southern suburbs, in a battered old black-and-yellow taxi. There's a 25% surcharge between 11pm and 5am. Some travellers have reported difficulty in persuading drivers to go to their intended hotel. Insist on your chosen destination and only surrender your voucher when you arrive where you want.

You can also book a prepaid taxi at the **Mega-cabs counter** (⌨011-41414141; www.megacabs.com) at both airport terminals. It costs ₹600 to ₹700 to the centre, but you get a cleaner car with air-con.

METRO

Delhi's **metro** (⌨011-23417910; www.delhimetro rail.com) is fast and efficient, with signs and arrival/departure announcements in Hindi and English. Trains run from around 6am to 11pm and the first carriage in the direction of travel is reserved for women only. Trains can get insanely busy at peak commuting times (around 9am to 10am and 5pm to 6pm) – avoid travelling with luggage during rush hour if at all possible.

Tokens (₹8 to ₹50) are sold at metro stations. There are also one-/three-day 'tourist cards' (₹150/300, ₹50 deposit, ₹30 refundable when you return it) for unlimited short-distance travel.

Because of security concerns, all bags are X-rayed and passengers must pass through an airport-style scanner.

TAXI & AUTORICKSHAW

Local taxis (recognisable by their black and yellow livery) and autorickshaws have meters but these are effectively ornamental as most drivers refuse to use them.

Delhi Traffic Police run a network of prepaid autorickshaw booths where you can pay a fixed fare, including at the New Delhi, Old Delhi and Nizamuddin train stations (all 24-hour), outside the **India Tourism Delhi office** (Map p48; 88 Janpath; ☺11am-8.30pm) and at **Central Park** (Map p48), Connaught Place. Elsewhere, you'll need to negotiate a fare before you set off. Fares are invariably elevated, especially for foreigners,

so haggle hard. If the fare sounds too outrageous, find another autorickshaw. Fares from Connaught Place should be around ₹30 to Paharganj, ₹60 to the Red Fort, ₹70 to Humayun's Tomb and ₹100 to Hauz Khas. However, it will be a struggle to get these prices. To report overcharging, harassment, or other problems take the licence number and call the Auto Complaint Line on ☏011-42400400/25844444.

Taxis typically charge twice the autorickshaw fare. From 11pm to 5am there's a 25% surcharge for both autorickshaws and taxis.

Kumar Tourist Taxi Service (Map p48; ☏011-23415930; www.kumarindiatours.com; 14/1 K-Block, Connaught Place; ☺9am-9pm) is a reliable company; a day of Delhi sightseeing costs from ₹2000 (an eight hour and 80km limit applies).

Metropole Tourist Service (☏011-24310313; www.metrovista.co.in; 224 Defence Colony Flyover Market; ☺7am-7pm) is another reliable, and long-running, taxi service, and good value, charging ₹1500 for up to 80km for one day's car-and-driver hire, plus ₹100/15 per hour/kilometre thereafter.

Where to Stay

Delhi has lively backpacker hostels, solid budget and midrange hotels, charmingly boutiquey guesthouses, and colonial-style and 21st-century luxury – all at very good prices by international standards.

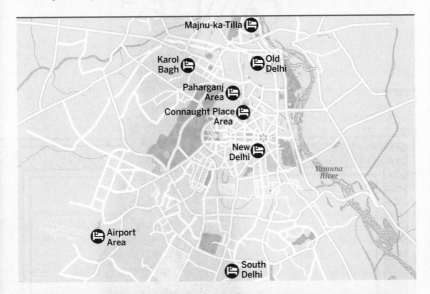

Neighbourhood	Atmosphere
Old Delhi	Has atmosphere in spades, and a growing number of varied accommodation choices.
Paharganj Area	Hectic traveller hub, convenient for New Delhi station and the Airport Express metro line.
Majnu-ka-Tilla	Tibetan enclave; more relaxed alternative to Paharganj.
Karol Bagh	Middle-class shopping district; most hotels served by agencies and touts are here.
Connaught Place Area	Unbeatably central, and close to shops, bars and restaurants, but busy and hassly.
New Delhi	Tree-lined boulevards, grand Raj-era buildings, upscale hotels, some boutique guesthouses.
South Delhi	Has some good guesthouses and hostels, especially in the attractive Hauz Khas area.
Airport Area	Aerocity is a convenient area of big hotels, only 4km from the airport.

AGRA &
TAJ MAHAL

In this Chapter
Taj Mahal 68
Fatehpur Sikri 76
Agra Fort 80
Sights 84
Eating 84

Agra & Taj Mahal at a Glance...

The Taj Mahal rises from Agra's haze as though from a dream. You've seen it in pictures, but experiencing it in person, you'll understand that it's not just a famous monument, but a love poem composed of stone.

But Agra is no one-sight town. For 130 years, this was the centre of India's great Mughal empire, and its legacy lives on in beautiful artwork, mouth-watering cuisine and magnificent architecture. The Taj is one of three places here with Unesco World Heritage status: the immense Agra Fort and the Fatehpur Sikri palace complex complete a superb trio of top-draw sights.

Agra in Two Days

Try to be at the **Taj Mahal** (p68) for dawn, a magical time. Later, explore **Agra Fort** (p80) and indulge with dinner at **Pinch of Spice** (p84).

On day two take a trip out to **Fatehpur Sikri** (p76), return for a second visit to the Taj, followed by dinner at **Esphahan** (p84).

Agra in Four Days

On day three enjoy a different visit view of the Taj Mahal from the exquisitely carved 'Baby Taj', the **Itimad-ud-Daulah** (p84), and dive into a local eating experience at **Mama Chicken** (p84).

On day four head 10km out of town to see **Akbar's Mausoleum** (p84), and return for a final visit to the Taj itself.

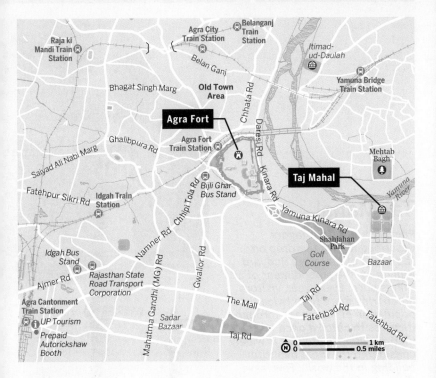

Arriving in Agra

Agra Cantonment station The main train station, west of the centre; trains to/from Delhi, Mumbai and elsewhere.

Agra Fort station Near the fort; for most trains to/from Rajasthan and Varanasi.

ISBT Bus Stand Luxury buses to/from Delhi and Varanasi.

Idgah Bus Stand Buses to/from Delhi, Jaipur, Fatehpur Sikri.

Sleeping

The main place for budget accommodation is the bustling area of Taj Ganj, immediately south of the Taj, while there's a high concentration of midrange hotels further south, along and near Fatehabad Rd. Sadar Bazaar, an area boasting good-quality restaurants, offers another option. Top-end places are scattered around all these areas.

Taj Mahal

Poet Rabindranath Tagore described it as 'a teardrop on the cheek of eternity'; Rudyard Kipling as 'the embodiment of all things pure'. Every year, visitors numbering more than twice the population of Agra pass through its gates to catch a once-in-a-lifetime glimpse of what is widely considered the most beautiful building in the world. Few leave disappointed.

Great For...

ℹ Need to Know

The Taj Mahal is open from dawn till dusk Saturday through to Thursday. Admission costs ₹40/1000 (Indian/foreigner), video ₹25.

★ Top Tip

Sunrise is a magical (and the most comfortable) time to visit, with far fewer crowds.

The Taj was built by the Mughal emperor Shah Jahan as a memorial for his third wife, Mumtaz Mahal, who died giving birth to their 14th child in 1631. The death of Mumtaz left the emperor so heartbroken that his hair is said to have turned grey virtually overnight. Construction of the Taj began the following year. Although the main building is thought to have been built in eight years, the whole complex was not completed until 1653.

Not long after it was finished Shah Jahan was overthrown by his son Aurangzeb and imprisoned in Agra Fort, where for the rest of his days he could only gaze out at his creation through a window. Following his death in 1666, Shah Jahan was buried here alongside his beloved Mumtaz.

In total, some 20,000 people from India and Central Asia worked on the building. Specialists were brought in from as far away as Europe to produce the exquisite marble screens and pietra dura (marble inlay work) made with thousands of semi-precious stones.

Entry

Note: the Taj is closed every Friday to anyone not attending prayers at the mosque.

The Taj can be accessed through the west, south and east gates. Tour groups tend to enter through the east and west gates. Independent travellers tend to use the south gate, which is nearest to Taj Ganj, the main area for budget accommodation, and generally has shorter queues than the west gate. The east gate has

Taj Mahal interior

the shortest queues of the lot, but this is because the ticket office is inconveniently located a 1km walk away at Shilpgram, a dire, government-run tourist centre. There are separate queues for men and women at all three gates. Once you have your ticket, foreigners can skip ahead of the lines of Indians waiting to get in – one perk of their pricey entry fee.

Cameras and videos are permitted but you can't take photographs inside the mausoleum itself, and the areas in which you can take videos are quite limited. Tripods are banned.

✕ Take a Break
Café Coffee Day (www.cafecoffeeday.com; 21/101 Taj East Gate; ⊙6am-8pm) **provides air-con and proper coffee just outside the Taj's East Gate.**

GRANT FAINT/GETTY IMAGES ©

Remember to retrieve your free 500mL bottle of water and shoe covers (included in Taj ticket price). If you keep your ticket you get small entry-fee discounts when visiting Agra Fort, Fatehpur Sikri, Akbar's Tomb or the Itimad-ud-Daulah on the same day. You can also pick up an audio guide (₹120). Bags much bigger than a money pouch are not allowed inside; free bag storage is available at the west gate. Any food or tobacco will be confiscated when you go through security.

From the south gate, entry to the inner compound is through a very impressive 30m red-sandstone gateway on the south side of the forecourt, which is inscribed with verses from the Quran.

Rickshaw Rumble

When taking an auto- or cycle-rickshaw to the Taj, make sure you're clear which gate you want to go to when negotiating the price. Otherwise, almost without fail, riders will take you to the roundabout at the south end of Shahjahan Gardens Rd – where expensive tongas (horse-drawn carriages) or camels wait to take tour groups to the west gate – and claim that's where they thought you meant. Only nonpolluting autos can go within a 500m radius of the Taj because of pollution rules, but they can get a lot closer than this.

Inside the Grounds

The ornamental gardens are set out along classical Mughal *charbagh* (formal Persian garden) lines – a square quartered by watercourses, with an ornamental marble plinth at its centre. When the fountains are not flowing, the Taj is beautifully reflected in the water.

☑ Don't Miss

The pietra dura (marble inlay work) inside the pishtaqs (large arched recesses) on the outer walls, and in the central chamber. Bring a torch for the latter.

The Taj Mahal itself stands on a raised marble platform at the northern end of the ornamental gardens, with its back to the Yamuna River. Its raised position means that the backdrop is only sky – a master stroke of design. Purely decorative 40m-high white minarets grace each corner of the platform. After more than three centuries they are not quite perpendicular, but they may have been designed to lean slightly outwards so that in the event of an earthquake they would fall away from the precious Taj. The red-sandstone mosque to the west is an important gathering place for Agra's Muslims. The identical building to the east, the jawab, was built for symmetry.

The central Taj structure is made of semitranslucent white marble, carved with flowers and inlaid with thousands of semiprecious stones in beautiful patterns. A perfect exercise in symmetry, the four identical faces of the Taj feature impressive vaulted arches embellished with pietra-dura scrollwork and quotations from the Quran in a style of calligraphy using inlaid jasper. The whole structure is topped off by four small domes surrounding the famous bulbous central dome.

Directly below the main dome is the Cenotaph of Mumtaz Mahal, an elaborate false tomb surrounded by an exquisite perforated marble screen inlaid with dozens of different types of semiprecious stones. Beside it, offsetting the symmetry of the Taj, is the Cenotaph of Shah Jahan, who was interred here with little ceremony by his usurping son Aurangzeb in 1666. Light is admitted into the central chamber by finely cut marble screens. The real tombs of Mumtaz Mahal and Shah Jahan are in a basement room below the main chamber and cannot be viewed.

Taj Museum

Within the Taj complex, on the western side of the gardens, is the small but excellent **Taj Museum** (☉9am-5pm Sat-Thu) **FREE**, housing a number of original Mughal miniature paintings, including a pair of 17th-century ivory portraits of Emperor Shah Jahan and his beloved wife Mumtaz Mahal. It also has some very well-preserved gold and silver coins dating from the same period, plus architectural drawings of the Taj and some nifty celadon plates, said to split into pieces or change colour if the food served on them contains poison.

Spa Mahal

After years of research, Indian and American scientists have identified the culprits behind the ongoing discolouration of the mausoleum, which was originally gleaming

Yamuna River

white. Agra's dust and air pollution have tarnished the surface of the Taj over the years, giving it a brownish hue. More recently, a greenish tint has begun to appear, due to the excrement of millions of insects that breed in the polluted Yamuna River and are drawn to the Taj's white-ish walls.

In an effort to restore the marble to some of its earlier glory, a mud-pack cleanse has been developed – based on a traditional recipe used by Indian women to restore their own facial radiance. The latest full treatment was scheduled to last from April 2017 to March 2018, using a newly improved formula that experts say won't mar the Taj's surface,

as previous applications may have done. If you visit during cleaning time, you'll find this wonder of the world covered by scaffolding. And of course, things may not go according to schedule...so if seeing the Taj in its full glory is a top priority, check that the work is complete before you book your flights.

★ Top Taj Viewpoints

- Inside the Taj grounds
- From Mehtab Bagh
- From the south bank of the Yamuna
- From a Taj Ganj rooftop cafe
- From Agra Fort

Taj Mahal

TIMELINE

1631 Emperor Shah Jahan's beloved third wife, Mumtaz Mahal, dies in Buhanpur while giving birth to their 14th child. Her body is initially interred in Buhanpur itself, where Shah Jahan is fighting a military campaign, but is later moved, in a golden casket, to a small building on the banks of the Yamuna River in Agra.

1632 Construction of a permanent mausoleum for Mumtaz Mahal begins.

1633 Mumtaz Mahal is interred in her final resting place, an underground tomb beneath a marble plinth, on top of which the Taj Mahal will be built.

1640 The white-marble mausoleum is completed.

1653 The rest of the Taj Mahal complex is completed.

1658 Emperor Shah Jahan is overthrown by his son Aurangzeb and imprisoned in Agra Fort.

1666 Shah Jahan dies. His body is transported along the Yamuna River and buried underneath the Taj, alongside the tomb of his wife.

1908 Repeatedly damaged and looted after the fall of the Mughal empire, the Taj receives some long-overdue attention as part of a major restoration project ordered by British viceroy Lord Curzon.

1983 The Taj is awarded Unesco World Heritage Site status.

2002 Having been discoloured by pollution in more recent years, the Taj is spruced up with an ancient recipe known as multani mitti – a blend of soil, cereal, milk and lime once used by Indian women to beautify their skin.

Today More than three million tourists visit the Taj Mahal each year. That's more than twice the current population of Agra.

ARIS ABDULLAH/SHUTTERSTOCK ©

GO BAREFOOT

Help the environment by entering the mausoleum barefoot instead of using the free disposable shoe covers.

Pishtaqs
These huge arched recesses are set into each side of the Taj. They provide depth to the building while their central, latticed marble screens allow patterned light to illuminate the inside of the mausoleum.

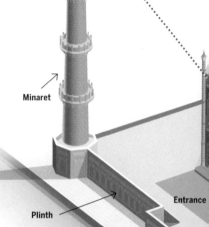

Minaret

Entrance

Plinth

Marble Relief Work
Flowering plants, thought to be representations of paradise, are a common theme among the beautifully decorative panels carved onto the white marble.

FABIOIM/SHUTTERSTOCK ©

LIGHT THE WAY

Bring a small torch into the mausoleum to fully appreciate the translucency of the white marble and semiprecious stones.

Filigree Screen
This stunning screen was carved out of a single piece of marble. It surrounds both cenotaphs, allowing patterned light to fall onto them through its intricately carved *jali* (latticework).

Central Dome
The Taj's famous central dome, topped by a brass finial, represents the vault of heaven, a stark contrast to the material world, which is represented by the square shape of the main structure.

Yamuna River

NORTH →

Pietra Dura
It's believed that 35 different precious and semi-precious stones were used to create the exquisite pietra dura (marble inlay work) found on the inside and outside of the mausoleum walls. Again, floral designs are common.

Calligraphy
The strips of calligraphy surrounding each of the four pishtaqs get larger as they get higher, giving the impression of uniform size when viewed from the ground. There's also calligraphy inside the mausoleum, including on Mumtaz Mahal's cenotaph.

Cenotaphs
The cenotaphs of Mumtaz Mahal and Shah Jahan, decorated with pietra dura inlay work, are actually fake tombs. The real ones are located in an underground vault closed to the public.

Fatehpur Sikri

This Indo-Islamic architectural masterpiece, 40km west of Agra, was capital of the Mughal empire between 1572 and 1585. It was abandoned shortly after the 1605 death of its creator, Emperor Akbar.

Great For...

☑ Don't Miss

The wonderfully intricate carving on the little Rumi Sultana palace.

Akbar built his capital near the village of Sikri because the Sufi saint Shaikh Salim Chishti there had correctly predicted the birth of an heir to the Mughal throne. The imperial complex included a stunning mosque, still in use today, and three palaces, one for each of Akbar's favourite wives – one believed to have been a Hindu, one a Muslim and one a Christian. Water shortages were apparently the reason for its early abandonment.

Palaces & Pavilions

Effectively an open-air courtroom, the Diwan-i-Am (Hall of Public Audiences) is where Akbar presided over trials. If legends can be believed, justice was dealt swiftly, with convicted criminals trampled to death on the spot by elephants.

Jama Masjid

Agra

Fatehpur Sikri

❶ Need to Know

Indian/foreigner ₹40/510, video ₹25;
⊙dawn-dusk

✕ Take a Break

You can get a decent, inexpensive meal at Hotel Goverdhan, about 200m east of the bus stand.

> ★ **Top Tip**
> The red-sandstone palace walls are at their most atmospheric and photogenic near sunset.

wife, said to be his favourite. It blends traditional Indian columns, Islamic cupolas and turquoise-blue Persian roof tiles.

Jama Masjid

This beautiful, immense mosque was completed in 1571 and contains elements of Persian and Indian design. Inside is the stunning white marble tomb of Shaikh Salim Cishti, completed in 1581, where women hoping to have children come to tie a thread to the *jalis* (carved lattice screens). The tomb is entered through an original door made of ebony. Inside are brightly coloured flower murals, while the sandalwood canopy is decorated with mother-of-pearl shell, and the marble *jalis* are among the finest in India.

The Pachisi Courtyard was designed for playing an ancestor to the game of ludo – the large, cross-shaped game board is visible in the middle. At the courtyard's north end, the Diwan-i-Khas (Hall of Private Audiences) is centred on a magnificently carved central column, which flares to create a flat-topped plinth linked to the room's corners by narrow stone bridges. From this plinth Akbar is believed to have debated with scholars and ministers who stood at the ends of the bridges.

The elegant five-storey Panch Mahal pavilion gives entrance to the imperial harem complex, where the Palace of the Christian Wife is believed to have been used by Akbar's Goan wife Mariam, who gave birth to Jehangir here in 1569. The Palace of Jodh Bai, set around an enormous courtyard, was the home of Akbar's Hindu

Getting to Fatehpur Sikri

Buses to Fatehpur Sikri (₹40, one hour) leave Agra's Idgah Bus Stand every 30 minutes, 6am to 6.30pm, returning every half-hour until 6.30pm.

Shuttle buses (₹10) run from the Gulistan Tourist Complex to Fatehpur Sikri's Diwan-i-Am entrance.

Fatehpur Sikri

A WALKING TOUR OF FATEHPUR SIKRI

You can enter this fortified ancient city from two entrances, but the northeast entrance at Diwan-i-Am (Hall of Public Audiences) offers the most logical approach to this remarkable Unesco World Heritage site. This large courtyard (now a garden) is where Emperor Akbar presided over the trials of accused criminals. Once through the ticket gate, you are in the northern end of the ❶ **Pachisi Courtyard**. The first building you see is ❷ **Diwan-i-Khas** (Hall of Private Audiences), the interior of which is dominated by a magnificently carved central stone column. Pitch south and enter ❸ **Rumi Sultana**, a small but elegant palace built for Akbar's Turkish Muslim wife. It's hard to miss the ❹ **Ornamental Pool** nearby – its southwest corner provides Fatehpur Sikri's most photogenic angle, perfectly framing its most striking building, the five-storey Panch Mahal, one of the gateways to the Imperial Harem Complex, where the ❺ **Lower Haramsara** once housed more than 200 female servants. Wander around the Palace of Jodh Bai and take notice of the towering ode to an elephant, the 21m-high ❻ **Hiran Minar**, in the distance to the northwest. Leave the palaces and pavilions area via Shahi Darwaza (King's Gate), which spills into India's second-largest mosque courtyard at ❼ **Jama Masjid**. Inside this immense and gorgeous mosque is the sacred ❽ **Tomb of Shaikh Salim Chishti**. Exit through the spectacular ❾ **Buland Darwaza** (Victory Gate), one of the world's most magnificent gateways.

Buland Darwaza

Most tours end with an exit through Jama Masjid's Victory Gate. Walk out and take a look behind you: Behold! The magnificent 15-storey sandstone gate, 54m high, is a menacing monolith to Akbar's reign.

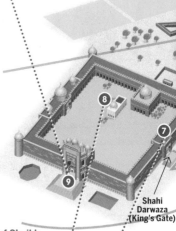

Shahi Darwaza (King's Gate)

Tomb of Shaikh Salim Chishti

Each knot in the strings tied to the 56 carved white marble designs of the interior walls of Shaikh Salim Chishti's tomb represents one wish of a maximum three.

Jama Masjid

The elaborate marble inlay work at the Badshahi Gate and throughout the Jama Masjid complex is said to have inspired similar work 82 years later at the Taj Mahal in Agra.

Hiran Minar

This bizarre, seldom-visited tower off the north-west corner of Fatehpur Sikri is decorated with hundreds of stone representations of elephant tusks. It is said to be the place where Minar, Akbar's favourite execution elephant, died.

Pachisi Courtyard

Under your feet just past Rumi Sultana is the Pachisi Courtyard where Akbar is said to have played the game *pachisi* (an ancient version of ludo) using slave girls in colourful dress as pieces.

Diwan-i-Khas

Emperor Akbar modified the central stone column inside Diwan-i-Khas to call attention to a new religion he called Din-i-Ilahi (God is One). The intricately carved column features a fusion of Hindu, Muslim, Christian and Buddhist imagery.

Panch Mahal

Diwan-i-Am (Hall of Public Audiences)

Rumi Sultana

Don't miss the headless creatures carved into Rumi Sultana's palace interiors: a lion, deer, an eagle and a few peacocks were beheaded by jewel thieves who swiped the precious jewels that originally formed their heads.

Ornamental Pool

Tansen, said to be the most gifted Indian vocalist of all time and one of Akbar's treasured nine *Navaratnas* (Gems), would be showered with coins during performances from the central platform of the Ornamental Pool.

Lower Haramsara

Akbar reportedly kept more than 5000 concubines, but the 200 or so female servants housed in the Lower Haramsara were strictly business. Knots were tied to these sandstone rings to support partitions between their individual quarters.

Agra Fort

With the Taj Mahal overshadowing it, one can easily forget that Agra has one of the finest Mughal forts in India. Walking through courtyard after courtyard of this palatial red-sandstone and marble fortress, your amazement grows as the scale of what was built here begins to sink in.

Great For...

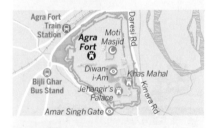

ⓘ Need to Know

Agra Fort is open dawn til dusk. Admission costs ₹40/550 (Indian/foreigner), and video ₹25.

★ Top Tip
If the Shish Mahal is still closed, you can glimpse its sparkling mirrors through cracks in the doors.

SMARTA/SHUTTERSTOCK ©

The fort's construction along the bank of the Yamuna River was begun by Emperor Akbar in 1565. Further additions were made, particularly by his grandson Shah Jahan, using his favourite building material – white marble. The fort was built primarily as a military structure, but Shah Jahan transformed it into a palace, and later it became his gilded prison for eight years after his son Aurangzeb seized power in 1658.

The ear-shaped fort's colossal double walls rise more than 20m in height and measure 2.5km in circumference. The Yamuna River originally flowed along the straight eastern edge of the fort, and the emperors had their own bathing ghats here. The fort contains a maze of buildings, forming a city within a city, including vast underground sections, though many structures were destroyed over the years by Nadir Shah, the Marathas, the Jats and finally the British, who used the fort as a garrison. Even today, much of the fort is used by the military and off-limits to the general public.

The Amar Singh Gate at the south end is the sole entry point to the fort these days. Its dog-leg design was meant to confuse attackers who made it past the first line of defence – the crocodile-infested moat.

A path leads straight up to the large Moti Masjid (Pearl Mosque), which is closed to the public. To your right, just before the Moti Masjid, is the large, open Diwan-i-Am (Hall of Public Audiences),

Diwan-i-Am

which was used by Shah Jahan for domestic government business.

A tiny staircase just to the left of the Diwan-i-Am's throne leads up to a large courtyard. To your left is the tiny but exquisite Nagina Masjid (Gem Mosque), built in 1635 by Shah Jahan for the ladies of the court.

On the far side of the large courtyard, along the fort's eastern wall, is the Diwan-i-Khas (Hall of Private Audiences), which was reserved for important dignitaries or foreign representatives. The hall once housed Shah Jahan's legendary Peacock Throne, which was inset with precious stones, including the famous Koh-i-noor diamond. Overlooking the river and the distant Taj Mahal is the Takhti-i-Jehangir, a huge slab of black rock that once supported a throne made for Akbar's son Jehangir when he was Prince Salim.

Off to your right from here (as you face the river) is the Shish Mahal (Mirror Palace), with walls inlaid with tiny mirrors. At the time of research it had been closed for some time due to restoration.

Further along the eastern edge of the fort you'll find Musamman Burj and the Khas Mahal, the wonderful white-marble octagonal tower and palace where Shah Jahan was imprisoned for eight years until his death in 1666, and from where he could gaze out at the Taj Mahal, the tomb of his wife. The now closed Mina Masjid, set back slightly from the eastern edge, was his private mosque.

The large courtyard here is the Anguri Bagh, a garden that has been brought back to life in recent years. An innocuous-looking entrance – now locked – leads down stairs into a two-storey labyrinth of underground rooms and passageways where Akbar kept his 500-strong harem.

Continuing south, the huge red-sandstone Jehangir's Palace was probably built by Akbar for Jehangir. It blends Indian and Central Asian architectural styles, a reminder of the Mughals' Afghani cultural roots. From here you can return to the main path back to Amar Singh Gate.

☑ **Don't Miss**

The Khas Mahal, from where the imprisoned Shah Jahan gazed out at his creation, the Taj Mahal.

ROOP_DEY/SHUTTERSTOCK ©

✗ **Take a Break**

For restaurants, you'll have to head to Taj Ganj or the Sadar Bazaar area of town.

Itimad-ud-Daulah

Nicknamed the Baby Taj, the **Itimad-ud-Daulah** (Indian/foreigner ₹20/210, video ₹25; ☉dawn-dusk), the exquisite tomb of Emperor Jehangir's chief minister Mizra Ghiyas Beg, shouldn't be missed. Built between 1622 and 1628, it doesn't have the same awesome beauty as the Taj, but it's arguably more delicate in appearance thanks to its particularly finely carved *jalis* (marble lattice screens).

ARTHIT KAEORATANAPATTAMA/SHUTTERSTOCK ©

⦿ SIGHTS

Mehtab Bagh
Park

(Indian/foreigner ₹15/200, video ₹25; ☉dawn-dusk) This park, originally built by Emperor Babur as the last in a series of 11 parks on the Yamuna's east bank (long before the Taj was conceived), fell into disrepair until it was little more than a huge mound of sand. To protect the Taj from the erosive effects of the sand blown across the river, the park was reconstructed and is now one the best places from which to view the great mausoleum.

Akbar's Mausoleum
Historic Building

(Indian/foreigner ₹15/300, video ₹25; ☉dawn-dusk) This outstanding sandstone and marble tomb commemorates the greatest of the Mughal emperors. The huge courtyard is entered through a stunning gateway. It has three-storey minarets at each corner and is built of red sandstone strikingly inlaid with white-marble geometric patterns.

The mausoleum is at **Sikandra**, 10km northwest of Agra Fort. Catch a bus (₹25, 45 minutes) headed to Mathura from **Bijli Ghar bus stand** (Agra Fort Bus Stand); they go past the mausoleum. Or else take a taxi (return trip about ₹800).

✖ EATING

A night out in Agra tends to revolve around sitting at a rooftop restaurant with a couple of beers. Taj Ganj restaurants aren't licensed, but they can find alcohol if you ask nicely, and don't mind you bringing drinks, as long as you're discreet.

Mama Chicken
Dhaba $

(Stall No 2, Sadar Bazaar; items ₹40-440; ☉noon-midnight) This superstar *dhaba* is a must: duelling veg and nonveg glorified street stalls employing 24 cooks during the rush, each of whom is handling outdoor tandoors or other traditional cookware. They whip up outrageously good *kathi* (flatbread wrap) rolls (try chicken tikka or paneer tikka), whole chickens numerous ways, curries and chow meins for a standing-room-only crowd hell-bent on sustenance.

Pinch of Spice
Modern Indian $$$

(www.pinchofspice.in; Fatehabad Rd; mains ₹280-410; ☉noon-11.30pm) This modern North Indian superstar is the best spot outside five-star hotels to indulge yourself in rich curries and succulent tandoori kebabs. The *murg boti masala* (chicken tikka swimming in a rich and spicy country gravy) and the paneer *lababdar* (unfermented cheese cubes in a spicy red gravy with sautéed onions) are outstanding. Located opposite the ITC Mughal Hotel.

Esphahan
North Indian $$$

(☎2231515; Taj East Gate Rd, Oberoi Amarvilas Hotel; mains ₹1550-3500; ☉dinner 6.30pm & 9pm) There are only two sittings each evening at Agra's finest restaurant, so booking a table is essential. The exquisite menu is chock-full of unique delicacies and rarely seen regional heritage dishes.

ℹ INFORMATION

UP Tourism (☎0562-2421204; www.up-tourism. com; Agra Cantonment Train Station; ⏱6.30am-9.30pm) The friendly train-station branch inside the Tourist Facilitation Centre on Platform 1 offers helpful advice and is where you can book day-long bus tours of Agra. This branch doubles as the Tourist Police.

ℹ GETTING THERE & AWAY

BUS

Ordinary buses leave **Idgah Bus Stand** (off National Hwy 2, near Sikandra) for Delhi (₹180, 4½ hours) and Jaipur (₹262, six hours) every 30 minutes from 5am to 11pm. A block east of Idgah, **Rajasthan State Road Transport Corp** (RSRTC; ☎0562-2420228; www.rsrtc.rajasthan.gov.in) runs more comfortable coaches to Jaipur (AC ₹440, five hours, 6.30am and 8.30am; luxury Volvo ₹530, 4½ hours, 11.30am and 2.30pm).

From the **ISBT Bus Stand** (☎0562-2603536), a ₹200 to ₹250 autorickshaw ride from town, luxury Volvo coaches leave for Delhi (₹595, four hours, 7am, 1pm, 3.30pm and 6.30pm).

TRAIN

Trains run to Delhi from Agra Cantonment (Cantt) station all day. If you can't reserve a seat, just buy a 'general ticket' for the next train (about ₹90), find a seat in sleeper class then upgrade when the ticket collector comes along.

ℹ GETTING AROUND

Agra's green-and-yellow autorickshaws run on CNG (compressed natural gas). Sample prices from the **prepaid autorickshaw booth** (⏱24hr) outside Agra Cantt station: Fatahabad Rd ₹150; Taj West Gate ₹100; Taj South Gate ₹130; four/eight-hour Agra tour ₹400/600. Usually, trips under 3km shouldn't cost more than ₹50.

Delhi–Agra Trains for Day Trippers

Trip	Train No & Name	Fare (₹)	Duration (hr)	Departures
New Delhi–Agra	12002 Shatabdi Exp	550/1010 (A)	2	6am
Agra–New Delhi	12001 Shatabdi Exp	690/1050 (A)	2	9.15pm
Hazrat Nizamuddin–Agra	12280 Taj Exp	100/370 (B)	2¾	7am
Agra–Hazrat Nizamuddin	12279 Taj Exp	100/370 (B)	3	6.55pm

Fares: (A) AC chair/ECC; (B) 2nd-class/AC chair

Other Useful Trains from Agra

Destination	Train No & Name	Fare (₹)	Duration (hr)	Departures
Jaipur*	12036 Shatabdi Exp	660/1225 (B)	3½	5.40pm (except Thu)
Mumbai (CST)	12138/7 Punjab Mail	580/1530/2215 (A)	23	8.35am
Varanasi*	14854/64/66 Marudhar Exp	340/930/1335 (A)	14	8.30pm

Fares: (A) sleeper/3AC/2AC; (B) AC chair/ECC; * leaves from Agra Fort station

JAISALMER

In this Chapter
Jaisalmer Fort 90
Camel Safaris 92
Sights 96
Activities 96
Shopping 97
Eating 98
Drinking & Nightlife 99

Jaisalmer at a Glance...

Jaisalmer's fort is a breathtaking sight: a huge sandcastle rising from the plains like a mirage from a bygone era. No place better evokes exotic camel-train trade routes and desert mystery. Ninety-nine bastions encircle the fort's twisting lanes. Beneath the ramparts, the old city's narrow streets conceal magnificent havelis (traditional, ornately decorated residence) carved from the same golden-honey sandstone – hence Jaisalmer's designation as the Golden City.

Don't miss the chance to climb aboard a camel and experience that camel-train mystique first hand on a safari in the Thar Desert.

Jaisalmer in Two Days

On day one organise an overnight **camel safari** (p92) to start the same afternoon. Wander the city at leisure followed by lunch before heading into the desert for your safari. You will return from safari in the morning, which will leave plenty of time for a detailed exploration of fascinating **Jaisalmer Fort** (p90) on day two.

Jaisalmer in Four Days

On day three visit the **Patwa-ki-Haveli** (p96) and other havelis, browse the shops and have a dinner with Rajasthani music and dancing at **Desert Boy's Dhani** (p98). Enjoy a second exploration of the fort (including a palace visit if you haven't already made one) on day four, and bid farewell with dinner at a rooftop restaurant.

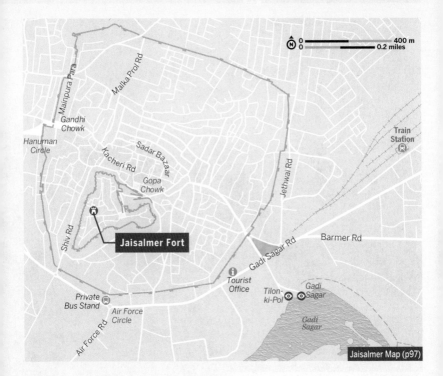

Jaisalmer Map (p97)

Arriving in Jaisalmer

Train station On the eastern edge of town (autorickshaw ₹40); two or three daily trains to/from Jodhpur, Jaipur and Delhi.

Private bus stand South of the fort; buses to/from Jodhpur, Jaipur and elsewhere; several companies have ticket offices at Hanuman Circle.

Main bus stand South of the fort; government buses to/from Jodhpur and elsewhere.

Sleeping

While staying in the fort might appear to be Jaisalmer's most atmospheric choice, habitation inside the fort – driven in no small part by tourism – is damaging the monument irreparably. Fortunately, there's a wide choice of good places to stay outside the fort. You'll get massive discounts between April and August, when Jaisalmer is hellishly hot.

DON MAMMOSER/SHUTTERSTOCK ©

Jaisalmer Fort

Jaisalmer's massive fort is not just a fairytale desert citadel but also a fascinatingly alive urban centre with about 4000 residents, honeycombed with narrow lanes lined with houses and temples.

Great For...

☑ **Don't Miss**

The 360-degree panorama over fort, city and desert from the palace rooftop.

You pass through four massive gates on the zigzag route up into the fort, emerging in Dashera Chowk at its centre. Along with its palace, temples and houses, the fort is home to a large number of handicraft shops, guesthouses and restaurants.

Founded in 1156 by the Bhati Rajput ruler Jaisal, Jaisalmer Fort was the focus of a number of battles between the Bhatis, the Mughals of Delhi and the Rathores of Jodhpur, but the Bhatis ruled Jaisalmer right through to Independence in 1947.

Fort Palace

Much of the former rulers' elegant seven-storey **palace** (Indian/foreigner incl compulsory audio guide ₹100/500, camera ₹100; ☺8am-6pm Apr-Oct, 9am-6pm Nov-Mar) is open to visitors. Floor upon floor of small rooms provide a fascinating sense of how

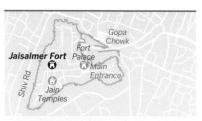

ℹ️ **Need to Know**

Entry to the fort is through the First Fort Gate, on its east side.

✕ **Take a Break**

Sun Set Palace (Vyas Para; mains ₹100-230; ⊗8am-10pm) serves good Indian vegetarian dishes on an airy terrace.

★ **Top Tip**

The Fort Palace's worthwhile 1½-hour audio guide is free with palace entry, but you must leave a ₹2000 deposit or your passport, driver's licence or credit card.

A Castle Built on Sand

A decade ago three of Jaisalmer Fort's ancient bastions had collapsed and the whole structure was in danger of being undermined by leaks from its antique drainage system. The main problem: material progress, in the form of piped water for the fort's inhabitants.

Much-needed conservation works have since been done – most importantly the renewal of the fort's drainage system, repaving of the streets and repair works inside the palace. Some conservationists, however, still believe the fort's structure is in danger, as was highlighted by a collapse of a wall being restored in 2016. Calls remain for the fort's inhabitants, and those who work in the fort, to be removed.

Vyas Chhatri (₹30, camera ₹20; ⊗4pm-dusk), an atmospheric assemblage of golden sandstone *chhatris* (a small, domed Mughal kiosk), in an old Brahmin cemetery on the northwestern edge of town, forms a popular sunset point from which to view the fort. Enter from Ramgarh Rd opposite the Himmatgarh Palace Hotel.

such buildings were designed for spying on the outside world. Top highlights include the mirrored and painted Rang Mahal (the bedroom of 18th-century ruler Mulraj II), a gallery of finely wrought 15th-century sculptures donated to the rulers by the builders of the fort's temples, and the spectacular views from the rooftop.

Jain Temples

Within the fort walls is a maze-like, interconnecting treasure trove of seven beautiful yellow sandstone **Jain temples** (Indian/foreigner ₹50/200, camera ₹50; ⊗Chandraprabhu, Rikhabdev & Gyan Bhandar 8am-noon, other temples 11am-noon), dating from the 15th and 16th centuries. The temples' intricate carving has an extraordinary quality because of the soft, warm stone. Shoes and all leather items must be removed before entering.

Camel Safaris

Trekking around by camel is the most evocative and fun way to sample Thar Desert life – and camping out in the desert, huddling around a tiny fire beneath the stars and listening to the camel drivers' songs, is a magical experience. Most trips now include 4WD rides to get you to less frequented areas.

Great For...

ℹ️ Need to Know

Competition between safari organisers is intense and standards vary. Check a few operators before deciding.

★ **Top Tip**
The camel drivers expect a tip at the trip's end: up to ₹100 per day is welcomed.

Trekking around the Thar Desert on a camel is a lot of fun, but don't expect great seas of dunes. The Thar is mostly arid scrubland sprinkled with villages and wind turbines, with dune areas popping out here and there. You'll often come across children herding flocks of sheep or goats, whose neck bells tinkle in the desert silence.

Which Safari?

Most hotels and guesthouses are very happy to arrange your camel safari. While many provide a good service, some may cut corners and take you for the kind of ride you didn't have in mind.

You can also organise a safari directly with one of the specialist agencies in Jaisalmer. Since these depend exclusively on safari business it's particularly in their interest to satisfy clients. Talk to other travellers and a few different operators.

The best-known dunes, at Sam, 40km west of Jaisalmer, are crowded in the evening and are more of a carnival than a back-to-nature experience. The dunes near Khuri, 48km southwest of Jaisalmer, are also quite busy at sunset, but quiet the rest of the time. Operators all sell trips now to 'nontouristy' and 'off the beaten track' areas.

Typical rates are between ₹1200 and ₹2500 per person for a one-day, one-night trip (leaving one morning and returning the next, with the camel riding usually done in two-hour batches, one before lunch, one after). Rates should include 4WD transfers, meals, mineral water, blankets and sometimes a thin mattress. Check that there will be one camel for each rider. Always get everything down in writing.

Costs are normally lower (₹1000 to ₹1500 per person) if you leave Jaisalmer in the afternoon and return the following morning. A quick sunset ride at Sam costs around ₹600 per person, including 4WD transfer. At the other end of the scale, you could take a 20-day trek to Bikaner. Expect to pay between ₹1200 and ₹2000 per person per day for multiday trips.

Sahara Travels

Run by the son of the late LN Bissa (aka Mr Desert), **Sahara Travels** (☏02992-252609; www.saharatravelsjaisalmer.com; Gopa Chowk; ⏱6am-8pm) is very professional and trans- parent. Trips are to 'nontouristy' areas only. Prices for an overnight trip (9am to 11am the following day) are ₹1900 per person, all inclusive.

Thar Desert Tours

Well-run **Thar Desert Tours** (☏91-9414365333; www.tharcamelsafarijaisalmer.com; Gandhi Chowk; ⏱8.30am-7.30pm) charges ₹1200 per person per day including water and meals, adjusting prices depending on trip times. It limits tours to five people max- imum, and we also receive good feedback about them. Customers pay 80% up front.

Trotters

Trotters (☏9828929974; www.trotters-jaisalmer.net; Gopa Chowk; ⏱5.30am-9.00pm) is transparently run with a clear price list showing everything on offer, including trips to 'nontouristy' areas as well as cheaper jaunts to Sam or Khuri. Prices for an overnight trip (8am to 10am the following day) are ₹1950 to ₹2450 per person, all inclusive.

What to Take

A wide-brimmed hat (or Lawrence of Arabia turban), long trousers, long-sleeved shirt, insect repellent, toilet paper, torch (flash- light), sunscreen, water bottle (with a strap), and some cash are recommended. Women should consider a sports bra, as a trotting camel is a bumpy ride. During summer, rain is not unheard of, so come prepared.

Precautions

Take care of your possessions, particu- larly on the return journey. Report any complaints to the **Superintendent of Police** (☏02992-252233) or the **tourist office** (☏02992-252406; Gadi Sagar Rd; ⏱9.30am-6pm).

> ★ **Don't Miss**
>
> An overnight safari, with a night on some dunes, is a minimum to get a feel for the experience.

AGF/UIG/GETTY IMAGES ©

> ✕ **Take A Break**
>
> There's always a long lunch stop during the hottest part of the day, with the camel drivers brewing chai and prepar- ing food.

◎ SIGHTS

Patwa-ki-Haveli   Historic Building
(Government sections Indian/foreigner ₹50/200; ⊙9am-6pm) The biggest fish in the *haveli* pond is Patwa-ki-Haveli, which towers over a narrow lane, its intricate stonework like honey-coloured lace. Divided into five sections, it was built between 1800 and 1860 by five Jain brothers who made their fortunes in brocade and jewellery. It's all very impressive from the outside; however, the first of the five sections, the privately owned **Kothari's Patwa-ki-Haveli Museum** (Indian/foreigner ₹100/250; ⊙9am-6pm), richly evokes 19th-century life and is the only one worth paying entry for.

Nathmal-ki-Haveli   Historic Building
(donation requested; ⊙8am-7pm) This late-19th-century *haveli,* once used as the prime minister's house, is still partly inhabited. It has an extraordinary exterior, dripping with carvings, and the 1st floor has some beautiful paintings using 1.5kg of gold leaf. The left and right wings were the work of two brothers, whose competitive spirits apparently produced this virtuoso work – the two sides are similar, but not identical. Sandstone elephants guard the entrance.

Thar Heritage Museum   Museum
(off Court Rd; ₹40, camera ₹20; ⊙10am-8pm) This private museum has an intriguing assortment of Jaisalmer artefacts, from turbans, musical instruments, fossils and kitchen equipment to displays on birth, marriage, death and opium customs. It's brought alive by the guided tour you'll get from its founder, local historian and folklorist LN Khatri. Look for the snakes and ladders game that acts as a teaching guide to Hinduism's spiritual journey. If the door is locked you'll find Mr Khatri at his shop, Desert Handicrafts Emporium, nearby on Court Rd.

Salim Singh-ki-Haveli   Historic Building
(incl guide ₹30, camera ₹20; ⊙8am-7pm May-Sep, to 6pm Oct-Apr) This 18th-century *haveli* has an amazing, distinctive shape. It's narrow for the first floors, and then the top storey spreads out into a mass of carving, with graceful arched balconies surmounted by pale-blue cupolas. The beautifully arched roof has superb carved brackets in the form of peacocks.

Desert Cultural Centre & Museum   Museum
(Gadi Sagar Rd; museum ₹50, camera ₹50, combined museum & puppet show ₹100; ⊙museum 10am-6pm, puppet show 6.30-8.30pm) This interesting little museum tells the history of Rajasthan's princely states and has exhibits on traditional Rajasthani culture. Features include Rajasthani music (with video), textiles, a *kavad* mobile temple, and a *phad* scroll painting depicting the story of the Rajasthani folk hero Pabuji, used by travelling singers as they recite Pabuji's epic exploits. It also hosts nightly half-hour puppet shows with English commentary. The ticket includes admission to the Jaisalmer Folklore Museum.

Gadi Sagar   Lake
This stately tank, southeast of the city walls, was Jaisalmer's vital water supply until 1965, and because of its importance it is surrounded by many small temples and shrines. The tank was built in 1367 by Maharawal Gadsi Singh, taking advantage of a natural declivity that already retained some water. It's a waterfowl favourite in winter, but can almost dry up before the monsoon.

✦ ACTIVITIES

After a camel trek you can soothe your jangled body with a spot of massage and herbal healing. Many places also offer henna painting and beauty treatments.

Baiju Ayurvedic Beauty Parlour   Ayurveda, Massage
(✆02992-250803; Dashera Chowk; ⊙10am-8pm) A friendly and trustworthy operation with two locations in the fort: this one near the main square and the other at the end of the street past the Jain temples.

Jaisalmer

Jaisalmer

◉ Sights
1 Desert Cultural Centre & Museum...........D3
2 Fort Palace...B2
3 Jain Temples...A3
4 Jaisalmer Fort..A2
5 Kothari's Patwa-ki-Haveli Museum...........B1
6 Nathmal-ki-Haveli.......................................B1
7 Patwa-ki-Haveli..B1
8 Salim Singh-ki-Haveli.................................C2
9 Thar Heritage Museum...............................A1

✚ Activities, Courses & Tours
10 Baiju Ayurvedic Beauty Parlour..............B2
11 Sahara Travels...B2

12 Thar Desert Tours......................................A1
13 Trotters...B2

🛍 Shopping
14 Bellissima...B2
15 Desert Handicrafts Emporium..................A1

✕ Eating
16 1st Gate Home Fusion................................C3
17 Jaisal Italy...B2
18 KB Cafe...B1
19 Natraj Restaurant.......................................C2
20 Saffron...A1
21 Sun Set Palace...A3

🔒 SHOPPING

Jaisalmer is famous for its stunning embroidery, bedspreads, mirror-work wall hangings, oil lamps, stonework and antiques.

There are several good *khadi* (homespun cloth) shops where you can find fixed-price tablecloths, rugs and clothes, with a variety of patterning techniques including tie-dye, block printing and embroidery. Try **Zila**

Khadi Gramodan Parishad (Malka Prol Rd; ⊙10am-6pm Mon-Sat), **Khadi Gramodyog Bhavan** (Dhibba; ⊙10am-6pm Mon-Sat) or **Gandhi Darshan Emporium** (near Hanuman Circle; ⊙11am-7pm Fri-Wed).

Bellissima   Arts & Crafts

(Dashera Chowk; ⊙8am-9pm) This small shop near the fort's main square sells beautiful patchworks, embroidery, paintings, bags, rugs, cushion covers and all types of Rajasthani art. Proceeds assist underprivileged women from surrounding villages, including those who have divorced or been widowed.

Desert Handicrafts
Emporium
Arts & Crafts

(Court Rd; ⊘9.30am-9.30pm) With some unusual jewellery, paintings, and all sorts of textiles, this is one of the most original of numerous craft shops around town.

EATING

Chandan Shree
Restaurant
Indian $

(near Hanuman Circle; mains ₹100-200; ⊘7am-11pm) An always busy (and rightfully so) dining hall serving up a huge range of tasty, spicy South Indian, Gujarati, Rajasthani, Punjabi and Bengali dishes.

1st Gate
Home Fusion
Italian, Indian $$

(☑02992-254462, 9462554462; First Fort Gate; mains ₹220-460; ⊘7.30-10.30am, noon-3pm & 7-11pm; ☜) Sitting atop the boutique hotel of the same name, this split-level, open-air terrace boasts dramatic fort views and a mouth-watering menu of authentic vegetarian Italian and Indian dishes. Also on offer are excellent wood-fired pizzas and good strong Italian coffee. Snacks and drinks are available outside meal times (7.30am to 11pm).

Saffron
Multicuisine $$

(Hotel Nachana Haveli, Goverdhan Chowk; mains ₹195-415; ⊘7am-11pm) On the spacious roof terrace of Hotel Nachana Haveli, the veg and nonveg food here is excellent. It's a particularly atmospheric place in the evening, with private and communal lounges and more formal seating arrangements. The Indian food is hard to beat, though the Italian isn't too bad either. Alcohol is served.

Desert Boy's Dhani
Indian $$

(Dhibba Para; mains ₹120-250, thali ₹400; ⊘11am-4pm & 7-11pm; ✸☜) A walled-garden restaurant where tables are spread around a large, stone-paved courtyard shaded by a big tree. There's

Indian patchwork quilt

KUJA PRUCHYATHAMRONG/SHUTTERSTOCK ©

also traditional cushion seating under-cover and in an air-con room. Rajasthani music and dance is performed from 8pm to 10pm nightly, and it's a very pleasant place to eat excellent, good-value Rajasthani and other Indian veg dishes.

KB Cafe   Multicuisine $$

(☏02992-253833; www.killabhawan.com; Patwa-ki-haveli Chowk; mains ₹140-380; ⏱7am-10.30pm) This delightfully stylish rooftop restaurant sits atop one of Jaisalmer's premier boutique hotels with views to the magnificent Patwa-ki-haveli. Enjoy excellent vegetarian pasta, pizza and curries, and finish off with an Italian coffee.

Natraj Restaurant   Multicuisine $$

(Aasani Rd; mains ₹120-180; ⏱10am-10pm; 🛜🖊) This rooftop restaurant has a satisfying view of the upper part of the Salim Singh-ki-Haveli next door. The pure veg food is consistently excellent and the service is great. The delicious South Indian dosas (paper-thin lentil-flour pancakes) are fantastic value.

Jaisal Italy   Italian $$

(First Fort Gate; mains ₹180-290; ⏱7.30am-11pm; ❄🛜) Just inside First Fort Gate, Jaisal Italy has a decent vegetarian Italian menu, including bruschetta, antipasti, pasta, pizza, salad and desserts, plus Spanish omelettes. All this is served up in an exotically decorated indoor restaurant (cosy in winter, deliciously air-conditioned in summer) or on a delightful terrace atop the lower fort walls, with cinematic views. Alcohol is served.

🍷 DRINKING & NIGHTLIFE

As the sun sets and the floodlights paint the bastions in bright light and dark shadows, head to a rooftop restaurant to enjoy a cold beer, wine or lassi. Most hotels have one with fort views and there are several independent restaurants near the First Fort Gate.

Beating the Hard Sell

Accommodation touts can be a big nuisance at the bus and train stations and on buses coming from Jodhpur. They're all best ignored if you can manage it. Many hotels offer pick-ups for arriving guests.

Some budget hotels are heavily into high-pressure camel-safari selling, and things can turn sour if you don't take up their propositions; room rates that sound too good to be true almost always are.

GETTING THERE & AWAY

BUS

Several private bus companies have ticket offices at Hanuman Circle. **Hanuman Travels** (☏9413362367) and **Swagat Travels** (☏02992-252557) are typical. The buses themselves leave from the **private bus stand** (Air Force Circle). There are two or three daily to Jaipur (seat/sleeper ₹400/500, 11 hours) and buses to Jodhpur (seat/sleeper ₹200/400, five hours) half-hourly from 6am to 10pm.

TRAIN

The **train station** (⏱ticket office 8am-8pm Mon-Sat, to 1.45pm Sun) is on the eastern edge of town. There's a reserved ticket booth for foreigners.

Delhi Sleeper/3AC ₹450/1205, 18 hours, two or three daily (12.45am, 1.10am, 5pm)

Jaipur Sleeper/3AC ₹350/935, 12 hours, three daily (12.45am, 5pm, 11.55pm)

GETTING AROUND

It's possible to hire taxis or 4WDs from the stand on Hanuman Circle. To Khuri or Sam Sand Dunes, expect to pay ₹1000 to ₹1200 return including a wait of about an hour or so.

JAIPUR

In this Chapter
Amber Fort 104
City Palace 106
Sights 110
Activities 110
Shopping 111
Eating 113
Drinking & Nightlife 114

Jaipur at a Glance...

Enthralling, historical Jaipur is the gateway to and capital of India's most flamboyant state, Rajasthan. The city's colourful, chaotic streets ebb and flow with a heady brew of old and new. Careering buses dodge dawdling camels while leisurely cycle-rickshaws frustrate swarms of motorbikes. In the midst of this mayhem, the splendours of Jaipur's majestic past are islands of relative calm. At the Old City's heart, the City Palace still houses the former royal family, and just out of sight, in the arid hills surrounding Jaipur, is the fairy-tale grandeur of Amber Fort, Jaipur's star attraction.

Jaipur in Two Days

Dive into the beating heart of Jaipur, the **Pink City** (p110), to explore its frenetic bazaars, the iconic **Hawa Mahal** (p110) and the fascinating **Jantar Mantar** (p110) and **City Palace** (p107). Wind up with dinner at classic **Niro's** (p113). On your second day explore magnificent **Amber Fort** (p105) then return to town for dinner at **Peacock Rooftop Restaurant** (p113) and more rooftop action at **Blackout club** (p114).

Jaipur in Four Days

On day three investigate the newer and outlying parts of Jaipur including the **Central Museum** (p110), **Nahargarh** (p110) and some of the excellent shops, including **Jaipur Modern** with its fine Mediterranean **cafe** (p114). Soar away on a **Sky Waltz balloon flight** (p110) day four, before returning to the Pink City's bazaars and winding down with an ayurvedic massage at **Kerala Ayurveda Kendra** (p111).

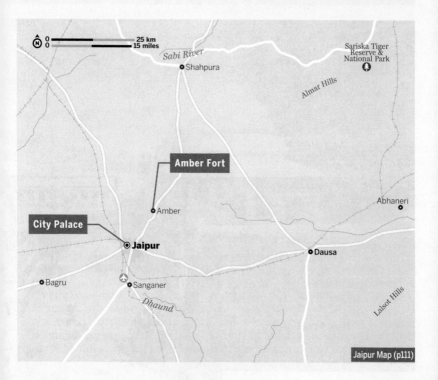

Jaipur Map (p111)

Arriving in Jaipur

Train station Trains to/from Sawai Madhopur (for Ranthambhore National Park; three hours), Agra (4½ hours), Delhi (six hours) and Jaisalmer (12 hours).

Jaipur International Airport Flights to/from Indian cities, Bangkok and Singapore.

Main bus station Government buses to/from Delhi (5½ hours), Agra (5½ hours) and Jaisalmer (14 hours).

Sleeping

Travellers are spoiled for choice in all budget categories. Many hotels will pick you up from the bus or train station if you ring ahead, saving you from being besieged on arrival by taxi/autorickshaw drivers acting as hotel touts. From May to September, most midrange and top-end hotels drop prices by 25% to 50%.

For more information on where to stay, see p115.

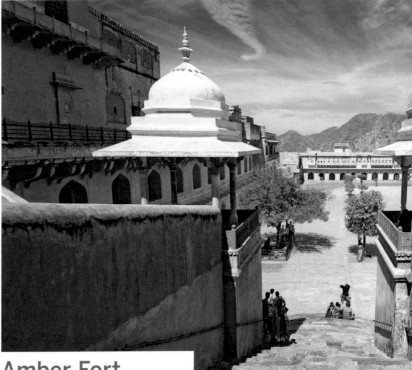

GENOVA-SHUTTERSTOCK ©

Amber Fort

The magnificent, formidable, honey-hued fort of Amber (pronounced 'amer'), an ethereal example of Rajput architecture, rises from a rocky mountainside about 11km northeast of Jaipur, and is the city's must-see sight.

This magnificent fort comprises an extensive palace complex, built from pale yellow and pink sandstone and white marble, and is divided into four main sections, each with its own courtyard. You can trudge up from the road in about 10 minutes, or take a 4WD (₹400 return for five passengers).

Entrances

If you walk or ride an elephant, you'll enter Amber Fort through the Suraj Pol (Sun Gate), which leads to the Jaleb Chowk (Main Courtyard), where returning armies would display their war booty to the populace. Women could view this area from the veiled windows of the palace. The ticket office is directly across the courtyard from the Suraj Pol. If you arrive by car you enter

Great For...

☑ **Don't Miss**

The delicate and quirky marble relief panels in the Jai Mandir, depicting cartoon-like insects and sinuous flowers.

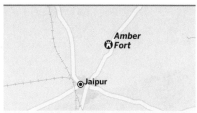

ℹ Need to Know

Indian/foreigner ₹100/500, night entry ₹100, guide ₹200, audio guide ₹200-250; ⊘8am-6pm, last entry 5.30pm, night entry 7-9pm

✕ Take a Break

There are cafes and restaurants in the palace complex, and street stalls in the town below.

★ Top Tip

Hiring a guide or grabbing an audio guide is highly recommended, as there are very few signs and many blind alleys.

through the Chand Pol (Moon Gate) on the opposite side of Jaleb Chowk.

Siladevi Temple

From Jaleb Chowk, an imposing stairway leads up to the main palace, but first it's worth taking the steps just to the right, to the small Siladevi Temple, with gorgeous silver doors featuring repoussé (raised relief) work.

Diwan-i-Am

The main stairway takes you up to the second courtyard and the Diwan-i-Am (Hall of Public Audience), which has a double row of columns, each topped by an elephant-shaped capital, and latticed galleries above.

Ganesh Pol & Maharaja's Apartments

The maharaja's apartments are set around the third courtyard. You enter through the fabulous Ganesh Pol, decorated with beautiful frescoed arches. The Jai Mandir (Hall of Victory) is noted for its inlaid panels and multimirrored ceiling. Opposite is the Sukh Niwas (Hall of Pleasure), with an ivory-inlaid sandalwood door and a channel that once carried cooling water through the room.

Amber's History

Amber Fort was built by the Kachhwaha Rajputs from Gwalior, in present-day Madhya Pradesh. Construction, financed with war booty, began in 1592 under Maharaja Man Singh, the Rajput commander of Mughal emperor Akbar's army. The fort was later extended and completed by the Jai Singhs before they shifted their capital to Jaipur.

City Palace

This fascinating complex of courtyards, gardens and buildings, a striking blend of Rajasthani, Mughal and European architecture, stands right at the heart of the Old City.

Great For...

☑ Don't Miss

The two enormous urns in the Diwan-i-Khas, reputedly the world's largest silver objects.

The palace's outer wall was built by Jaipur's 18th-century founder Jai Singh II. The palace within has been enlarged and adapted with buildings added right up to the 20th century.

Mubarak Mahal

Entering through Virendra Pol, you'll see the Mubarak Mahal (Welcome Palace), built in the late 19th century for Maharaja Madho Singh II as a reception centre for dignitaries. Its multiarched, colonnaded construction was cooked up in an Islamic/Rajput/European stylistic stew by architect Sir Swinton Jacob. It forms part of the Maharaja Sawai Mansingh II Museum, containing royal costumes and superb shawls. One remarkable exhibit is Sawai Madho Singh I's capacious clothing; it's said he was a cuddly 2m tall, 1.2m wide and 250kg.

❶ Need to Know

☎0141-4088888; www.royaljaipur.in; Indian/
foreigner incl camera ₹130/500, guide from
₹300, audio guide free, Royal Grandeur tour
Indian/foreigner ₹2000/2500; ⏰9.30am-5pm

✕ Take a Break

Air-conditioned **LMB** (p113), going
strong since 1954, serves up top-class
all-vegetarian thalis (traditional 'all-you-
can-eat' plate meal) and sweets.

> ### ★ Top Tip
>
> **For foreigners the admission price
> includes entry to the Royal Gaitor,
> the Cenotaphs of the Maharanis, and
> Jaigarh at Amber. This ticket is valid
> for two days.**

Armoury

The Armoury in the Anand Mahal Sileg
Khana (the Maharani's Palace) has one of
India's best collections of weapons. Many
of the ceremonial items are elegantly
engraved and inlaid, belying their grisly
purpose.

Diwan-i-Khas (Sarvatobhadra)

At the centre of the Sarvatobhadra courtyard is a pink-and-white, marble-paved
gallery that served as the Diwan-i-Khas
(Hall of Private Audience), where maharajas would consult their ministers. Two
enormous silver vessels here, each 1.6m
tall, were made for Maharaja Madho Singh
II to transport holy Ganges water to England for bathing, on a visit in 1902.

Diwan-i-Am Art Gallery

Within the lavish Diwan-i-Am (Hall of Public
Audience), this gallery's exhibits include a
copy of the entire Bhagavad Gita (a Hindu
sacred text) handwritten in tiny script, and
miniature copies of other Hindu scriptures.
These were small enough to be hidden in
the event that zealot Mughal armies tried to
destroy the sacred texts.

Pitam Niwas Chowk & Chandra Mahal

Towards the palace's inner courtyard is Pitam
Niwas Chowk. Here four glorious gates repre-
sent the seasons – the Peacock Gate depicts
autumn, the Lotus Gate signifies summer, the
Green Gate represents spring, and the Rose
Gate embodies winter.

Beyond is the Chandra Mahal palace, still
the residence of the descendants of the royal
family, where you can take a 45-minute Royal
Grandeur guided tour of select areas.

Pink City

Jaipur's Old City was painted pink in 1876 to welcome the Prince of Wales. In among the seethingly busy market streets are the city's major monuments.
Start New Gate
Distance 4.5km
Duration Three to five hours

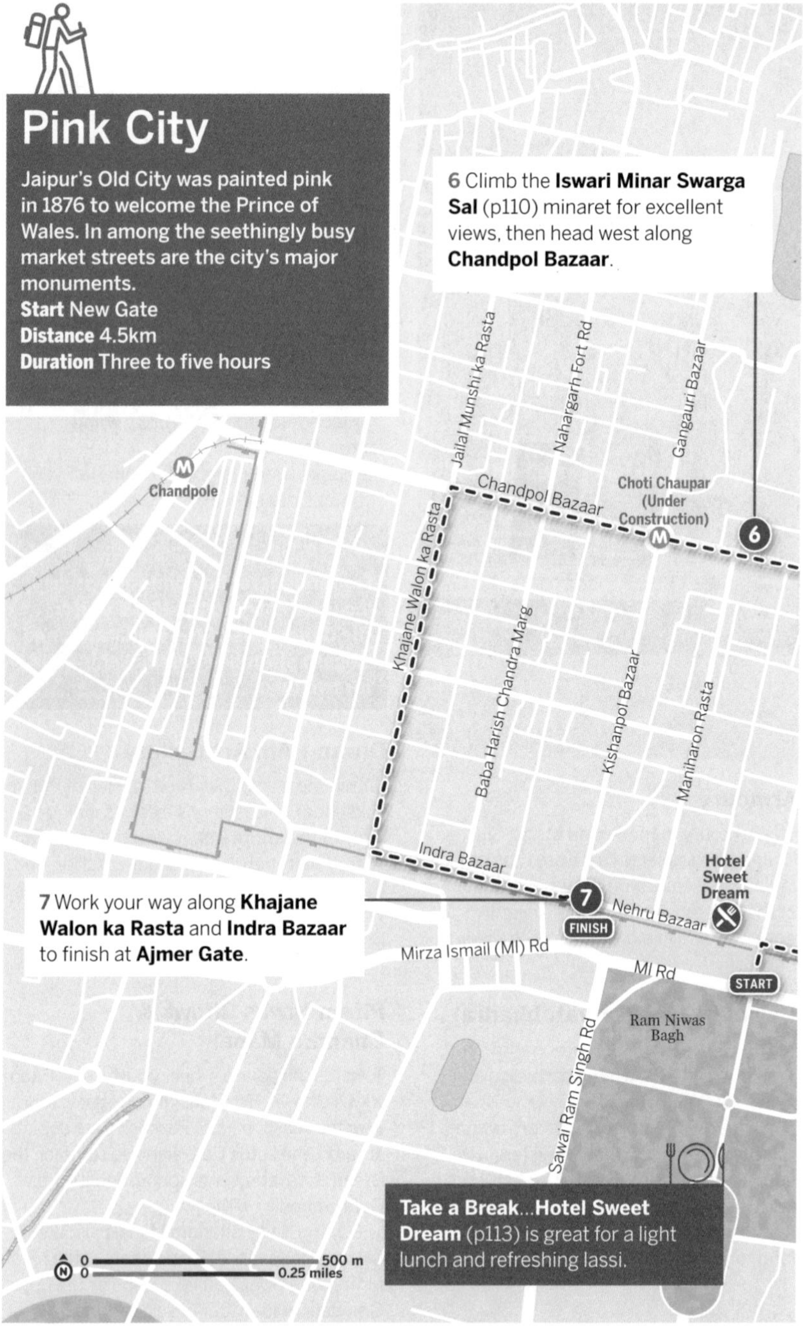

6 Climb the **Iswari Minar Swarga Sal** (p110) minaret for excellent views, then head west along **Chandpol Bazaar**.

Jalal Munshi ka Rasta

Nahargarh Fort Rd

Gangauri Bazaar

Chandpole Ⓜ

Chandpol Bazaar

Choti Chaupar (Under Construction)

6

Khajane Walon ka Rasta

Baba Harish Chandra Marg

Kishanpol Bazaar

Maniharon Rasta

Indra Bazaar

7 Work your way along **Khajane Walon ka Rasta** and **Indra Bazaar** to finish at **Ajmer Gate**.

7
FINISH

Nehru Bazaar

Hotel Sweet Dream

START

Mirza Ismail (MI) Rd

MI Rd

Sawai Ram Singh Rd

Ram Niwas Bagh

Take a Break...**Hotel Sweet Dream** (p113) is great for a light lunch and refreshing lassi.

Ⓝ
0 — 500 m
0 — 0.25 miles

4 The **City Palace** (p106) is a fascinating conglomeration of palaces within palaces, galleries, gateways and courtyards.

5 The 1728 observatory **Jantar Mantar** (p110) resembles a group of bizarre sculptures but genuinely measures the heavens.

Classic Photo The beehive-like geometry of the **Hawa Mahal** (p110) offers lots of interesting angles.

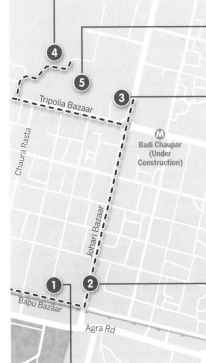

3 The extraordinary **Hawa Mahal** (p110) was constructed in 1799 to enable royal ladies to watch city life.

Tripolia Bazaar

Chaura Rasta

Ⓜ Badi Chaupar (Under Construction)

Johari Bazaar

Bapu Bazaar

Agra Rd

2 In **Johari Bazaar** you'll find jewellers, goldsmiths and artisans doing highly glazed meenakari (enamelwork).

1 Bright fabrics, perfumes and jootis (traditional, often pointy-toed, slip-in shoes) make **Bapu Bazaar** a favourite with Jaipur's women.

4 DOMINIC DUDLEY/SHUTTERSTOCK © 7 NILA NEWSOM/SHUTTERSTOCK ©

◉ SIGHTS

◉ Old City (Pink City)

The Old City is both a marvel of 18th-century town planning and the heart of the city today. Avenues divide it into neat rectangles, each specialising in certain crafts, as ordained in the Shilpa Shastra (ancient Hindu texts).

Hawa Mahal   Historic Building

(Sireh Deori Bazaar; Indian/foreigner incl camera ₹50/200, guide ₹200, audio guide Hindi/English ₹115/170; ⊙9am-5.30pm) Jaipur's most distinctive landmark, the Hawa Mahal is an extraordinary pink-painted delicately honeycombed hive that rises a dizzying five storeys. It was constructed in 1799 by Maharaja Sawai Pratap Singh to enable ladies of the royal household to watch the life and processions of the city. The top offers stunning views over Jantar Mantar and the City Palace in one direction and over Sireh Deori Bazaar in the other.

Jantar Mantar   Historic Site

(Indian/foreigner ₹50/200, guide ₹200, audio guide ₹100; ⊙9am-4.30pm) Adjacent to the City Palace is Jantar Mantar, an observatory begun by Jai Singh II in 1728 that resembles a collection of bizarre giant sculptures. Built for measuring the heavens, the name is derived from the Sanskrit *yanta mantr,* meaning 'instrument of calculation', and in 2010 it was added to India's list of Unesco World Heritage Sites. Paying for a local guide is highly recommended if you wish to learn how each fascinating instrument works.

Iswari Minar Swarga Sal   Notable Building

(Heaven-Piercing Minaret; Indian/foreigner ₹50/200; ⊙9am-4.30pm) Piercing the skyline near the City Palace is this unusual minaret, erected in the 1740s by Jai Singh II's son and successor Iswari. The entrance is around the back of the row of shops fronting Chandpol Bazaar – take the alley 50m west of the minaret along the bazaar or go via the Atishpol entrance to the City Palace compound, 150m east of the minaret. You can spiral to the top of the minaret for excellent views.

◉ Other Areas

Central Museum   Museum

(Albert Hall; J Nehru Marg; Indian/foreigner ₹40/300, audio guide Hindi/English ₹115/175; ⊙9am-6pm) This museum is housed in the spectacularly florid Albert Hall, south of the Old City. The building was designed by Sir Swinton Jacob, and combines elements of English and North Indian architecture, as well as huge friezes celebrating the world's great cultures. It was known as the pride of the new Jaipur when it opened in 1887. The grand old building hosts an eclectic array of tribal dress, dioramas, sculptures, miniature paintings, carpets, musical instruments and even an Egyptian mummy.

Nahargarh   Fort

(Tiger Fort; Indian/foreigner ₹50/200; ⊙10am-5pm) Built in 1734 and extended in 1868, this sturdy fort overlooks the city from a sheer ridge to the north. The story goes that the fort was named after Nahar Singh, a dead prince whose restless spirit was disrupting construction. Whatever was built in the day crumbled in the night. The prince agreed to leave on condition that the fort was named for him. The views are glorious and there's a restaurant that's perfect for a beer.

Royal Gaitor   Historic Site

(Gatore ki Chhatriyan; Indian/foreigner ₹40/100; ⊙9am-5pm) The royal cenotaphs, just outside the city walls, beneath Nahargarh, are an appropriately restful place to visit and feel remarkably undiscovered. The stone monuments are beautifully and intricately carved. Maharajas Pratap Singh, Madho Singh II and Jai Singh II, among others, are honoured here. Jai Singh II has the most impressive marble cenotaph, with a dome supported by 20 carved pillars.

❸ ACTIVITIES

Sky Waltz Ballooning   Ballooning

(www.skywaltz.com; ☎9560 387222) Sky Waltz offers spectacular early-morning balloon flights over Amber Fort and the surround-

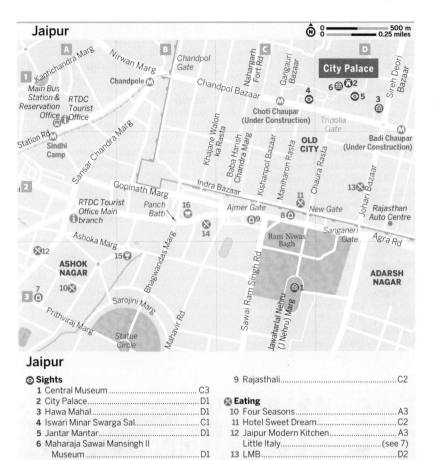

Jaipur

◉ Sights
1 Central Museum C3
2 City Palace D1
3 Hawa Mahal D1
4 Iswari Minar Swarga Sal C1
5 Jantar Mantar D1
6 Maharaja Sawai Mansingh II
   Museum D1

🔒 Shopping
7 Anokhi A3
8 Gem-Testing Laboratory C2
   Jaipur Modern .... (see 12)

9 Rajasthali C2

✖ Eating
10 Four Seasons A3
11 Hotel Sweet Dream C2
12 Jaipur Modern Kitchen A3
   Little Italy .... (see 7)
13 LMB D2
14 Niro's B2

◉ Drinking & Nightlife
15 Blackout B3
16 Lassiwala B2

ing countryside. The package includes pick-up and drop off from your Jaipur hotel, hot refreshments, watching the balloon inflation, and the hour-long flight itself.

Kerala Ayurveda Kendra Massage
(www.keralaayurvedakendra.com; 32 Indra Colony, Bani Park; 📞 0141- 4022446; 55min massage from ₹500; ⏰ 9am-9pm) Is Jaipur making your nerves jangle? Get help through

ayurvedic massage and therapy. Treatments include sirodhara (₹1500/2400) where medicated oil is steadily streamed over your forehead to reduce stress, tone the brain and help with sleep disorders.

🔒 SHOPPING

Jaipur is a shopper's paradise. Commercial buyers come from all over the world to stock up on the amazing range of jewellery, gems, textiles and crafts from all over Rajasthan. You'll have to bargain hard, particularly around major tourist sights.

Anokhi — Clothing, Textiles

(www.anokhi.com; 2nd fl, KK Square, C-11 Prithviraj Marg; 9.30am-8pm Mon-Sat, 11am-7pm Sun) Anokhi is a classy, upmarket boutique selling stunning high-quality textiles such as block-printed fabrics, tablecloths, bed covers, cosmetic bags and scarves, as well as a range of well-designed, beautifully made clothing that combines Indian and Western influences. There's a wonderful little cafe on the premises and an excellent bookshop in the same building.

Rajasthali — Arts & Crafts

(MI Rd; 11am-7.30pm Mon-Sat) This state-government-run emporium, opposite Ajmer Gate, is packed with quality Rajasthani artefacts and crafts, including enamelwork, embroidery, pottery, woodwork, jewellery, puppets, block-printed sheets, miniatures, brassware, mirror-work and more. Scout out prices here before launching into the bazaar; items can be cheaper at the markets, but the quality is often higher at the emporium for not much more money.

Jaipur Modern — Fashion & Accessories

(0141-4112000; www.jaipurmodern.com; 51 Sardar Patel Marg, C-Scheme; 11am-11pm) This contemporary showroom offers local arts and crafts, clothing, homewares, stationary and fashion accessories. The staff are relaxed (no hard sell here) and if you are not in the mood to shop, there's a great cafe serving Lavazza coffee and Mediterranean snacks.

Silver Shop — Jewellery

(Hotel Pearl Palace, Hari Kishan Somani Marg; 6-10pm) A trusted jewellery shop backed by the hotel management that hosts the store. A money-back guarantee is offered on all items. Find it under the peacock canopy in the hotel's Peacock Rooftop Restaurant.

Jewellery on sale in a bazaar

SARAWUT/SHUTTERSTOCK ©

⊗ EATING

Peacock Rooftop Restaurant
Multicuisine $$

(☎0141-2373700; Hotel Pearl Palace, Hari Kishan Somani Marg; mains ₹175-340; ☺7am-11pm) This multilevel rooftop restaurant at the Hotel Pearl Palace gets rave reviews for its excellent yet inexpensive cuisine (Indian, Chinese and Continental) and fun ambience. The attentive service, whimsical furnishings and romantic view towards Hathroi Fort make it a first-rate restaurant. In addition to the dinner menu, there are healthy breakfasts and great-value burgers, pizzas and thalis (traditional 'all-you-can-eat' plate meal) for lunch.

It's wise to make a booking for dinner.

Four Seasons
Multicuisine $$

(☎0141-2375450; D43A Subhash Marg; mains ₹125-295; ☺11am-3.30pm & 6.30-11pm) Four Seasons is one of Jaipur's best vegetarian restaurants. It's a popular place with dining on two levels and a glass wall to the busy kitchens. There's a great range of dishes on offer, including tasty Rajasthani specialities, South Indian dosas (paper-thin lentil-flour pancakes), Chinese fare, and a selection of thalis and pizzas. No alcohol.

LMB
Indian $$

(☎0141-2560845; Johari Bazaar; mains ₹210-320; ☺8am-11pm) Laxmi Misthan Bhandar, LMB to you and me, is a vegetarian restaurant in the Old City that's been going strong since 1954. A welcoming air-conditioned refuge from frenzied Johari Bazaar, LMB is also an institution with its singular decor, attentive waiters and extensive sweet counter. No longer *sattvik* (pure vegetarian), you can now order meals with onion and garlic.

Popular with both local and international tourists, try the Rajasthan thali (₹540) followed by the signature *kulfa* (₹100, a fusion of *kulfi* and *falooda* with dry fruits and saffron).

Hotel Sweet Dream
Multicuisine $$

(☎0141-2314409; www.hotelsweetdreamjaipur.in; Nehru Bazaar; mains ₹130-285) This hotel in the Old City has a splendid restaurant on the roof

Jaipur Gems

Jaipur is famous for precious and semiprecious stones. Many shops offer bargain prices, but you do need to know your gems. The main gem-dealing area is around the Muslim area of Pahar Ganj.

You can get an authenticity certificate for gems at the **gem-testing laboratory** (☎0141-2568221; www.gtljaipur. info; Rajasthan Chamber Bhawan, MI Rd; ☺10am-4pm Mon-Sat). The service costs ₹1050 per stone for next-day service, or ₹1650 for same-day service if deposited before 1pm.

with views down to bustling Nehru Bazaar. It's a great place to break the shopping spree and grab a light lunch or a refreshing *makhania* lassi (₹140) made with fresh fruits and curd. The menu includes pizza and Chinese, but the Indian is best.

Niro's
Indian $$$

(☎0141-2374493; MI Rd; mains ₹250-500; ☺10am-11pm) Established in 1949, Niro's is a long-standing favourite on MI Rd that, like a good wine, only improves with age. Escape the chaos of the street by ducking into its cool, clean, mirror-ceilinged sanctum to savour veg and nonveg Indian cuisine with professional service. Classic Chinese and Continental food are available, but the Indian menu is definitely the pick.

Little Italy
Italian $$$

(☎0141-4022444; 3rd fl, KK Square, Prithviraj Marg; mains ₹300-500; ☺noon-10pm) The best Italian restaurant in Jaipur, Little Italy is part of a small national chain that offers excellent vegetarian pasta, risotto, and wood-fired pizzas in cool, contemporary surroundings. The menu is extensive and includes some Mexican items, plus first-rate Italian desserts. It's licensed and there's an attached sister concern, Little India, with an Indian and Chinese menu.

Bar-restaurant, City Palace (p106)

Jaipur Modern
Kitchen   Mediterranean $$$

(📞0141-411 300; www.jaipurmodern.com;51 Sardar Patel Marg, C-Scheme, ⊙11am-11pm; mains ₹300-550) Jaipur Modern boasts this super Mediterranean cafe showcasing organic ingredients and supporting local sustainable agriculture. The tasty pizzas, pastas, momos and wraps are all made in-house. There's even a special emphasis on locally grown quinoa; the Q menu features soups. appetisers, mains and desserts, all containing the versatile seed.

🍸 DRINKING & NIGHTLIFE

Most upper-end hotel bars are good for casual drinking.

Bar Palladio   Bar

(📞0141-2565556; www.bar-palladio.com; Narain Niwas Palace Hotel, Narain Singh Rd; cocktails ₹500-700; ⊙6-11pm) This cool bar-restaurant boasts an extensive drinks list and an Italian food menu (mains ₹350 to ₹400). The vivid blue theme of the romantic Orientalist interior flows through to candlelit outdoor seating,

making this a very relaxing place to sip a drink, snack on bruschetta and enjoy a conversation. Il Teatro is an occasional live-music event at the bar – see the website for dates.

Blackout   Club

(📞0141-3319497; www.facebook.com/blackout-jaipur; Hotel Golden Oak, Ahinsa Circle, C-Scheme; cocktails from ₹225; ⊙1pm-2am) This popular spot is spread over three levels, including the rooftop, which boasts great views of the city. There's ample seating, good food (mains ₹225 to ₹400), a DJ and a dance floor. It's more of a restaurant during the week and a club on the weekends. Thursday night (from 8pm) is Ladies' Night, with free cocktails for women.

Lassiwala   Cafe

(Ml Rd; lassi small/large ₹25/50; ⊙7.30am until sold out) This famous, much-imitated institution is a simple place that whips up fabulous, creamy lassis in clay cups. Get here early to avoid disappointment! Will the real Lassiwala please stand up? It's the one that says 'Shop 312' and 'Since 1944', directly next to the alleyway. Imitators spread to the right as you face it.

 INFORMATION

RTDC Tourist Office (0141-5155137; www.rajasthantourism.gov.in; former RTDC Tourist Hotel, MI Rd; ⊕9.30am-6pm Mon-Fri) Has maps and brochures on Jaipur and Rajasthan. Additional branches at the **airport** (0141-2722647; ⊕9am-5pm Mon-Fri), **Amber Fort** (0141-2530264; ⊕9.30am-5pm Mon-Fri), **Jaipur train station** (0141-2200778; platform 1; ⊕24hr) and the **main bus station** (0141-5064102; platform 3; ⊕10am-5pm Mon-Fri).

 GETTING THERE & AWAY

AIR

Jaipur International Airport (0141-2550623; www.jaipurairport.com), 12km southeast of the city, has daily flights to Delhi and Mumbai with the following:

Air India (0141-2743500, airport 0141-2721333; www.airindia.com; Nehru Place, Tonk Rd)

IndiGo (9212783838; www.goindigo.in; Terminal 2, Jaipur International Airport) Also flies to Bengaluru.

Jet Airways (0141-2725025, 1800 225522; www.jetairways.com; ⊕5.30am-9pm)

Scoot (8000016354; www.scoot.com) Flies to Singapore.

SpiceJet (9871803333; www.spicejet.com; Terminal 2; ⊕6am-7pm).

Thai Smile (Thailand +662-1188888; www.thaismileair.com) Flies to Bangkok.

BUS

Rajasthan State Road Transport Corporation (RSRTC, aka Rajasthan Roadways) buses all leave from the **main bus station** (Station Rd; left luggage per bag per 24hr ₹10), picking up passengers at Narain Singh Circle (where you can also buy tickets).

Ordinary buses are known as 'express' buses. 'Deluxe' buses (from platform 3) are generally much more expensive and comfortable (usually

 Where to Stay

There are plenty of pickings along and near Mirza Ismail (MI) Rd, plus options in the Old City, the Rambagh area and the relatively peaceful Bani Park area about 2km west of the Old City.

with air-con), and can be booked in advance at the **reservation office** (0141-5116032; Main Bus Station).

Destinations include Agra (₹261 to ₹289, AC ₹470 to ₹573, 5½ hours, 11 buses daily), Delhi (₹273, AC ₹800, 5½ hours, at least hourly) and Jaisalmer (₹593, 14 hours, two buses daily).

TRAIN

The **reservation office** (enquiries 131, reservations 135; ⊕8am-2pm & 3-8pm) is to your left as you enter Jaipur train station. It's open for advance reservations only (more than five hours before departure). Services include the following:

Agra Sleeper ₹185, 3½ to 4½ hours, nine daily.

Delhi Sleeper ₹245, 4½ to six hours, at least nine daily (1am, 2.50am, 4.40am, 5am, 6am, 2.35pm, 4.25pm, 5.50pm and 11.15pm), more on selected days.

Jaisalmer Sleeper ₹350, 12 hours, three daily (11.10am, 4.15pm and 11.45pm)

Ranthambhore NP (Sawai Madhopur) Sleeper ₹180, two to three hours, at least nine daily (12.30am, 5.40am, 6.40am, 11.05am, 2pm, 4.50pm, 5.35pm, 7.35pm and 8.45pm), more on selected days.

 GETTING AROUND

There are no bus services from the airport. An autorickshaw/taxi costs at least ₹350/450. There's a prepaid taxi booth inside the terminal.

Autorickshaw drivers at the bus and train stations might just be the pushiest in Rajasthan. Use the fixed-rate prepaid autorickshaw stands instead.

If you have the apps, both Uber and Ola operate in Jaipur and both offer cheaper services than autorickshaws, without the need to haggle.

Ranthambhore National Park

Sighting a tiger in the wild is an incomparable thrill and India has about 70% of the world's wild tigers. Ranthambhore presents some of the best chances of spotting these majestic jungle beasts.

Great For...

☑ Don't Miss

Historic Ranthambhore Fort, with peerless hilltop panoramas, makes a great complement to wildlife safaris.

Ranthambhore's 1334 sq km of wild jungle scrub is home to around 50 to 55 tigers. Spotting any is partly a matter of luck, so allow time for two or three safaris to maximise your chances. Even if no tigers appear, there's plenty of other wildlife to see, including more than 300 bird species.

The park's gateway town is Sawai Madhopur, about 150km southeast of Jaipur. From here it's 10km to the first park gate, and another 3km to the main gate.

Safaris

Safaris start between 6am and 7am and between 2pm and 3.30pm, depending on the time of year. Each safari lasts for around three hours. Mornings can be exceptionally chilly in the open vehicles, so bring warm clothes.

Royal Bengal tigers

❶ Need to Know

www.rajasthanwildlife.in; ⊙Oct-Jun

✗ Take a Break

Between safaris it's convenient to eat at your hotel. Many hotels offer full-board packages.

> ★ **Top Tip**
>
> **Arrange your safaris as far ahead as possible. Three or even four months is ideal.**

If all else fails, a limited number of vehicles (one gypsy and five canters at research time) are kept for in-person booking at the **safari booking office** (⊙5.30am-3.30pm) in Sawai Madhopur. To be sure of getting a seat, start queuing at least an hour (if not two) before safaris are due to begin – meaning a very early start for morning safaris!

Getting There & Away

Sawai Madhopur is poorly served by buses, but Sawai Madhopur Junction train station (near Hammir Circle, which leads to Ranthambhore Rd) has services to/from Agra (Agra Fort Station; sleeper ₹210, six hours, three daily), Delhi (2nd-class/sleeper/3AC ₹190/260/660, 5½ to eight hours, 13 daily) and Jaipur (2nd-class seat/sleeper/3AC ₹100/180/560, two hours, 11 to 13 daily).

Many hotels will pick you up from the train station for free if you call ahead.

The best option is to travel by **gypsy** (six-person, open-topped 4WD; Indian/foreigner ₹730/1470). You still have a chance of seeing a tiger from a **canter** (20-seat, open-topped truck; ₹510/1250), but other passengers can be rowdy.

The rules for booking safaris (and prices) are prone to change. Safaris can be booked online through the park's website, but the process is fraught with complications and difficulties. It's far better to get hotels to arrange things, even though they charge commission. Try to book well ahead as safari seats can sell out very early. The area's nicest accommodation is stretched out along Ranthambhore Rd, between Sawai Madhopur and the park, and all these hotels can help with safari bookings.

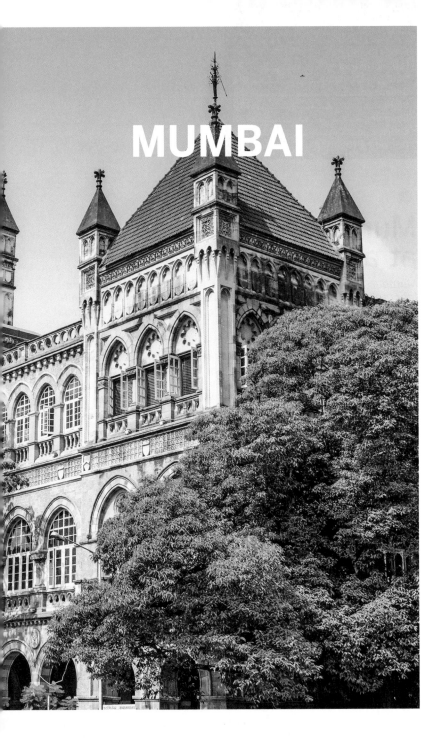
MUMBAI

In this Chapter
Bazaar District.................................122
Dining in Mumbai 124
Bollywood...126
Sights 130
Shopping..132
Eating 132
Drinking & Nightlife.......................136

Mumbai at a Glance...

Mumbai, formerly Bombay, is big. It's full of dreamers and hard-labourers, starlets and gangsters, fisherfolk and crorepatis (millionaires), and many millions of other people. It's India's financial powerhouse and fashion epicentre, it's home to India's most prolific film industry and it has some of Asia's biggest slums.

Mumbai's furious energy and punishing pollution are challenging, but it isn't a threatening place. It contains some of the world's grandest colonial-era architecture, and you'll uncover unique bazaars, hidden temples and India's premier restaurants and nightlife.

Mumbai in Two Days

Begin at **Chhatrapati Shivaji Maharaj Vastu Sangrahalaya** (p130), before lunch at **Samrat** (p133). Tour the **Gateway of India** (p130) and **Taj Mahal Palace** (p130), then fine-dine at **Indigo** (p124).

On day two visit the **Chhatrapati Shivaji Terminus** (p130) and unique **Crawford Market** (p122) and wander the lanes of Khotachiwadi. Hip Lower Parel beckons for dinner and craft beers at **Woodside Inn** (p138).

Mumbai in Four Days

Sail to **Elephanta Island** (p136) on your third day, returning for lunch in artsy Kala Ghoda. In the evening, head north for exquisite seafood at **Bastian** (p135), followed by bar action in Bandra.

On day four visit the **Mahalaxmi Dhobi Ghat** (p137), **Mahalaxmi Temple** (p137) and **Haji Ali Dargah** (p137). Call it a night after exploring modern Indian fare at **Masala Library** (p125).

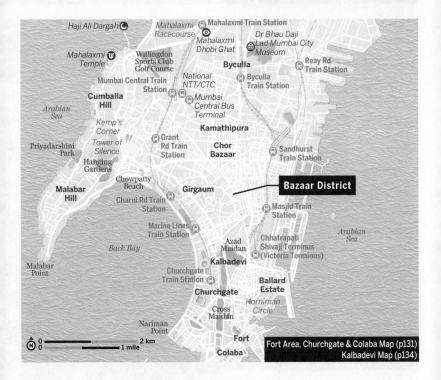

Haji Ali Dargah

Mahalaxmi Racecourse

Mahalaxmi Train Station

Dr Bhau Daji Lad Mumbai City Museum

Mahalaxmi Temple

Willingdon Sports Club Golf Course

Mahalaxmi Dhobi Ghat

Byculla

Reay Rd Train Station

Mumbai Central Train Station

National NTT/CTC

Byculla Train Station

Arabian Sea

Cumballa Hill

Mumbai Central Bus Terminal

Kemp's Corner

Kamathipura

Priyadarshini Park

Tower of Silence

Grant Rd Train Station

Chor Bazaar

Sandhurst Train Station

Hanging Gardens

Chowpatty Beach

Malabar Hill

Charni Rd Train Station

Girgaum

Bazaar District

Masjid Train Station

Marine Lines Train Station

Arabian Sea

Back Bay

Azad Maidan

Chhatrapati Shivaji Terminus (Victoria Terminus)

Malabar Point

Kalbadevi

Churchgate Train Station

Ballard Estate

Churchgate

Horniman Circle

Cross Maidan

Nariman Point

Fort

Fort Area, Churchgate & Colaba Map (p131)
Kalbadevi Map (p134)

N 0 2 km
0 1 mile

Colaba

Arriving in Mumbai

Chhatrapati Shivaji International Airport International flights at Terminal 2; domestic flights at Terminal 2 or 1B.

Chhatrapati Shivaji Terminus (CST) Trains to/from the east and south and a few to/from the north.

Mumbai Central station (BCT) Trains to/from the north.

Mumbai Central Bus Terminal Government-run buses.

Dr Anadrao Nair Rd Private buses.

Sleeping

Mumbai has the most expensive accommodation in India; you'll never quite feel you're getting your money's worth. Always book ahead.

Compact Colaba has the liveliest tourist scene and many budget and midrange options. Neighbouring Fort area is convenient for train stations and is a dining and shopping epicentre. Most top-end places are along Marine Dr or in the western suburbs.

Bazaar District

Mumbai's main market district is one of Asia's most fascinating, an incredibly dense combination of humanity and commerce that's a total assault on the senses.

If you've just got off a plane from the West, or a taxi from Bandra – hold on tight!

This working-class district stretches north of Crawford Market up as far as Chor Bazaar, a 2.5km walk away. Such are the crowds (and narrowness of the lanes) that progress through the markets is never quick.

You can buy just about anything here, but as the stores and stalls are very much geared to local tastes, most of the fun is simply taking in the street life and investigating the souk-like lanes rather than buying souvenirs. The markets merge into each other in an amoeba-like mass, but there are some key landmarks so you can orientate yourself.

Crawford Market

Crawford Market (Map p134; Mahatma Phule Market; cnr DN & Lokmanya Tilak Rds;

Great For...

☑ Don't Miss

If you're in Crawford Market during Alphonso mango season (May to June) be sure to indulge.

Crawford Market

ℹ Need to Know

The markets are open daily, about 10am to 9pm. Some individual shops close on Sunday.

✗ Take a Break

Stop into **Badshah Snacks & Drinks** (Map p134; 52/156 Umrigar Bldg, Lokmanya Tilak Marg; snacks & drinks ₹55-240; ⏱7am-12.30am) for its famous *falooda* (rose-flavoured drink).

★ Top Tip

You need at least two to three hours to explore the market district thoroughly.

⏱10.30am-9pm) is the largest in Mumbai, and contains the last whiff of British Bombay before the tumult of the central bazaars begins. Bas-reliefs by Rudyard Kipling's father, Lockwood Kipling, adorn the Norman Gothic exterior. Fruit and vegetables, meat and fish are mainly traded, but it's also an excellent place to stock up on spices.

Mangaldas Market

Mangaldas Market (Map p134), traditionally home to traders from Gujarat, is a mini-town, complete with lanes of fabrics.

Zaveri Bazaar

Wander the narrow lanes of Mumbai's **jewellery market** (Map p134) in search of gems, jewels and gold – 65% of India's gold trade emerges from here. Notable jewellers include Tribhovandas Bhimji Zaveri and Dhirajlal Bhimji Zaveri.

Bhuleshwar Market

Bhuleshwar Market (Map p134; cnr Sheikh Memon St & M Devi Marg; ⏱10am-9pm) has fruit and veg. Just a few metres further along Sheikh Memon St are a Jain pigeon-feeding station, a flower market and a religious market.

Chor Bazaar

Chor Bazaar (Map p134; Mutton St, Kumbharwada) is known for antiques, though nowadays many of them are reproductions. The main area of activity is Mutton St, where shops specialise in these 'antiques' and miscellaneous junk. Dhabu St, to the east, is lined with fine leather goods.

Dining in Mumbai

Mumbai is India's culinary capital, with flavours from all over India colliding with international trends. You can feast like a maharaja or snack on an infinite array of street foods.

Great For...

☑ **Don't Miss**

Dabeli, a street-food flavour bomb of potatoes, spices, peanuts and pomegranate, on bread.

Top Dining Experiences

Peshawri

Make the Northwest Frontier restaurant **Peshawri** (☎022-28303030; www.itchotels.in; ITC Maratha, Sahar Rd, Andheri East; mains ₹1600-3000; ⏰12.45-2.45pm & 7-11.45pm), outside the international airport, your first or last stop in Mumbai. Folks flock here for the buttery dhal bukhara (a 24-hour simmered black dhal; ₹800), but its kebabs are sublime: try the Murgh Malai (tandoor-grilled chicken marinated in cream cheese, malt vinegar, green chilli and coriander).

Indigo

The incredibly classy Colaba institution **Indigo** (Map p131; ☎022-66368980; www.foodindigo.com; 4 Mandlik Marg; mains ₹885-2185; ⏰noon-3pm & 7-11.45pm; 📶) is a colonial-era property converted into a

Bhelpuri

❶ Need to Know

Reservations are always a good idea, and sometimes essential, at high-end and trendy restaurants.

✕ Take a Break

Need to slow things down? Sip organic, ayurvedic and exotic teas at **Cha Bar** (Map p131; Oxford Bookstore, Apeejay House, 3 Dinsha Vachha Marg, Churchgate; ☺11am-8pm).

★ Top Tip

North Mumbai is home to the city's trendiest dining, centred on Bandra West and Juhu.

Street Food

Mumbai's street cuisine is more vast than many Western culinary traditions. Stalls tend to get started in the late afternoon; items are ₹10 to ₹80.

Most street food is vegetarian. Chowpatty Beach is a great place to try Mumbai's famous *bhelpuri* (a delectable combination of crisp papadis, puffed rice, crunchy *sev* noodles, onions, potatoes, mango and chutneys). Stalls offering samosas, *pav bhaji* (spiced vegetables and bread), *vada pav* (deep-fried spiced lentil-ball sandwich) and *bhurji pav* (scrambled eggs and bread) are spread through the city.

Mohammed Ali and Merchant Rds in Kalbadevi are famous for meaty kebabs. In Colaba, **Bademiya Seekh Kebab Stall** (Map p131; www.bademiya.com; Tulloch Rd; light meals ₹110-220; ☺5pm-4am) is a late-night Mumbai rite of passage, renowned for its chicken tikka rolls.

temple of fine dining. It serves inventive, expensive European and Asian cuisine and offers a long wine list, sleek ambience and a gorgeous rooftop deck. Favourites include creamed pumpkin and sage ravioli and maple orange-glazed duck breast.

Masala Library

Daring and imaginative **Masala Library** (☎022-66424142; www.masalalibrary.co.in; ground fl, First International Financial Centre, G Block, Bandra East; mains ₹500-900, tasting menu ₹2300-2500, with wine ₹3800-4000; ☺noon-2.15pm & 7-11pm) challenges us to rethink our notions of subcontinent cuisine. The tasting menus are an exotic culinary journey – think pan-tossed mushrooms with black pepper, dill crust and truffle haze; and kashmiri chilli duck; and *jalebi* caviar.

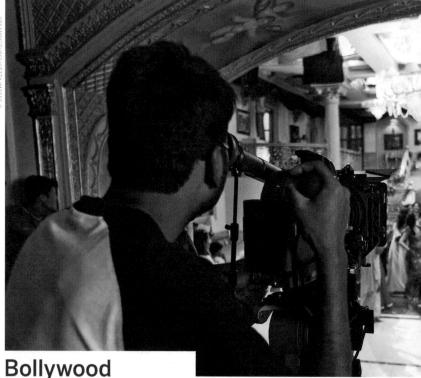

Bollywood

Mumbai is the glittering epicentre of India's gargantuan Hindi-language film industry, entrancing the nation with more than 1000 films a year.

Great For...

☑ Don't Miss

To experience Bollywood blockbusters in situ, try **Eros Cinema** (Maharshi Karve Rd, Churchgate; www.eroscinema.co.in; tickets ₹130-180).

The Lumière brothers screened the first film ever shown in India at the Watson Hotel in Mumbai in 1896. Beginning with the 1913 silent epic *Raja Harishchandra* (with an all-male cast, some in drag) and the first talkie, *Lama Ara* (1931), Bollywood now churns out more than 1000 films a year – doubling Hollywood's output, and not surprising considering it has a captive audience of one-sixth of the world's population.

Every part of India has its regional film industry, but Bollywood continues to entrance the nation with its escapist formula in which all-singing, all-dancing lovers fight and conquer the forces keeping them apart. These days, Hollywood-inspired thrillers and action extravaganzas vie for moviegoers' attention alongside the more family-oriented saccharine formulas.

Bollywood film set

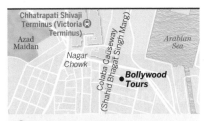

Bollywood stars can attain near godlike status in India and star-spotting is a favourite activity.

Bollywood Tours

You can see the stars' homes as well as a film/TV studio with **Bollywood Tours** (☏9820255202; www.bollywoodtours.in; 8 Lucky House, Goa St, Fort; per person 4/8hr tour ₹8000/10,000), but you're not guaranteed to see a dance number and you may spend much of your time in traffic.

Indian Hippy

Indian Hippy (☏8080822022; www.hippy. in; 17C Sherly Rajan Rd, Bandra West, off Carter Rd; ⊘by appointment) will put your name in lights, with custom-designed vintage Bollywood posters hand-painted on canvas by original studio artists (a dying breed since

the advent of digital illustrating). Bring (or email) a photo and your imagination (or let them guide you). Also sells vintage film posters and all manner of (frankly bizarre) Bollywood-themed products. Portraits cost ₹7500 to ₹15,000. Ships worldwide.

Extra, Extra!

Studios sometimes want Westerners as extras to add a whiff of international flair (or provocative dress, which locals often won't wear) to a film. If you're game, just hang around Colaba (especially the Salvation Army hostel) where studio scouts will find you.

A day's work, which can be up to 16 hours, pays around ₹500 (more for speaking roles). You'll get lunch, snacks and (usually) transport. The day can be long and hot with loads of standing around the set. Before agreeing to anything, always ask for the scout's identification and go with your gut.

Architectural Mumbai

Mumbai's defining visual feature is its distinctive mix of colonial-era architecture, including gorgeous art-deco creations from the 1920s and '30s.

Start Gateway of India
Distance 2.5km
Duration 1½ hours

7 Cross the Oval Maidan for the art-deco beauties along its west side, especially **Eros cinema** (p126).

Cross Maidan

Marine Dr

Churchgate Train Station

Veer Nariman Rd

FINISH **7**

Oval Maidan

Bhaurao Patil Marg

6

Maharshi Karve Rd

Madame Cama

6 Backtrack past Flora Fountain and south to the august High Court and the ornate **University of Mumbai** (Bhaurao Patil Marg).

Woodhouse Rd (Nathalal Parekh Marg)

Arabian Sea

Take a Break...Stop for the legendary breakfasts at **Pantry** (Yashwanth Chambers, Military Sq Ln, B Bharucha Marg, Kala Gh).

N
0   500 m
0   0.25 miles

4 Continue to the Flora Fountain and turn east down Veer Nariman Rd to **St Thomas' Cathedral** (Veer Nariman Rd, Churchgate; ⊘7am-6pm).

5 Ahead lies stately **Horniman Circle**, an arcaded ring of 1860s buildings around a beautifully kept botanical garden.

Chhatrapati Shivaji Terminus (Victoria Terminus)

Sir P Mehta Rd

Mahatma Gandhi (MG) Rd

Homi Modi St

Nagindas Master Rd

M Samachar Marg

Shahid Bhagat Singh Marg

K Dubash Marg

❌ Pantry

Rd

MB Marg

Pj Ramchandani Marg (Strand Rd)

Classic Photo The Chhatrapati Shivaji Maharaj Vastu Sangrahalaya, a blend of Islamic, Hindu and British styles fronted by tall palms.

3 VICTOR JIANG-SHUTTERSTOCK © · 6 RACHEL MOON-SHUTTERSTOCK ©

3 Continue up Mahatma Gandhi (MG) Rd, passing the glorious Indo-Saracenic **Chhatrapati Shivaji Maharaj Vastu Sangrahalaya** (p130).

2 Walk to **Regal Circle** to admire buildings such as the art-deco Regal Cinema.

Arabian Sea

START 1

1 Start at the **Gateway of India** (p130), with the world-famous Taj Mahal Palace hotel behind it.

⊙ SIGHTS

Gateway of India   Monument

(Map p131) This bold basalt arch of colonial triumph faces out to Mumbai Harbour from the tip of Apollo Bunder. Incorporating Islamic styles of 16th-century Gujarat, it was built to commemorate the 1911 royal visit of King George V, but wasn't completed until 1924. Ironically, the British builders of the gateway used it just 24 years later to parade the last British regiment as India marched towards independence.

Taj Mahal Palace, Mumbai   Landmark

(Map p131; https://taj.tajhotels.com; Apollo Bunder) Mumbai's most famous landmark, this stunning hotel is a fairy-tale blend of Islamic and Renaissance styles, and India's second-most photographed monument. It was built in 1903 by the Parsi industrialist JN Tata, supposedly after he was refused entry to nearby European hotels on account of being 'a native'. Dozens were killed inside the hotel when it was targeted during the 2008 terrorist attacks, and images of its burning facade were beamed worldwide. The fully restored hotel reopened on Independence Day 2010.

Chhatrapati Shivaji Maharaj Vastu Sangrahalaya   Museum

(Map p131; Prince of Wales Museum; www.csmvs.in; 159-161 Mahatma Gandhi Rd, Fort; Indian/foreigner ₹70/500, mobile/camera ₹50/100; ⊙10.15am-6pm) Mumbai's biggest and best museum displays a mix of India-wide exhibits. The domed behemoth, an intriguing hodgepodge of Islamic, Hindu and British architecture, is a flamboyant Indo-Saracenic design by George Wittet (who also designed the Gateway of India). Its vast collection includes impressive Hindu and Buddhist sculpture, terracotta figurines from the Indus Valley, Indian miniature paintings and some particularly vicious-looking weaponry.

Marine Drive   Waterfront

(Map p131; Netaji Subhashchandra Bose Rd) Built on reclaimed land in 1920, Marine Dr arcs along the shore of the Arabian Sea from Nariman Point past Girgaum Chowpatty and continues to the foot of Malabar Hill. Lined with flaking art-deco apartments, it's one of Mumbai's most popular promenades and sunset-watching spots. Its twinkling night-time lights earned it the nickname 'the Queen's Necklace'.

Chhatrapati Shivaji Terminus   Historic Building

(Map p134; Victoria Terminus) Imposing, exuberant and overflowing with people, this monumental train station is the city's most extravagant Gothic building and an aphorism for colonial-era India. It's a meringue of Victorian, Hindu and Islamic styles whipped into an imposing Daliesque structure of buttresses, domes, turrets, spires and stained glass.

Fort Area, Churchgate & Colaba

⊙ **Sights**
1 Chhatrapati Shivaji Maharaj Vastu
    Sangrahalaya C5
2 Gateway of India D6
3 Marine Drive A2
4 St Thomas' Cathedral D3
5 Taj Mahal Palace, Mumbai D6
6 University of Mumbai C4

🛍 **Shopping**
7 Contemporary Arts & Crafts D1
8 Cottonworld Corp C6
9 Fabindia C4
10 Fashion Street C1

🍴 **Eating**
11 Bademiya Seekh Kebab Stall D6
12 Indigo C6
13 Khyber C4
14 Pantry C4
15 Samrat B3

🍷 **Drinking & Nightlife**
16 Cha Bar B4
17 Colaba Social C6
18 Harbour Bar D6

🎭 **Entertainment**
19 Eros B3

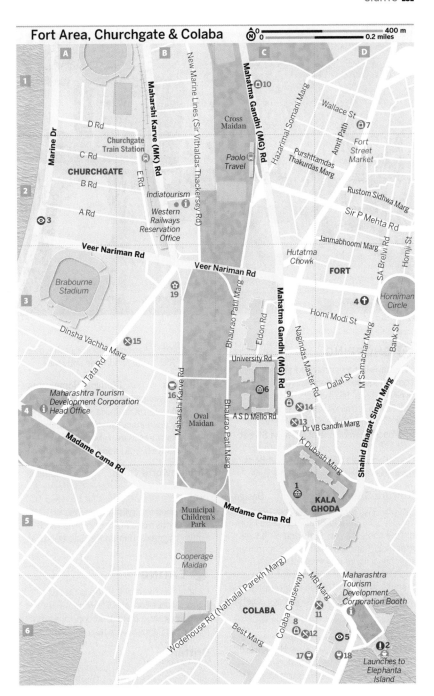

Fort Area, Churchgate & Colaba

N 0 — 400 m
0 — 0.2 miles

Marine Dr

D Rd

C Rd

CHURCHGATE

B Rd

A Rd

Maharshi Karve (MK) Rd

Churchgate Train Station

E Rd

New Marine Lines (Sir Vithaldas Thackersey Rd)

Mahatma Gandhi (MG) Rd

10

Cross Maiden

Paolo Travel

Indiatourism

Western Railways Reservation Office

Wallace St

7

Fort Street Market

Hazarimal Somani Marg

Amrit Path

Purshttamdas Thakurdas Marg

Rustom Sidhwa Marg

Sir P Mehta Rd

Janmabhoomi Marg

3

Veer Nariman Rd

Veer Nariman Rd

Hutatma Chowk

FORT

SA Brelvi Rd

Homji St

Brabourne Stadium

19

Bhaurao Patil Marg

Eldon Rd

Mahatma Gandhi (MG) Rd

4

Homi Modi St

Horniman Circle

Bank St

Dinsha Vachha Marg

15

J Tata Rd

Nagindas Master Rd

Dalal St

M Samachar Marg

Maharashtra Tourism Development Corporation Head Office

16

Maharshi Karve Rd

University Rd

6

9

14

Bhaurao Patil Marg

A S D Mello Rd

Oval Maidan

13

Dr VB Gandhi Marg

Shahid Bhagat Singh Marg

Madame Cama Rd

K Dubash Marg

1

KALA GHODA

Municipal Children's Park

Madame Cama Rd

Cooperage Maiden

Wodehouse Rd (Nathalal Parekh Marg)

Best Marg

Colaba Causeway

MB Marg

COLABA

8

12

11

Maharashtra Tourism Development Corporation Booth

5

17

18

2

Launches to Elephanta Island

Fashion Street

WIN INITIATIVE/GETTY IMAGES ©

🔒 SHOPPING

Mumbai is India's great marketplace, with some of the best shopping in the country. Spend a day at the markets north of Chhatrapati Shivaji Terminus for the classic Mumbai shopping experience. Snap up a bargain backpacking wardrobe at **Fashion Street** (Map p131; Mahatma Gandhi Rd). The Kemp's Corner and Kala Ghoda neighbourhoods have good shops for designer threads.

Kulture Shop — Design

(www.kultureshop.in; 241 Hill Rd, Bandra West; ⏰11am-8pm) Behold Bandra's – and Mumbai's – coolest shop, featuring exclusive graphic art and illustrations sourced from a global army of Indian artists. You'll find thought-provoking and conceptually daring T-shirts, art prints, coffee mugs, notebooks, stationery and other cutting-edge objets d'art.

Contemporary Arts & Crafts — Homewares

(Map p131; www.cac.co.in; 210 Dr Dadabhai Naoroji Rd, Fort; ⏰10.30am-7.30pm) Modish, high-quality takes on traditional crafts: these are not your usual handmade souvenirs.

Fabindia — Clothing, Homewares

(Map p131; www.fabindia.com; Jeroo Bldg, 137 Mahatma Gandhi Rd, Kala Ghoda; ⏰10am-9pm) 🌿 Ethically sourced cotton and silk fashions and homewares in everybody's favourite modern-meets-traditional Indian shop.

Cottonworld Corp — Clothing

(Map p131; www.cottonworld.net; Mandlik Marg, Colaba; ⏰10.30am-8pm Mon-Sat, noon-8pm Sun) A great shop for stylish Indian-Western-hybrid goods made from cotton, linen and natural materials. Think Indian Gap, but cooler.

✖ EATING

Colaba has most of the cheap tourist haunts, while Fort and Churchgate are more upscale, a trend that continues in Mahalaxmi and the western suburbs.

Brittania — Parsi $$

(Wakefield House, Ballard Estate; mains ₹250-900; ⏰noon-4pm Mon-Sat) This Parsi institution is the domain of 95-year-old Boman Kohinoor, who will warm your heart with his stories (and he still takes the orders!). The signature dishes are the *dhansak* (meat with curried lentils and rice) and the berry *pulao* – spiced and boneless mutton or chicken, veg or egg, buried in basmati rice and tart barberries imported from Iran.

Samrat   Gujarati $$
(Map p131; www.prashantcaterers.com; Prem Ct, J Tata Rd; thali lunch/dinner ₹330/415; ⊘noon-11pm) Samrat has an à la carte menu but most rightly opt for the famous Gujarati thali (traditional 'all-you-can-eat' plate meal) – a cavalcade of taste and texture, sweetness and spice that includes four curries, three chutneys, curd, rotis and other bits and pieces. Samrat is air-conditioned and beer is available.

Dakshinayan   South Indian $$
(Anand Hotel, Gandhigram Rd, Juhu; mains ₹130-250; ⊘11am-11pm Mon-Sat, from 8am Sun) With *rangoli* (elaborate coloured powder design) on the walls, servers in lungis and sari-clad women lunching (*chappals* off

 Mumbai: Getting Your Bearings

Mumbai is an island connected by bridges to the mainland. The city's commercial and cultural centre is at the southern, claw-shaped end of the island known as South Mumbai. The southernmost peninsula is Colaba, traditionally the travellers' nerve centre, a bustling district with elegant colonial-era mansions.

North of Colaba is the busy commercial area known as Fort, where many majestic Victorian buildings still stand. Kala Ghoda is a hip, atmospheric sub-neighbourhood of Fort with many of Mumbai's museums, galleries, boutiques, restaurants and cafes.

Continuing north you enter 'the suburbs', which contain the airport and many of Mumbai's best restaurants, shops and nightspots. The upmarket districts Bandra, Juhu and Lower Parel are key areas.

Samrat restaurant

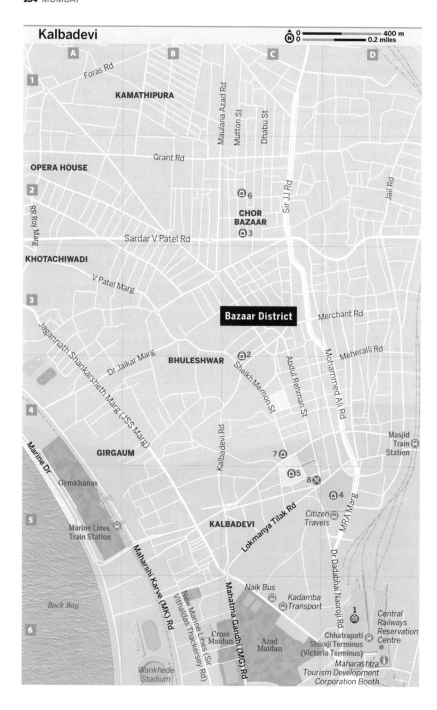

Kalbadevi

N 0 ——————— 400 m
0 ——————— 0.2 miles

A **B** **C** **D**

1

Foras Rd

KAMATHIPURA

Maulana Azad Rd

Mutton St

Dhabu St

Grant Rd

OPERA HOUSE

2

RR Roy Marg

Sir JJ Rd

🏛6

CHOR BAZAAR

Sardar V Patel Rd

🏛3

KHOTACHIWADI

V Patel Marg

3

Jagannath Shankarsheth Marg (JSS Marg)

Dr Jaikar Marg

Bazaar District

Merchant Rd

Meheralli Rd

BHULESHWAR

🏛2

Sheikh Memon St

Abdul Rehman St

Mohammed Ali Rd

4

Kalbadevi Rd

GIRGAUM

7🏛

Masjid Train Station

Marine Dr

Gymkhanas

🏛5

8🍴

KALBADEVI

🏛4

MRA Marg

5

Marine Lines Train Station

Lokmanya Tilak Rd

Citizen Travels

Dr Dadabhai Naoroji Rd

Maharshi Karve (MK) Rd

Naik Bus

Kadamba Transport

New Marine Lines (Sir Vithaldas Thackersey Rd)

Mahatma Gandhi (MG) Rd

1

6

Back Bay

Cross Maidan

Azad Maidan

Chhatrapati Shivaji Terminus (Victoria Terminus)

Central Railways Reservation Centre

Maharashtra Tourism Development Corporation Booth

Wankhede Stadium

Jail Rd

Kalbadevi

◎ **Sights**
  1 Chhatrapati Shivaji Terminus D6

🏬 **Shopping**
  2 Bhuleshwar Market C3
  3 Chor Bazaar... C2
  4 Crawford Market..D5

  5 Mangaldas Market C5
  6 Mini Market/Bollywood
     Bazaar/Super Sale C2
  7 Zaveri Bazaar..C4

🍴 **Eating**
  8 Badshah Snacks & Drinks.......................... C5

under the table), Dakshinayan channels Tamil Nadu. There are delicately textured dosas, *idli* (spongy, round, fermented rice cake) and *uttapam* (thick, savoury South Indian rice pancake with finely chopped onions, green chillies, coriander and coconut), village-fresh chutneys and perhaps the best *rasam* (tomato soup with spices and tamarind) in Mumbai. Finish off with a South Indian filter coffee, served in a stainless-steel set.

Khyber   Mughlai, Indian $$$

(Map p131; ☏022-40396666; www.khyberrestaurant.com; 145 Mahatma Gandhi Rd; mains ₹510-1100; ⊗12.30-4pm & 7.30-11.30pm) The much-acclaimed Khyber has a Northwest Frontier–themed design that incorporates murals depicting turbaned Mughal royalty, lots of exposed brickwork and oil lanterns – just the sort of place an Afghan warlord might feel at home. The meat-centric menu features gloriously tender kebabs, rich curries and lots of tandoori favourites roasted in the Khyber's famous red masala sauce.

Bastian   Seafood $$$

(www.facebook.com/BastianSeafood; B/1, New Kamal Bldg, Linking Rd, Bandra West; mains for 2 people ₹700-2600; ⊗7pm-12.45am Tue-Sun; 🛜) All the praise bestowed upon this trendy seafooder is indisputably warranted. Chinese-Canadian chef Boo Kwang Kim and his culinary sidekick, American-Korean

Thali meal

Elephanta Island

Out in Mumbai Harbour, the rock-cut temples on **Elephanta Island** (Gharapuri; Indian/foreigner ₹30/500; ☺caves 9am-5pm Tue-Sun) are a Unesco World Heritage Site. Created between AD 450 and 750, the labyrinth of temples represents some of India's most impressive temple carving. Its magnum opus is a 6m-tall statue of Sadhashiva, depicting a three-faced Shiva as the destroyer, creator and preserver of the universe.

Launches (economy/deluxe ₹145/180) head to Elephanta from the Gateway of India every half-hour from 9am to 3.30pm. The voyage takes about an hour.

Kelvin Cheung, have forged an East-meets-West gastronomic dream. Go with the market-fresh side menu: choose your catch (prawns, fish, mud crab or lobster) then pick from an insanely difficult list of impossibly tasty Pan-Asian sauces.

🍷 DRINKING & NIGHTLIFE

Mumbai is a city that really knows how to enjoy itself. Whatever your tipple and whatever your taste, you'll find it here. Colaba is rich in unpretentious pub-like joints, while Bandra, Juhu and Andheri are home turf for the film and model set. Some of the most intriguing new places are opening in midtown areas like Lower Parel, where a craft-beer revolution has taken hold.

Colaba Social   Bar

(Map p131; www.socialoffline.in; ground fl, Glen Rose Bldg, BK Boman Behram Marg, Apollo Bunder; ☺9am-1.30am; ☎) Colaba is the best of the locations of the hip Social chain, which combines a restaurant-bar with a collaborative work space. The happening bar nails the cocktails (₹295 to ₹450) – the

Harbour Bar (p138)

Aer bar

PETER ADAMS/GETTY IMAGES ©

Acharroska is the perfect East-meets-West marriage of Indian pungency and Brazilian sweet. The food (mains ₹160 to ₹360) spans everything from fish and chips and *poutine* to Punjabi and Mangalorean (with great Parsi dishes for breakfast).

There are also Social locations in **Lower Parel** (Todi Mill; www.socialoffline.in; 242 Mathuradas Mill Compound, Todi Mills, Lower Parel; 🕙9am-1am; 🛜) and **Khar** (www.socialoffline. in; Rohan Plaza, 5th Rd, Ram Krishna Nagar, Khar West; mains ₹160-360; 🕙9am-1am; 🛜).

Aer   Lounge

(www.fourseasons.com/mumbai; Four Seasons Hotel, 34th fl, 114 Dr E Moses Rd, Worli; 🕙5.30pm-midnight; 🛜) Boasting astounding sea, sunset and city views, Aer is Mumbai's premier sky bar. Drink prices are steep (cocktails ₹1000 to ₹1500), but that's kind of the point. DJs spin house and lounge tunes nightly, including over groovy happy-hour sundowner specials, concocted by some of Mumbai's best mixologists.

 ## Mahalaxmi Dhobi Ghat

The 140-year-old **Mahalaxmi Dhobi Ghat** (Dr E Moses Rd, Mahalaxmi; 🕙4.30am-dusk) is Mumbai's biggest human-powered washing machine: every day hundreds of people beat the dirt out of thousands of kilograms of soiled Mumbai clothes and linen in 1026 open-air troughs. The best view is from the bridge across the railway tracks near Mahalaxmi train station.

You can combine a visit here with the colourful **Mahalaxmi Temple** (off V Desai Chowk), dedicated to the goddess of wealth; the **Haji Ali Dargah** (www. hajialidargah.in; off V Desai Chowk), a hugely popular Islamic shrine reachable only by a long causeway at low tide; and the excellent **Dr Bhau Daji Lad Mumbai City Museum** (www.bdlmuseum.org; Dr Babasaheb Ambedkar Rd; Indian/foreigner ₹10/100; 🕙10am-6pm Thu-Tue).

Woodside Inn — Craft Beer

(www.facebook.com/WoodsideInn; Mathuradas Mills Compound, NM Joshi Marg, Lower Parel; ⊙11am-1am Mon-Fri, from 10am Sat & Sun) Colaba classic Woodside Inn's third outlet in the city is its most beer-focused yet – 25 taps in total easily make it Mumbai's most exhaustive craft-beer destination (pints from ₹445). You can knock back many of Mumbai's best here – Gateway Brewing Company, Independence Brewing Company, Doolally, Brewbot and White Owl – along with Nitro coffee and elevated gastro-grub.

Harbour Bar — Bar

(Map p131; Taj Mahal Palace, Apollo Bunder; ⊙11am-11.45pm) With unmatched views of the Gateway of India and harbour, this timeless bar inside the Taj Mahal Palace is an essential visit. Drinks aren't uber-expensive (from ₹450/670/900 for a beer/wine/cocktail) given the surrounds and the fact that they come with very generous portions of nibbles (including jumbo cashews).

INFORMATION

Indiatourism (Government of India Tourist Office; ☏022-22074333; www.incredibleindia.com; Western Railways Reservation Complex, 123 Maharshi Karve Rd; ⊙8.30am-6pm Mon-Fri, to 2pm Sat) Provides information for the entire country, as well as contacts for Mumbai guides and homestays.

Maharashtra Tourism Development Corporation Head Office (MTDC; ☏022-22845678; www.maharashtratourism.gov.in; Madame Cama Rd, Nariman Point; ⊙10am-5.30pm) The MTDC's head office has helpful staff and lots of pamphlets and information on Maharashtra and bookings for MTDC hotels. There are additional booths at **Apollo Bunder** (☏022-22841877; ⊙9am-4pm Tue-Sun) and **Chhatrapati Shivaji Terminus** (☏022-22622859; ⊙10am-5pm Mon-Sat).

GETTING THERE & AWAY

AIR

Chhatrapati Shivaji International Airport (☏022-66851010; www.csia.in) is about 30km north of the city centre. The impressive, remodelled international Terminal 2 (T2) handles all international and some domestic flights. Other domestic flights operate out of the older Terminal 1B (T1B), 5km away, also known as Santa Cruz Airport. A fixed-rate taxi service operates between the terminals (₹230 from T1B to T2, ₹245 vice-versa).

BUS

Long-distance government-run buses depart from the **Mumbai Central bus terminal** (☏enquiries 022-23024075; Jehangir Boman Behram Marg, RBI Staff Colony).

Private buses are usually more comfortable and simpler to book (if a bit more costly). Most depart from Dr Anadrao Nair Rd near Mumbai Central train station. Check departure times and prices with **Citizen Travels** (☏022-23459695; www.citizenbus.com; G Block, Sitaram Bldg, Palton Rd) or **National NTT/CTC** (☏022-23074854, 022-23015652; Dr Anadrao Nair Rd; ⊙6.20am-11.30pm).

Private buses to Goa (14 hours) cost from as little as ₹450 (a bad choice) to ₹1000. **Naik Bus** (☏022-23676840; www.naibus.com; ⊙6pm, 7pm, 8.30pm & 9pm), **Paolo Travel** (☏022-26433023; www.paulotravels.com; ⊙5.30pm & 8pm) and government-run **Kadamba Transport** (☏9969561146; www.goakadamba.com; 6pm) are convenient for the city centre, leaving from in front of Azad Maidan.

TRAIN

Central Railways (☏139; www.cr.indianrailways.gov.in), handling services to the east and south, plus a few trains to the north, operates from CST (Chhatrapati Shivaji Terminus; also known as 'VT'). Foreign-tourist-quota tickets can be bought at Counter 52 on the 1st floor of the **reservation centre** (www.cr.indianrailways.gov.in; ⊙8am-8pm Mon-Sat, to 2pm Sun). There is a prepaid taxi scheme near the MTDC booth (₹160 to Colaba, ₹360 to Bandra).

Western Railways (☏139; www.wr.indian railways.gov.in) has services to the north from

Major Trains from Mumbai

Destination	Train No & Name	Fare (₹)	Duration (hr)	Departures
Agra	12137 Punjab Mail	613/1596/2281/3856 (A)	22	7.40pm CST
Bengaluru	11301 Udyan Exp	533/1416/2031/3421 (A)	24	8.05am CST
Delhi	12951 Mumbai Rajdhani	1856/2641/4481 (C)	16	5pm BCT
Jaipur	12955 Bct Jp Sf Exp	568/1481/2106/3546 (A)	18	6.50pm BCT
Kochi	16345 Netravati Exp	648/1711/2481 (B)	25½	11.40am LTT
Madgaon (Goa)	10103 Mandovi Exp 12133 Mangalore Exp 12133 Mangalore Exp	423/1131/1601/2661(A) 453/1176/1646 (B)	12 9	7.10am CST 10pm CST

Station abbreviations: CST (Chhatrapati Shivaji Terminus); BCT (Mumbai Central); LTT (Lokmanya Tilak)

Fares: (A) sleeper/3AC/2AC/1AC; (B) sleeper/3AC/2AC; (C) 3AC/2AC/1AC

Mumbai Central train station, usually called Bombay Central (BCT). The **reservation office** (www.wr.indianrailways.gov.in; ⊙8am-8pm Mon-Sat, to 2pm Sun), opposite Churchgate station, has foreign-tourist-quota tickets.

Tickets for either system can be bought from any station with computerised ticketing.

GETTING AROUND

TO/FROM THE AIRPORT

TERMINAL 2

Prepaid taxi fares are ₹680/820 (non-AC/AC; including one piece of luggage) to Colaba and Fort and ₹400/480 to Bandra. The journey to Colaba takes about an hour at night and 1½ to two hours during the day.

The trip from South Mumbai to the international airport in an AC taxi should cost from ₹650 to ₹850. Allow two hours if you travel between 4pm and 8pm. From Colaba, an UberGo is around ₹385 off-peak.

TERMINAL 1B

There's a prepaid taxi counter in the arrivals hall. A non-AC/AC taxi costs ₹560/683 to Colaba or Fort and ₹283/340 to Bandra (a bit more at night).

TAXI & AUTORICKSHAW

Mumbai's black-and-yellow taxis are the most convenient way to get around southern Mumbai; drivers *almost* always use the meter without prompting. The minimum fare is ₹22 (for up to 1.5km); a 5km trip costs about ₹80.

Game-changing taxi apps include **Uber** (www.uber.com) and **Ola** (www.olacabs.com); the latter is good for booking autorickshaws as well – no more rickshaw-wallah price gouging!

Autorickshaws are the name of the game north of Bandra. The minimum fare is ₹18, up to 1.5km; a 3km trip is about ₹36 during daylight.

TRAIN

Mumbai's suburban train network is one of the world's busiest; forget travelling during rush hours. The Western Line runs from Churchgate north to Charni Rd (for Girgaum Chowpatty), Mumbai Central, Mahalaxmi, Bandra, Vile Parle (for the domestic airport) and Andheri (for the international airport).

From Churchgate, 2nd-/1st-class fares are ₹5/50 to Mumbai Central and ₹10/55 to Vile Parle.

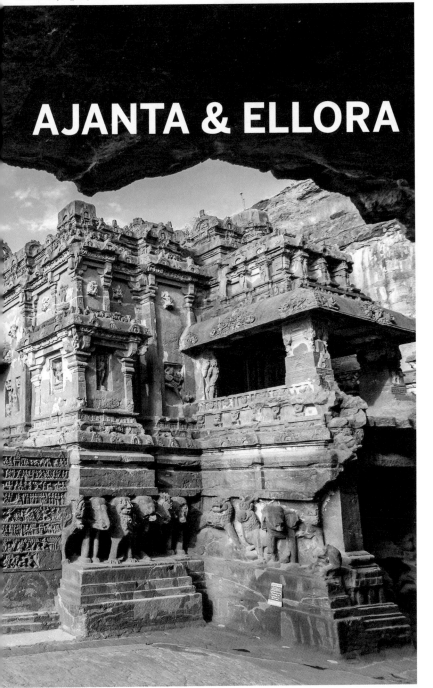

AJANTA & ELLORA

In this Chapter
Ajanta Caves.....................................144
Ellora Caves 148
Sights 154
Tours...155
Eating 155
Drinking & Nightlife.......................156

Ajanta & Ellora at a Glance...

The World Heritage–listed caves of Ajanta and Ellora, situated within 100km of each other in Maharashtra in central India, are stunning galleries of ancient art in remote settings, replete with historic sculptures, rock-cut shrines and natural-dye paintings.

The Ellora caves were laboriously chipped out by generations of Buddhist, Hindu and Jain monks over about four centuries (roughly AD 600 to 1000). The Buddhist caves at Ajanta are even older: they were carved out of a sheer rock face between about the 2nd century BC and the 6th century AD.

Ajanta & Ellora in Two Days

Start early from Aurangabad to visit **Daulatabad Fort** (p155) en route to **Ellora** (p148). Explore Ellora and return to Aurangabad. Start early again on day two for the longer trip to **Ajanta** (p143). When you get back to Aurangabad, reward yourself with a thali dinner at **Bhoj** (p155). Note that Ajanta is closed on Mondays and Ellora on Tuesdays.

Ajanta & Ellora in Four Days

Instead of returning to Aurangabad at the end of day two, stay at the **MTDC Ajanta Tourist Resort** (p147), allowing for a second caves visit before returning to Aurangabad. On day four visit the **Bibi-qa-Maqbara** (p154) and **Aurangabad Caves** (p154) and see some specialist weavers in action at the **Paithani Silk Weaving Centre** (p157).

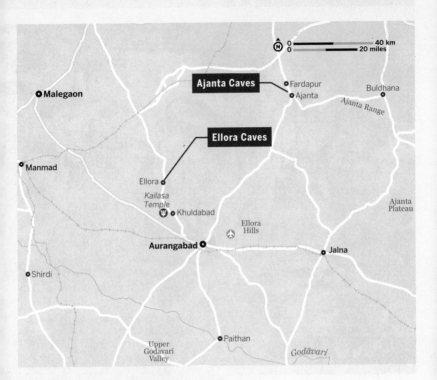

Arriving in Ajanta & Ellora

The usual jumping-off point for Ellora and Ajanta is Aurangabad, which has frequent bus connections with both sites. Aurangabad has daily flights from Delhi and Mumbai, and four daily trains plus AC overnight buses from Mumbai. Coming from the north, head first for Jalgaon, with trains from Delhi and Varanasi. From Jalgaon it's about two hours by bus to Ajanta.

Sleeping

There are just a few reasonable overnight options near the cave sites, including the **MTDC Ajanta Tourist Resort** (p143) in Fardapur and **Hotel Kailas** (p153) at Ellora. There's a far bigger range of options for all budgets, at better prices than you might expect, in Aurangabad.

Ajanta Caves

Superbly set in a remote river valley 105km northeast of Aurangabad, the remarkable cave temples of Ajanta were among the earliest monastic institutions to be constructed in India.

Great For...

☑ **Don't Miss**

Ajanta's excellent **visitor centre** (⊘9am-5.30pm Tue-Sun) features impressive cave replicas, and galleries on Buddhism in India.

Ajanta's caves line a steep face of a horseshoe-shaped gorge on the Waghore River. Five of the caves are *chaityas* (prayer halls) while others are *viharas* (monasteries). Caves 8, 9, 10, 12, 13 and part of 15 are early Buddhist caves, while the others date from around the 5th century AD (Mahayana period). In the austere early Buddhist school, the Buddha was never represented directly but always alluded to by a symbol such as the footprint or wheel of law.

During busy periods, viewers are allotted 15 minutes in the caves, which have to be entered barefoot (socks/shoe covers allowed; flip-flops will make your life a lot easier).

Ajanta's 'Frescoes'

Few other paintings from ancient times match the artistic excellence and fine execution of the renowned 'frescoes' (actually

Wall painting, Cave 2 (p146)

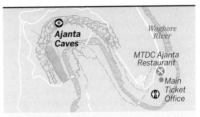

ℹ Need to Know

Indian/foreigner ₹30/500, video ₹25, author-
ised guide ₹1370; 🕘9am-5.30pm Tue-Sun)

✕ Take a Break

MTDC Ajanta Restaurant (mains ₹160-
450, thalis ₹150-280; 🕘9am-6pm Tue-Sun),
by the ticket office, serves vegetarian
thali (traditional 'all-you-can-eat' plate
meal) and cold drinks.

> ★ **Top Tip**
>
> **Most tour buses don't arrive until
> noon. To avoid crowds stay locally
> in Fardapur or start early from
> Aurangabad.**

temperas) adorning many of the Ajanta
caves' interiors.

The paintings in most caves remain
finely preserved and many attribute this to
their relative isolation from humanity for
centuries. However, it would be a tad opti-
mistic to say that decay hasn't set in.

It's believed the natural pigments for
these paintings were mixed with animal
glue and vegetable gum to bind them to
the dry surface. Many caves have small,
craterlike holes in their floors, which acted
as palettes during paint jobs.

Ajanta Lost and Found

Much older than Ellora, the Ajanta caves
date from around the 2nd century BC to
the 6th century AD. Ironically, it was Ellora's
rise that brought about Ajanta's downfall

and historians believe the site was abandoned once the focus shifted to Ellora.

As the Deccan forest claimed and shielded
the caves, with roots and shoots choking the
sculptures, Ajanta remained deserted for
about a millennium, until 1819 when a British
hunting party led by officer John Smith stumbled upon them purely by chance.

Viewpoints

Two lookouts offer picture-perfect views of
the whole horseshoe-shaped gorge. The first
is a short walk beyond the river, crossed by
a bridge below Cave 8. A further 40-minute
uphill walk (not to be attempted during the
monsoons) leads to the lookout where the
British party first spotted the caves.

Cave 1

Cave 1, a Mahayana *vihara*, was one of the
last to be excavated and is the most beautifully decorated. This is where you'll find
a rendition of the *Bodhisattva Padmapani*,

the most famous and iconic of the Ajanta artworks. A verandah in front leads to a large congregation hall housing sculptures and narrative murals known for their splendid perspective and elaborate detailing of dress, daily life and facial expressions.

The colours in the paintings were created from local minerals, with the exception of the vibrant blue made from Central Asian lapis lazuli. Look up to the ceiling to see the carving of four deer sharing a common head.

Cave 2

Cave 2 is a late Mahayana *vihara* with deliriously ornamented columns and capitals and some fine paintings. The ceiling is decorated with geometric and floral patterns. The murals depict scenes from the Jataka tales, including Buddha's mother's dream of a six-tusked elephant, which heralded his conception.

Cave 4

Cave 4, Ajanta's largest *vihara*, is supported by 28 pillars. Although never completed, the cave has some impressive sculptures, such as the four statues surrounding a huge central Buddha. There are also scenes of people fleeing from the 'eight great dangers' to the protection of Avalokitesvara.

Cave 10

Cave 10, the largest *chaitya*, is thought to be the oldest cave (200 BC) and was the first to be spotted by the British hunting party. The facade has collapsed and the paintings inside have been damaged, in some cases by graffiti dating from soon after their rediscovery. One pillar to the right bears the engraved name of Smith, who left his mark here for posterity.

Reclining Buddha, Cave 26

Cave 16

Cave 16, a *vihara*, is thought to have been the original entrance to the entire complex. The best known of very fine paintings is of the 'dying princess', Sundari, wife of the Buddha's half-brother Nanda, who is said to have fainted at the news her husband was renouncing the material life (and her) in order to become a monk.

Carved figures appear to support the ceiling and there's a statue of the Buddha seated on a lion throne teaching the Noble Eightfold Path.

ℹ Need to Know

Flash photography is prohibited within the caves. Rows of tiny, pigment-friendly lights help to illuminate minute details, but you'll need long exposures for photographs.

BHASKAR DUTTA/GETTY IMAGES ©

Cave 17

With carved dwarves supporting the pillars, cave 17 has Ajanta's best-preserved and most varied paintings. Famous images include a princess applying make-up, a seductive prince using the old trick of plying his lover with wine and the Buddha returning home from his enlightenment to beg from his wife and astonished son.

Cave 19

Cave 19, a magnificent *chaitya*, has a remarkably detailed facade; its dominant feature is an impressive horseshoe-shaped window. Two fine standing Buddha figures flank the entrance. Inside is a three-tiered dagoba with a figure of the Buddha on the front. Outside the cave, to the west, sits a striking image of the Naga king with seven cobra hoods around his head. His wife, hooded by a single cobra, sits by his side.

Cave 26

A largely ruined *chaitya*, cave 26 is now dramatically lit and contains some fine sculptures that shouldn't be missed. On the left wall is a huge figure of the reclining Buddha. Other scenes include a lengthy depiction of the Buddha's temptation by Maya.

Getting to Ajanta

Buses from Aurangabad or Jalgaon will drop you at Fardapur T-junction, 4km from the site. After paying an 'amenities' fee (₹10), walk to the departure point for the buses that zoom up to the caves (with/without AC ₹22/16). Buses return half-hourly to the T-junction until 5pm.

Taxis from Fardapur cost about ₹1500/2500 to Jalgaon/Aurangabad.

★ MTDC Ajanta Tourist Complex

Located just behind the shopping 'plaza' and the bus stand, the five **cottages** (☏02438-244033; www.maharashtratourism. gov.in; cottage ₹2140) nestled in grassy lawns have some charm, though they could be better maintained. Note there's no restaurant.

Ellora Caves

The pinnacle of ancient Indian rock-cut architecture, Ellora's cave temples, 30km northwest of Aurangabad, served as monasteries, chapels or temples for Buddhists, Hindus and Jains and were embellished with a profusion of remarkably detailed sculptures. In their midst stands the awesome Kailasa Temple – the world's largest monolithic sculpture, hewn from a cliff face over 150 years by thousands of labourers.

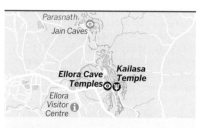

Great For...

ℹ Need to Know

Indian/foreigner ₹30/500; ⊘6am-6pm Wed-Mon

YIN YANG/GETTY IMAGES ©

Ellora has 34 caves in all: 12 Buddhist (AD 600–800), 17 Hindu (AD 600–900) and five Jain (AD 800–1000) – though the exact time scales of their construction are the subject of academic debate.

Unlike the caves at Ajanta, which are carved into a sheer rock face, the Ellora caves line a 2km-long escarpment, whose gentle slope allowed architects to build elaborate courtyards in front of the shrines and adorn them with sculptures of a surreal quality.

The established academic theory is that Ellora represents the renaissance of Hinduism under the Chalukya and Rashtrakuta dynasties, the subsequent decline of Indian Buddhism and a brief resurgence of Jainism under official patronage. However, due to the absence of inscriptions, accurately dating most of Ellora's monuments is impossible, and some scholars argue that some Hindu temples predate the Buddhist group. What is certain is that their coexistence at one site indicates a lengthy period of religious tolerance.

Visitor Centre & Guides

Ellora's impressive **visitor centre** (◔9am-5pm Wed-Mon), 750m west of the site, is well worth dropping by. It features modern displays and information panels, a 15-minute video and a Kailasa Temple gallery (with diorama).

Official guides can be hired at the ticket office in front of the Kailasa Temple for ₹1370 (up to five people). They have an extensive knowledge of cave architecture so are worth the investment.

Buddhas in meditation, Cave 12 (p152)

Kailasa Temple

One of Incredible India's greatest monuments, this astonishing temple, carved from solid rock by 7000 labourers over a period of 150 years in the 8th and 9th centuries, was built to represent Mt Kailasa (Kailash), Shiva's Himalayan abode. To say that the assignment was daring would be an understatement. Three huge trenches were bored into the sheer cliff face, a process that entailed removing 200,000 tonnes of rock by hammer and chisel, before the temple could begin to take shape

✕ Take a Break

MTDC Ellora Restaurant & Beer Bar (mains/thali from ₹110/140; ☺9am-5pm), within the temple complex, is an easy place for lunch and a cold Kingfisher.

JEREMY RICHARDS/ALAMY ©

and its remarkable sculptural decoration could be added.

Covering twice the area of the Parthenon in Athens and being half as high again, Kailasa is an engineering marvel that was executed straight from the head with zero margin for error. Modern draughtsmen might have a lesson or two to learn here.

The temple houses several intricately carved panels, depicting scenes from the Ramayana, the Mahabharata and the adventures of Krishna. Also worth admiring are the immense monolithic pillars that stand in the courtyard, flanking the entrance on both sides, and the southeastern gallery that has 10 giant and fabulous panels depicting the different avatars of Lord Vishnu.

After you're done with the main enclosure, bypass the hordes of snack-munching day trippers to explore the temple's many dank, bat-urine-soaked corners with their numerous forgotten carvings.

Buddhist Caves

Calm and contemplation infuse the 12 Buddhist caves, which stretch to the south of the Kailasa Temple. Nearly all are Buddhist *viharas* (monasteries) used for study and worship, but these multistoreyed structures also included cooking, living and sleeping areas. While the earliest caves are simple, Caves 11 and 12 are on a par with Ellora's more impressive Hindu temples.

Cave 2 is notable for its ornate pillars and the imposing seated Buddha that faces the setting sun.

Cave 5 is the largest *vihara* in this group at 18m wide and 36m long; the rows of stone benches hint that it may once have been an assembly hall.

Cave 6 is an ornate *vihara* with wonderful images of Tara, consort of the Bodhisat-

❶ Don't Miss

The bird's-eye view of Kailasa Temple from its top perimeter, reached by an overgrown trail to its south (or bypass the scaffolding to walk up sturdier rock).

tva Avalokitesvara, and of the Buddhist goddess of learning, Mahamayuri, looking remarkably similar to Saraswati, her Hindu equivalent. **Cave 9**, above Cave 8, is notable for its wonderfully carved fascia.

Cave 10 is the only *chaitya* (assembly hall) in the Buddhist group and one of the finest in India. Its ceiling features ribs carved into the stonework; the grooves were once fitted with wooden panels. The balcony and upper gallery offer a closer view of the ceiling and a frieze depicting amorous couples. A decorative window gently illuminates an enormous figure of the teaching Buddha.

Cave 11, the Do Thal (Two Storey) Cave, is entered through its third basement level, not discovered until 1876. Like Cave 12, it possibly owes its size to competition with Hindu caves of the same period.

Cave 12, the huge Tin Thal (Three Storey) Cave, is entered through a courtyard. The locked shrine on the top floor contains a large Buddha figure flanked by his seven previous incarnations. The walls are carved with relief pictures.

Hindu Caves

Drama and excitement characterise the Hindu group (Caves 13 to 29). In terms of scale, creative vision and skill of execution, these caves are in a league of their own.

All these temples were cut from the top down, so it was never necessary to use scaffolding – the builders began with the roof and moved down to the floor.

Cave 14, the Ravana-ki-Khai, is a Buddhist *vihara* converted to a temple dedicated to Shiva some time in the 7th century.

Cave 15, the Das Avatara (Ten Incarnations of Vishnu) Cave, is one of the finest at Ellora. The two-storey temple contains a mesmerising Shiva Nataraja and a Shiva emerging from a lingam (phallic image) while Vishnu and Brahma pay homage.

Cave 21, known as the Rameshvara Cave, features interesting interpretations of familiar Shaivite scenes depicted in the earlier temples. The figure of the goddess Ganga standing on her Makara (mythical sea creature) is particularly notable.

The large **Cave 29**, the Dumar Lena, is thought to be a transitional model between the simpler hollowed-out caves and the fully developed temples exemplified by the Kailasa. It has views over a nearby waterfall, though the path was inaccessible at the time of writing. It's best reached via the MSRTC bus that shuttles to the **Jain Caves**.

Jain Caves

The five Jain caves may lack the ambitious size of the best Hindu temples, but they are exceptionally detailed, with remarkable paintings and carvings.

The caves are 1km north of the last Hindu temple (Cave 29) at the end of the bitumen road; an MRSTC bus (₹21 return) runs back and forth from in front of the Kailasa Temple.

Cave sculpture, Cave 32

Cave 30, the Chhota Kailasa (Little Kailasa), is a poor imitation of the great Kailasa Temple and stands some distance from the other Jain temples. It's reached via the unmarked stairway between caves 31 and 32.

Cave 32, the Indra Sabha (Assembly Hall of Indra), is the finest of the Jain temples. Its ground-floor plan is similar to that of the Kailasa, but the upstairs area is as ornate and richly decorated as the downstairs is plain. There are images of the Jain *tirthankars* (great teachers) Parasnath and Gomateshvara, the latter surrounded by wildlife. Inside the shrine is a seated figure of Mahavira, the last *tirthankar* and founder of the Jain religion.

Cave 33, the Jagannath Sabha, is similar in plan to Cave 32 and has some well-preserved sculptures. The final temple, the small **Cave 34**, also has interesting sculptures. On the hilltop over the Jain temples, a 5m-high image of Parasnath looks down on Ellora.

Getting to Ellora

Buses to Ellora leave Aurangabad every half-hour (AC/non-AC ₹251/32, 30 minutes, 5am to 12.30am); the last bus back leaves Ellora at 9pm.

★ **Did You Know?**

If you wish to stay close to the caves the **Hotel Kailas** (www.hotelkailas.com; ☏02437-244446; r with/without AC ₹3570/2500) offers attractive air-con stone cottages in leafy surrounds. The restaurant (mains ₹90 to 280) is excellent, but the wi-fi charges are ridiculous.

Aurangabad

Aurangabad (population 1.28 million) only hit the spotlight when the Mughal emperor, Aurangzeb, made it his capital from 1653 to 1707. The brief period of glory saw the building of some fascinating monuments, including Bibi-qa-Maqbara, a Taj Mahal replica. Silk fabrics were once Aurangabad's chief revenue generator and the city is still known for its hand-woven Himroo and Paithani saris.

Aurangabad's train station, cheap hotels and restaurants are clumped together in the south of the town along Station Rd East and Station Rd West. The MSRTC/Central Bus Stand is 1.5km north of the train station. Northeast of the bus stand is the buzzing old town, with its narrow streets and Muslim quarter.

◉ SIGHTS

Bibi-qa-Maqbara   Monument
(Indian/foreigner ₹15/200; ⊙6am-8pm) Built by Aurangzeb's son Azam Khan in 1679 as a mausoleum for his mother Rabia-ud-Daurani,

Bibi-qa-Maqbara is widely known as the poor man's Taj. With its four minarets flanking a central onion-domed mausoleum, the white structure certainly does bear a striking resemblance to Agra's Taj Mahal.

It is much less grand, however, and apart from having a few marble adornments, namely the plinth and dome, much of the structure is finished in lime mortar.

Apparently the prince conceived the entire mausoleum in white marble, but was thwarted by his frugal father who opposed his extravagant idea of draining state coffers for the purpose. Despite the use of cheaper material and the obvious weathering, it's a sight far more impressive than the average gravestone.

The Bibi's formal gardens are a delight to explore, with the Deccan hills providing a scenic backdrop. It's located 3km north of the bus stand.

Aurangabad Caves   Cave
(Indian/foreigner ₹15/200; ⊙6am-6pm) Architecturally speaking, the Aurangabad Caves aren't a patch on Ellora or Ajanta, but they do shed light on early Buddhist architec-

Bibi-qa-Maqbara

SAIKO3P/SHUTTERSTOCK ©

ture and make for a quiet and peaceful outing. Carved out of the hillside in the 6th or 7th century AD, the 10 caves, comprising two groups 1km apart (retain your ticket for entry into both sets), are all Buddhist.

Cave 7, with its sculptures of scantily clad lovers in suggestive positions, is a perennial favourite.

The caves are about 2km north of Bibi-qa-Maqbara. A return autorickshaw from the mausoleum shouldn't cost more than ₹250, including waiting time.

Shrimat Chatrapati
Shivaji Museum   Museum
(Dr Ambedkar Rd; ₹5; ⊙10.30am-6.30pm Fri-Wed) This simple museum is dedicated to the life of the Maratha hero Shivaji. Its collection includes a 500-year-old chain-mail suit and a copy of the Quran, handwritten by Aurangzeb.

🕓 TOURS
Ashoka Tours &
Travels   Sightseeing
(✏9890340816, 0240-2359102; www.tourist aurangabad.com; Hotel Panchavati, Station Rd West; ⊙7am-8pm) The stand-out Aurangabad agency, with excellent city and regional tours and decent car hire at fair rates. Prices for an AC car for up to four people are ₹1450 for Ellora and ₹2450 for Ajanta. Run by Ashok T Kadam, a knowledgeable former autorickshaw driver.

✕ EATING
Kailash   Indian $
(Station Rd East; mains ₹50-150; ⊙8am-11pm; ❄) This bustling pure-veg restaurant looks and feels vaguely like a half-hearted Indian take on an American diner, with big portions of food in familial surrounds. There's lots of Punjabi and South Indian food, as well as rice and noodle dishes, and an extensive list of *pav bhaji* options, a Mumbai street-food staple. It's rightfully popular.

Bhoj   Indian $$
(Station Rd West; thali ₹210; ⊙11am-3pm & 7-11pm) Rightly famous for its delicious,

 Daulatabad Fort

No trip to Aurangabad is complete without a pit-stop at the ruined but truly magnificent fortress of **Daulatabad** (Indian/foreigner ₹15/200; ⊙6am-6pm), sitting atop a 200m-high craggy outcrop about 15km northwest of town (on the route of Ellora-bound buses). A 5km battlement surrounds this fort, originally built in the 12th century and given its current name ('City of Fortune') in 1328 by Delhi sultan Mohammed Tughlaq, who decided to shift his capital here from Delhi. Tughlaq even marched the entire population of Delhi 1100km south to populate it. Ironically, Daulatabad soon proved untenable as a capital due to an acute water crisis.

The climb to the summit leads past multiple doorways designed with odd angles and spike-studded doors to prevent elephant charges. You can walk into the Chini Mahal, where Abul Hasan Tana Shah, king of Golconda, was held captive for 12 years before his death in 1699. Part of the ascent goes through a pitch-black, bat-infested, water-seeping, spiralling tunnel. Guides (₹1368) are available near the ticket counter, and their torch-bearing assistants will lead you through the dark passageway for a small tip.

As the fort is in ruins (with crumbling staircases and sheer drops) and involves a steep ascent, some will find it a tough challenge. Allow 2½ hours to explore it, and bring water and a torch.

AJITSINGH CHAUHAN/SHUTTERSTOCK ©

Local cuisine

unlimited Rajasthani and Gujarati thalis, Bhoj is a wonderful place to refuel and relax after a hard day on the road (or rail). It's on the 1st floor of a somewhat scruffy little shopping arcade, but the decor, ambience, service and presentation are all first rate. Best thali in Maharashtra!

Green Leaf   Indian $$
(www.greenleafpureveg.com; Shop 6-9, Fame Tapadiya Multiplex, Town Centre; mains ₹140-280; ⊘noon-11pm; 🛜) Aurangabad's favourite modern vegetarian is loved for delectable pure-veg dishes that really pop with flavour (try the veg *handi* or *paneer Hyderabadi*) and come with spice-level indicators (one chilli pepper equals medium!). Teal-trousered servers gracefully navigate the clean, contemporary surrounds. So clean, in fact, the kitchen is open for all to see. It's 400m from CIDCO Bus Stand.

Tandoor   North Indian $$
(Station Rd East, Shyam Chambers; mains ₹150-380; ⊘11am-11pm) Offers fine tandoori dishes, flavoursome North Indian veg and nonveg options and an extensive beer list

(for Aurangabad) in a weirdly Pharaonic atmosphere. Try the wonderful sizzler kebabs. A few Chinese dishes are also on offer, but patrons clearly prefer the dishes coming out of...well...the tandoor.

Swad Restaurant   Indian $$
(Station Rd East, Kanchan Chamber; thali ₹200) Though prices are similar, always-packed Swad is the simpler, more local and slightly greasier counterpart to some of our other favourite spots in town. Waiters clad in bright Rajasthani-style turbans sling spicy *sabzi* (vegetables), dhal and other Gujarati-Rajasthani thali delights – an endless flavour train under the benevolent gaze of patron saint swami Yogiraj Hanstirth.

🍷 DRINKING & NIGHTLIFE

For a city with more than one million residents, Aurangabad's nocturnal options leave something to be desired. Many hotels have bars, but your best bet for a convivial traveller atmosphere is grabbing a drink at **Hotel Panchavati** (📞0240-2328755; www.hotelpanchavati.com; Station Rd West;

s/d ₹1000/1130, r with AC ₹1250; ✱@🛜). If you want to mingle with hip locals over cocktails, **KA Lounge** (Satya Dharam Complex, Akashwari Cir, Jalna Rd; cocktails from ₹320; ☺noon-11pm Mon-Fri, to 1am Sat & Sun; 🛜) is Aurangabad's one trendy bar. It's brand spankingly new and caters to the city's up-wardly hip who plop down on cosy lounges amid brick exposed walls. You can easily make an evening of it - the modern fusion menu (mains ₹220 to ₹690) features loads of interesting Indian/Asian/Continental-hybrid cuisine.

 ## GETTING THERE & AWAY

AIR

Aurangabad Airport (Chikkalthana Airport) is 10km east of town. Daily direct flights go to Delhi and Mumbai with both **Air India** (📞0240-2483392; www.airindia.in; Airliens House, Town Centre, Jalna Rd; ☺10am-1pm & 2-5pm Mon-Sat) and **Jet Airways** (📞0240-2441392; www.jetairways.com; 4, Santsheel, Vidyanagar 7 Hills, Jalna Rd).

BUS

Private bus agents mainly cluster on Dr Rajendra Prasad Marg and Court Rd. There's deluxe overnight service to Mumbai (AC sleeper ₹774 to ₹1400, 7½ to 9½ hours).

Ordinary buses head to Ellora from the **MSRTC/Central Bus Stand** (📞0240-2242164; Station Rd West) every half-hour (AC/non-AC ₹251/32, 30 minutes, 5am to 12.30am), and to Jalgaon (non-AC ₹177, four hours, 5am to 8pm) via Fardapur (₹120, three hours), which is the drop-off point for Ajanta.

TRAIN

Aurangabad's **train station** (Station Rd East) is not on a main line, but it has four daily direct trains to/from Mumbai. The Tapovan Express (2nd class/chair ₹173/571, 7½ hours) departs Aurangabad at 2.35pm. The Janshatabdi Express (2nd class/chair ₹223/686, 6½ hours) departs Aurangabad at 6am. To reach northern or eastern India, take a bus to Jalgaon and board a train there.

 ## Himroo & Paithani

Himroo material is a traditional Aurang-abad speciality made from cotton, silk and metallic threads. Most of today's Himroo shawls and saris are produced using power looms, but some show-rooms still stock hand-loomed cloth.

Himroo saris start at around ₹2000 for a cotton and silk blend. Paithani sa-ris, which are of superior quality, range from ₹8000 to ₹150,000 – but some of them take more than a year to make. If you're buying, make sure you get authentic Himroo, not 'Aurangabad silk'.

One of the best places to come and watch weavers at work is the **Paithani Silk Weaving Centre** (www.paithanisilk.com; 54, P-1, Town Center, Lokmat Nagar; ☺9.30am-9pm) where you'll find good quality products for sale. It's about 6km east of Kranti Chowk (behind the Air India office), so take a taxi.

Silk weaving
ORAPIN JOYPHUEM/SHUTTERSTOCK ©

 ## GETTING AROUND

Autorickshaws are common here and are bookable (along with taxis) with **Ola Cabs** (www.olacabs.com). The taxi stand is next to the MSRTC/Central Bus Stand; shared 4WDs also depart from here for Ellora and Daulatabad but are usually very packed. Renting a car and driver is a much better option.

GOA

In this Chapter
Day in Old Goa 162
Best Goan Beaches 164
Yoga in Its Homeland......................168
Panaji...170
Palolem..172
Anjuna 174

Goa
at a Glance...

Pint-sized Goa is much more than beaches and trance parties. A kaleido-scopic blend of Indian and Portuguese cultures, sweetened with sun, sea, sand, seafood and spirituality, there's nowhere in India quite like it.

While Goa's biggest draw is undoubtedly its string of golden-sand beaches, each with its own personality, it also stands out for the charm of its Portuguese heritage; for the scents, spices and flavours of its tantalising cuisine; and as a spiritual sanctuary where options for yoga, t'ai chi, meditation and healing grow more bountiful each year.

Goa in Three Days

Spend day one in Goa's cultural heartland, **Panaji** (p170) and **Old Goa** (p162), ideally staying in a quaint Panaji heritage hotel.

Then head down to **Palolem** (p172) and spend days two and three enjoying the palm-fringed sands, safe swimming and maybe a spot of yoga, spa pampering, kayaking, a cooking class or a silent headphone party.

Goa in Five Days

You might be so happy in Palolem you don't want to move on...but if you do, head up to North Goa's all-round best beach base, **Anjuna** (p174), where something of the old hippie vibe lingers but there are also plenty of daytime activities for days four and five: a good **yoga scene** (p168), happening nightclubs and a good range of budget and midrange accommodation.

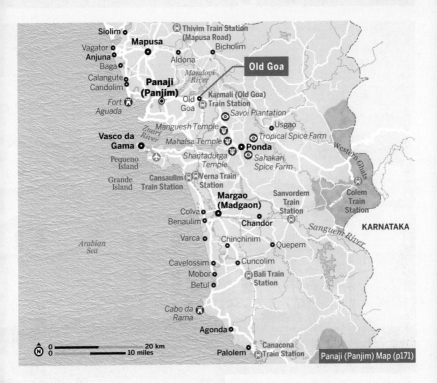

Siolim o
Thivim Train Station (Mapusa Road)
Vagator o
Mapusa
Bicholim
Anjuna o
Aldona
Baga o
Old Goa
Calangute
Candolim
Panaji (Panjim)
Mandovi River
Fort Aguada
Old Goa
Karmali (Old Goa) Train Station
Savoi Plantation
Manguesh Temple
Usgao
Zuari River
Vasco da Gama o
Mahalsa Temple
Tropical Spice Farm
Ponda
Pequeno Island
Shantadurga Temple
Sahakari Spice Farm
Western Ghats
Grande Island
Cansaulim Train Station
Verna Train Station
Margao (Madgaon)
Sanvordem Train Station
Colem Train Station
Arabian Sea
Colva o
Chandor
Sanguem River
KARNATAKA
Benaulim o
Varca o
Chinchinim
Quepem
Cavelossim o
Cuncolim
Mobor o
Bali Train Station
Betul o
Cabo da Rama
Agonda o
Canacona Train Station
Palolem
Panaji (Panjim) Map (p171)

0   20 km
0   10 miles

Arriving in Goa

Dabolim Airport Domestic flights, plus international charter flights (November to March); prepaid taxi booth to all Goan destinations.

Madgaon Railway Station, Margao
Main stop on Mumbai–Mangaluru line; prepaid taxi booth to all Goan destinations.

Karmali Railway Station, Old Goa
Closest station to Panaji.

Buses From Mumbai and other cities to Panaji, Margao (Madgaon) and Mapusa.

Sleeping

Goa's accommodation ranges from basic beach huts, hostels and budget guesthouses, found at a great many beaches and in Panaji; through midrange hotels and guesthouses (everywhere); to charming boutique and heritage havens (in Panaji and scattered around elsewhere); and opulent five-star beachfront resorts, many of which are clustered along the northern part of the southern coast, especially in the Varca-Cavelossim-Mobor stretch.

HARSHIL PATEL/ALAMY ©

A Day in Old Goa

The 17th-century Portuguese capital of Old Goa once rivalled Lisbon and London in size and importance. Today all that remains is a handful of amazingly well-preserved churches and cathedrals – but what a handful!

Great For...

☑ **Don't Miss**

The 'incorrupt' body of St Francis Xavier in the Basilica of Bom Jesus.

From the 16th to the 18th centuries Goa's former capital was considered the 'Rome of the East'. You can still sense that grandeur today. Old Goa's rise under the Portuguese, from 1510, was meteoric, but cholera and malaria forced its abandonment in the 17th century.

Basilica of Bom Jesus

Famous throughout the Roman Catholic world, the imposing late-Renaissance style **Basilica of Bom Jesus** (⊘7.30am-6.30pm), built between 1594 and 1605, contains the tomb and mortal remains of St Francis Xavier, the so-called Apostle of the Indies. St Francis Xavier's missionary voyages throughout the East became legendary. His 'incorrupt' body is in the mausoleum to the right of the altar, in a glass-sided coffin amid a shower of gilt stars.

Church of St Francis of Assisi

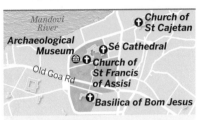

Need to Know

Frequent buses to Old Goa (₹10, 25 minutes) leave from Panaji's Kadamba bus stand; a return taxi is around ₹400.

✕ Take a Break

A string of little tourist restaurants near the bus stop offers snacks, chai and thalis (traditional 'all-you-can-eat' plate meal).

★ Top Tip

Old Goa can get crowded with visitors: consider coming on a weekday morning.

Sé Cathedral

More than 76m long and 55m wide, the cavernous **Sé Cathedral** (⊙9am-6pm; Mass 7am & 6pm Mon-Sat, 7.15am, 10am & 4pm Sun) is the largest church in Asia. Building lasted from 1562 to the 1650s. Its rather lopsided look results from the loss of one bell tower to lightning in 1776. The remaining tower houses the famous Sino de Ouro (Golden Bell), the largest in Asia.

The interior is surprisingly plain, apart from the huge gilded reredos (ornamental screen), above the main altar, and some of the side chapels – notably the gorgeously gilded and decorated Chapel of the Blessed Sacrament.

Church of St Cajetan

This impressive **church** (⊙9am-5.30pm) was built by Italian friars sent to preach Christianity in the kingdom of Golconda (near Hyderabad). The friars were refused entry to Golconda, so they settled instead at Old Goa in 1640. This is the only domed church remaining in Goa.

Church of St Francis of Assisi

West of the Sé Cathedral, the **Church of St Francis of Assisi** (⊙9am-5pm) is no longer used for worship, and consequently exudes a more mournful air than its neighbours. It dates from 1661, with the ornate Manueline-style doorway of an earlier church on the site incorporated into the much plainer new facade.

The interior, though now rather ragged and faded, is nevertheless beautiful, in a particularly 'folk art' type style.

TETIANA VITSENKO/ALAMY ©

Best Goan Beaches

With more than 100km of sand-fringed coastline, Goa's beaches can exude the feel of a tropical island. Each spot has a different character. The question is: which beach?

Great For...

☑ **Don't Miss**

Goan sunsets – visible from *all* of Goa's beaches!

Deciding which Goan beach to visit isn't just a matter of the aesthetics of sand and sea: it's about choosing the beach community that suits your style of travel and sense of place. The villages and resorts vary in character, depending on the types of people who congregate there, the standards of accommodation, restaurants and nightlife and the activities on offer.

Locating the perfect beach is the secret to making the most of your stay. It could be backpacker-filled beach huts, five-star luxury, yoga shalas or the party crowd. Goa is small so you can easily jump on a scooter or in a taxi and explore.

Swimming & Water Sports

Most of Goa's main beaches offer water sports in season – parasailing, jet skis and speed-

Market, Vagator beach

boat rides. Swimming is safest at patrolled beaches.

○ **Palolem** (p172) Calm waters offer the safest ocean swimming. Also the best place for kayaking and stand-up paddleboarding.

○ **Calangute & Candolim** Several water-sports operators offer a full range of activities on Goa's busiest beach strip. Also has scuba-diving outfits.

○ **Arambol** Another relatively gentle beach for swimming, with a surf club and paragliding.

○ **Colva & Benaulim** Not as busy as Calangute but all of the adrenalin sports are on offer at respective beach entrances; Colva is popular with domestic tourists.

○ **Aswem** A good choice mainly for its excellent surfing and kite-surfing school and kayaking on the river.

Family Fun

Families will find a lot to like about Goa's beaches.

○ **Vagator** Rock pools and calm waters make Vagator's three pretty little bays excellent for kids. Food and drink vendors gather at the beach entrance. Good for day trips.

○ **Palolem** (p172) One of the best all-round beaches for families with plenty of activities, safe swimming and beach-facing huts.

○ **Patnem** Similar to Palolem but smaller and quieter, Patnem is very family-friendly with a large expat community, and schools and kindergartens nearby.

○ **Arambol** A popular beach with long-staying families, Arambol has a relaxed backpacker vibe, good budget accommodation and relatively safe waters.

Partying & Drinking

Goa loves to party and there's a liberal attitude to drinking, but it's not quite Ibiza on the subcontinent. The all-night trance parties on beaches and in coconut groves are largely consigned to history but EDM (electronic dance music) parties, raves, dance festivals and nightclubs still happen in season.

○ **Anjuna** (p174) Late-night parties are legendary at Anjuna's southern beach shacks, especially popular Curlies.

○ **Baga** Tito's Lane is the place of choice for many young Indians on a weekend away from their IT jobs, as well as package tourists staying in the area.

○ **Vagator** Some traces of Goa trance and hippie heyday remain in Vagator and Chapora.

○ **Candolim** Two of Goa's most upmarket nightclubs are found here, along with busy bar-restaurants along Fort Aguada Rd.

○ **Palolem** (p172) Silent headphone parties happen most nights and the huge Leopard Valley dance club is nearby.

Backpackers & Budget Travellers

○ **Arambol** Huts and rooms along the clifftop path remain some of the cheapest in Goa, making this popular with backpackers.

○ **Anjuna** (p174) A wide range of accommodation, two backpacker hostels, good cafes and plenty of bikes to rent for commuting to neighbouring beaches.

Agonda beach

○ **Vagator & Chapora** Picturesque beach, cool fort; these laid-back villages attract budget travellers who like to chill *and* party.

○ **Palolem** (p172) **& Patnem** There's a hut to suit all tastes and budgets here, along with a genuine traveller vibe.

> ### ❶ Safe Swimming
>
> One of the most deceptive dangers in Goa is to be found right in front of you. The Arabian Sea, with its strong currents, often steeply shelving sands and dangerous undertows, claims lives each year. Goa's main beaches are patrolled by lifeguards during 'swimming season' (November to March). Be vigilant with children, avoid swimming after drinking alcohol and don't even consider swimming during the monsoon.

Five-Star Treatment

Goa has more five-star resorts and boutique hotels per square kilometre than anywhere else in India. Even if you're not staying, you can almost always book a table at a fancy in-house restaurant or an afternoon at a spa, or even pay to use the pool.

○ **Varca, Cavelossim & Mobor** South Goa's five-star strip includes the Leela, Holiday Inn and Radisson Blu.

○ **Candolim & Sinquerim** Two sprawling Taj Vivanta resorts plus some fine boutique hotels such as Aashyana Lakhanpal.

○ **Mandrem & Aswem** The high standard of beach-hut operations has turned Mandrem and Aswem into one of the classiest beach strips in the north.

Beach Huts

○ **Palolem** Where the beach-hut craze really took off – Palolem still has some of the best in Goa.

○ **Agonda** Beach-hut design is taken to another level at some of Agonda's mini-resorts.

○ **Patnem** A smaller version of Palolem with some nice, laid-back hut villages.

○ **Mandrem** Fabulous hut resorts connected to the beach by bamboo bridges make Mandrem a popular choice.

○ **Arambol** Backpacker-friendly Arambol has a string of beach-facing huts on the main strip.

PAVEL LAPUTSKOV/SHUTTERSTOCK ©

Yoga in its Homeland

India is regarded as the birthplace of yoga and there are few better places than Goa to downward dog or salute to the sun.

Great For...

☑ Don't Miss

The chance to learn or practise yoga in the land of its birth.

Yoga Season

Yoga centres and retreats are open, and courses in full swing, from mid-November to early April. A handful of smaller classes operate year-round.

Palolem, Agonda and Patnem in south Goa, and Arambol, Mandrem, Anjuna and Assagao in the north, are particularly great places to take classes or longer courses. At most beach centres you'll find no shortage of classes.

Teachers and practitioners are largely an ever-changing parade of foreign or Indian teachers who set up shop in Goa when the monsoon subsides.

Which Yoga Class?

○ **Ashtanga** Often referred to as 'power yoga', active and physically demanding, good for some serious toning.

◦ **Hatha** Covers a gamut of styles, but generally refers to yoga focused on breath work (pranayama), and slow, gentle stretching, making it good for beginners.

◦ **Iyengar** Slow and steady, often using 'props' in the form of blocks, balls and straps.

◦ **Kundalini** Aims to free the base of the spine, to unleash energy hidden there, and usually involves lots of core, spine and sitting work.

◦ **Vinyasa** An active, fluid series of changing poses characterises Vinyasa, also called 'flow yoga'.

Yoga Centres

Respected options for yoga classes, courses, retreats and teacher certification are scattered across Goa. Many hotels and resorts also offer classes.

◦ **Bamboo Yoga Retreat** (🖉9637567730; www.bamboo-yoga-retreat.com; s/d from ₹6500/10,000; 🛜) In Patnem.

◦ **Brahmani Yoga** (p174) In Anjuna.

◦ **Himalayan Iyengar Yoga Centre** (www. hiyogacentre.com; Madhlo Vaddo; 5-day yoga course ₹4000; ⊘9am-6pm Tue-Sun Nov-Mar) In Arambol.

◦ **Purple Valley Yoga Retreat** (🖉0832-2268363; www.yogagoa.com; 142 Bairo Alto; dm/s 1 week from £690/820, 2 weeks £1100/1350) In Assagao.

◦ **Love the Green Retreat** (🖉07507715975; www.lovethegreenretreat.com; Sadolxem Village; yoga classes ₹500; ⊘9.30am & 4pm Mon-Fri) In Patnem.

◦ **Swan Yoga Retreat** (🖉0832-2268024, 8007360677; www.swan-yoga-goa.com; drop-in classes ₹350, 1 week from ₹23,300) In Assagao.

◦ **Yoga Magic** (🖉0832-6523796; www.yoga magic.net; Mapusa-Chapora Rd, Anjuna; lodge s/d ₹6750/9000, ste ₹9000/12,000) ✎ In Anjuna.

◦ **Bhakti Kutir** (🖉0832-2643469, 9823627258; www.bhaktikutir.com; Colomb Bay; cottage ₹2200-3500; @) In Palolem.

Panaji

Central Goa is the state's historic and cultural heart and soul. No visit to Goa is really complete without visiting the Latin Quarter (Fontainhas, Sao Tomé and Mala) in the laid-back state capital, Panaji, or the state's major cultural attraction, Old Goa.

SIGHTS & ACTIVITIES

Church of Our Lady of the Immaculate Conception   Church
(cnr Emilio Gracia & Jose Falcao Rds; ⊗10am-12.30pm & 3-5.30pm Mon-Sat, 11am-12.30pm & 3.30-5pm Sun, English Mass 8am daily) Panaji's spiritual, as well as geographical, centre is this elevated, pearly white church, built in 1619 over an older, smaller 1540 chapel, and stacked like a fancy white wedding cake. When Panaji was little more than a sleepy fishing village, this church was the first port of call for sailors from Lisbon, who would give thanks for a safe crossing, before continuing to Ela (Old Goa) further east up the river. The church is beautifully illuminated at night.

Fontainhas & Sao Tomé   Area
The oldest, and by far the most atmospheric, Portuguese-flavoured districts of Panaji are squeezed between the hillside of Altinho and the banks of Ourem Creek, and make for attractive wandering with their narrow streets, overhanging balconies and quaint air of Mediterranean yesteryear.

Altinho Hill   Area
On the hillside above Panaji is the well-to-do residential district of Altinho. Apart from good views over the city and river, the main attraction here is the Bishop's Palace, an imposing building completed in 1893.

EATING & DRINKING

A stroll down 18th June or 31st January Rds will turn up a number of cheap but tasty canteen-style options, many of them pure veg. The Latin Quarter has a developing foodie scene.

Viva Panjim   Goan $$
(☏0832-2422405; 31st January Rd; mains ₹130-220; ⊗11.30am-3.30pm & 7-11pm Mon-Sat, 7-11pm Sun) Well known to tourists, this little side-street eatery, in an old Portuguese house and with a few tables out on the laneway, still delivers tasty Goan classics at reasonable prices. There's a whole page devoted to pork dishes, along with tasty *xacuti* and *cafreal*-style dishes, seafood such as kingfish vindaloo and crab *xec xec*, and desserts such as *bebinca* (richly layered Goan dessert made from egg yolk and coconut).

Cafe Bodega   Cafe $$
(☏0832-2421315; Altinho; mains ₹140-340; ⊗10am-7pm Mon-Sat, 10am-4pm Sun; 🛜) It's well worth a trip up to Altinho Hill to visit this serene cafe-gallery in a lavender-and-white Portuguese mansion in the grounds of Sunaparanta Centre for the Arts. Enjoy good coffee, juices and fresh-baked cakes around the inner courtyard or lunch on super pizzas and sandwiches.

Black Sheep Bistro   European $$$
(☏0832-2222901; www.blacksheepbistro.in; Swami Vivekanand Rd; tapas ₹190-280, mains ₹320-650; ⊗noon-4pm & 7-10.45pm) Among the best of Panaji's burgeoning boutique restaurants, Black Sheep's impressive pale-yellow facade gives way to a sexy dark-wood bar and loungey dining room. The tapas dishes are light, fresh and expertly prepared in keeping with their farm-to-table philosophy. Salads, pasta, seafood and dishes such as lamb osso bucco grace the menu, while an internationally trained sommelier matches food to wine.

❶ GETTING THERE & AWAY

AIR

Dabolim Airport (DABOLIM, Goa International Airport; ☏0832-2540806) is around 30km south of Panaji. From the airport, the prepaid taxi fare is ₹870 (₹920 for AC). There are no direct buses, though some higher-end hotels offer a minibus service.

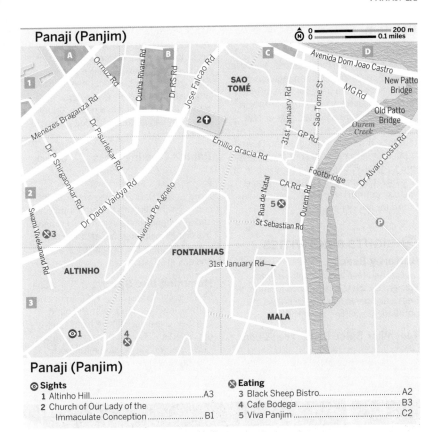

Panaji (Panjim)

◎ **Sights**
1 Altinho Hill...A3
2 Church of Our Lady of the
   Immaculate Conception B1

✖ **Eating**
3 Black Sheep Bistro..................................... A2
4 Cafe Bodega B3
5 Viva Panjim C2

BUS

All local buses depart from Panaji's **Kadamba bus stand** (☏interstate 0832-2438035, local 0832-2438034; www.goakadamba.com; ⏱reservations 8am-8pm), with frequent services heading out every few minutes, including to Mapusa (₹30, 30 minutes) in the north and Margao (₹30, 45 minutes) to the south. For the beaches in South Goa including Palolem, take an express bus to Margao and change there; for Anjuna and other beaches north of Baga, head to Mapusa and change there.

State-run long-distance services also depart from the Kadamba bus stand, but private operators, such as reliable **Paulo Travels** (☏0832-2438531; www.paulobus.com; G1, Kardozo Bldg), offer greater choice in type of bus and departure times, for similar fares. Many private operators have booths outside the bus stand entrance, but their buses mostly depart from the interstate bus stand across the highway next to the New Patto Bridge.

TRAIN

The closest station to Panaji is Karmali (Old Goa), 12km east. A number of long-distance trains stop here, including services to and from Mumbai, and many trains coming from Margao also stop here – but check in advance. Panaji's **Konkan Railway Reservation Office** (☏0832-2712940; www.konkanrailway.com; ⏱8am-8pm Mon-Sat) is on the 1st floor of the Kadamba bus stand – not at the train station.

Palolem

Palolem is undoubtedly one of Goa's most postcard-perfect beaches: a gentle curve of palm-fringed sand facing a calm bay. In season the beachfront is transformed into a toy town of colourful and increasingly sophisticated timber and bamboo huts fronted by palm-thatch restaurants. It's still a great place to be and is popular with backpackers, long-stayers and families. The protected bay is one of the safest swimming spots in Goa and you can comfortably kayak and paddle-board for hours here.

◎ SIGHTS & ACTIVITIES

Butterfly Beach   Beach
(from ₹1700) Hire a local boatman from Palolem Beach to ferry you up to Butterfly Beach and back, relishing the views of untouched coastline along the way.

Tanshikar Spice Farm   Food & Drink
(✆0832-2608358, 9421184114; www.tanshikar spicefarm.com; Netravali; tour incl lunch ₹500;

⊙10am-4pm) Tanshikar Spice Farm is a working, family-run organic spice farm with crops including vanilla, cashews, pepper, nutmeg and chillies, as well as beekeeping. There are no tour buses out here and the amiable young owners give a personalised tour of the plantation and nearby bubble lake. They can also offer guided jungle treks to nearby waterfalls.

Rahul's Cooking Class   Cooking
(✆07875990647; www.rahulcookingclass.com; Palolem Beach Rd; per person ₹1500; ⊙11am-2pm & 6-9pm) Rahul's is one of the original cooking schools, with three-hour morning and afternoon classes each day. Prepare five dishes including chapati and coconut curry. Minimum two people; book at least one day in advance.

Humming Bird Spa   Spa
(Ciaran's; 1hr massage from ₹1900) For sheer pampering, Palolem's best all-round spa is at Ciaran's. Choose from ayurvedic, Swedish, Balinese, Thai or aroma massage, waxing or even a full-body chocolate wrap.

Cafe on Palolem beach

MISHAKOV VALERY/SHUTTERSTOCK ©

EATING

In season every hut operation lining the beach has its own restaurant, often with tables and umbrellas on the sand. They all serve fresh seafood, so just check a few and find the ambience that suits.

Space Goa   Cafe $$

(✆80063283333; www.thespacegoa.com; mains ₹150-280; ⏰8.30am-5.30pm; 🛜) On the Agonda road, Space Goa combines an excellent organic whole-food cafe with a gourmet deli, craft shop and a wellness centre offering meditation, ayurvedic treatments and zen cosmic healing. The food is fresh and delicious, with fabulous salads, paninis and meze, and the desserts – such as chocolate beetroot cake – are divine. Drop-in morning yoga classes are ₹500.

Magic Italy   Italian $$

(✆8805767705; Palolem Beach Rd; mains ₹260-480; ⏰5pm-midnight) On the main beach road, Magic Italy has been around for a while and the quality of its pizza and pasta remains high, with imported Italian ingredients including ham, salami, cheese and olive oil, imaginative wood-fired pizzas and homemade pasta. Sit at tables, or Arabian-style on floor cushions. The atmosphere is busy but chilled.

Ourem 88   Fusion $$$

(✆8698827679; mains ₹540-750; ⏰6-10pm Tue-Sun) British-run Ourem 88 is a gastro sensation with just a handful of tables and a small but masterful menu. Try baked brie, tender calamari stuffed with Goan sausage, braised lamb shank or fluffy souffle. Worth a splurge.

DRINKING & NIGHTLIFE

Palolem doesn't party like the northern beaches but it's certainly not devoid of nightlife. Some of the beach bars stay open 24 hours in season and there are silent headphone parties four nights a week.

🎫 Silent Discos

Neatly sidestepping Goa's statewide ban on loud music in open spaces after 10pm, Palolem's 'silent parties' are the way to dance the night away without upsetting the neighbours.

Turn up around 10pm, don your headphones with a choice of two or three channels featuring Goan and international DJs playing trance, house, hip hop, electro and funk, and then party the night away in inner bliss but outer silence.

Silent Noise (www.silentnoise.in; On the Rocks; cover charge ₹600; ⏰9pm-4am Sat Nov-Apr)

Neptune Point Headphone Disco (www.neptunepoint.com; Neptune's Point, Colomb Bay; cover charge ₹600; ⏰9.30am-4am Sat Nov-Apr)

Silent disco in Palolem, Goa
DAVID PEARSON/ALAMY ©

Leopard Valley   Club

(www.leopardvalley.com; Palolem-Agonda Rd; entry from ₹600; ⏰9pm-4am Fri) South Goa's biggest outdoor dance club is a sight (and sound) to behold, with 3D laser light shows, pyrotechnics and state-of-the-art sound systems blasting local and international DJs on Friday nights.

GETTING THERE & AWAY

Hourly buses run to Margao (₹40, one hour) from the bus stop on the corner of the road down to the beach. At Margao you can change for Panaji.

Anjuna Flea Market

Anjuna's weekly Wednesday **flea market** (⊙8am-late Wed, Nov-Apr) is as much part of the Goan experience as a day on the beach. More than three decades ago, it was conceived and created by hippies smoking jumbo joints, convening to compare experiences on the heady Indian circuit and selling jeans or handmade jewellery to help fund their stay.

Nowadays things are far more mainstream and the merchandise comes from all over India: sculptures and jewellery courtesy of Tibetan and Kashmiri traders; colourful saris, bags and bedspreads from Rajasthan; spices from Kerala; and the hard-to-miss tribal girls from Karnataka pleading passers-by to 'come look in my shop'. Weaving in among this are the remaining hippies, backpackers and weekenders from Mumbai.

Such purchasing power has pushed prices up but you can still find bargains. The market sprawls back from the beach to the entrance road in the paddy fields. For a rest from shopping there are chai stalls and a couple of restaurant-bars: Cafe Looda has a fabulous sunset beachfront location and live music from 5pm.

The best time to visit is early (from 8am) or late afternoon (around 4pm till close just after sunset). The market operates from around mid-November till the end of April. Watch out for pickpockets.

The closest train station is Canacona, 2km from Palolem's beach entrance. A taxi to Dabolim Airport is around ₹1500.

Anjuna

Good old Anjuna has been a stalwart of the hippie scene since the 1960s and continues to pull in droves of backpack-

ers – but midrange and domestic tourists are increasingly making their way here for a dose of hippie-chic. Anjuna continues to evolve, with a heady beach party scene and a flowering of new restaurants and bars. Unless you're drawn to the thumping nightclubs and wall-to-wall drinking of the Calangute-Baga package-holiday party strip, this is North Goa's all-round best beach base, with plenty of daytime activities, a good yoga scene shared with nearby Assagao and Vagator, plus happening nightclubs of its own and a famous Wednesday market.

The village is spread over a wide area. Do as most do: hire a scooter or motorbike and explore the back lanes and southern beach area and you'll find a place that suits. Anjuna will grow on you.

✈ ACTIVITIES

Anjuna's charismatic, narrow beach runs for almost 2km from the rocky, low-slung cliffs at the northern village area right down beyond the flea market in the south. In season there are water sports here, including jet skis (₹400), banana boats (₹1000 for four people) and parasailing (₹700).

Lots of yoga, ayurveda and other alternative therapies and regimes are on offer in season; look out for noticeboards at popular cafes such as Artjuna Cafe.

Brahmani Yoga   Yoga
(☎9545620578; www.brahmaniyoga.com; Tito's White House, Aguada-Siolim Rd; class ₹700, 10-class pass ₹5000; ⊙classes 9.30am) This friendly drop-in centre offers daily classes from late November to April in ashtanga, vinyasa, hatha and dynamic yoga, as well as pranayama meditation. No need to book: just turn up 15 minutes before the class.

EATING

Anjuna has a good range of eating options, from clifftop restaurant-bars and cafes hidden in the back lanes to the big beachfront places near the market site. New places are popping up all the time, keeping things fresh.

Artjuna Cafe — Cafe $$

(0832-2274794; www.artjuna.com; Market Rd; mains ₹130-350; 8am-10.30pm;) Artjuna is right up there with our favourite cafes in Anjuna. Along with all-day breakfast, outstanding espresso coffee, salads, sandwiches and Middle Eastern surprises like baba ganoush, tahini and felafel, this sweet garden cafe has an excellent craft and lifestyle shop, yoga classes and a useful noticeboard. Great meeting place.

Burger Factory — Burgers $$

(Anjuna-Mapusa Rd; burgers ₹300-450; 11.30am-3.30pm & 6.30-10.30pm Thu-Tue) There's no mistaking what's on offer at this little alfresco diner. The straightforward menu of burgers isn't cheap, but they are interesting and expertly crafted. Choose between beef or chicken burgers and toppings such as cheddar or beetroot and aioli.

Elephant Art Cafe — Beach Cafe $$

(mains ₹190-370; 8am-10pm;) A standout among the restaurants lining the beach, Elephant Art Cafe does a great range of tapas, sandwiches, fish and chips and speciality breakfasts.

DRINKING & NIGHTLIFE

Anjuna vies with Vagator as the trance party capital of Goa and the southern end of the beach has several nightclubs that are the most happening places in North Goa when the night is right. Market day is always fun, with live music at one or both of the two bars there.

Purple Martini — Cocktail Bar

(9823772890; Sunset Point; 9pm-midnight) The clifftop sunset views, blue-and-white colour scheme and swanky bar at this beautifully situated restaurant-bar could easily transport you to Santorini. Come for a sundowner cocktail and check out the menu of Greek kebabs and Mediterranean salads.

Where to Stay

Panaji Has some of Goa's better mid-range boutique and heritage hotels and guesthouses, mostly in the Fontainhas area. Fontainhas also has budget guesthouses and a hostel.

Palolem Most accommodation is of the seasonal beach-hut variety. It's still possible to find a basic palm-thatch hut or plywood cottage somewhere near the beach for as little as ₹800, but many huts these days are more thoughtfully designed – the very best have air-con, flat-screen TV and sea-facing balcony.

Anjuna Has a good range of budget and midrange accommodation spread over a wide area. Dozens of basic rooms are strung along the northern clifftop, while pricier places front the main beach. Plenty of small, family-run guesthouses are also tucked back from the main beach strip, offering nicer double rooms for a similar price; look for 'rooms to let' or 'house to let' signs.

Curlies — Bar

(www.curliesgoa.com; 9am-3am) Holding sway at South Anjuna Beach, Curlies mixes laid-back beach-bar vibe with sophisticated night spot – the party nights here are notorious and loud. There's a rooftop lounge bar and an enclosed late-night dance club. Thursday and Saturday are big nights, as are full moon nights.

GETTING THERE & AWAY

Buses to Mapusa (₹15, 30 minutes) depart every half-hour or so from the main bus stand at the end of the Anjuna–Mapusa road near the beach.

Plenty of motorcycle taxis and autorickshaws gather at the main crossroads and you can also easily hire scooters and motorcycles here from ₹250 to ₹400 – most Anjuna-based travellers get around on two wheels.

KERALA

In this Chapter
Backwater Boat Trips.................180
Ayurvedic Resorts.....................182
Best Keralan Beaches...............184
Kathakali.................................186
Trivandrum..............................188
Kovalam...................................189
Alleppey 190
Kochi.......................................192

Kerala at a Glance...

For many travellers, Kerala is South India's most serenely beautiful state. Behind 600km of glorious Arabian Sea coast extends a languid network of glistening backwaters, and behind them rise the spice- and tea-covered hills of the Western Ghats. Kerala is a world away from the frenzy of elsewhere.

Besides its famous backwaters, elegant houseboats, ayurvedic treatments and taste-bud-tingling cuisine, vibrant traditions such as Kathakali plays, temple festivals and snake-boat races frequently bring even the smallest villages to life.

Kerala in Three Days

Spend the first day and night enjoying the sights, smells, food, shops and quaint colonial atmosphere of the age-old trading port **Kochi** (Cochin; p192), then start early for **Alappuzha** (Alleppey; p190) and kick back on a two-day houseboat cruise drifting lazily through Kerala's famed backwaters (p180).

Kerala in Five Days

On day four head south, with a stop in Kerala's capital **Thiruvananthapuram** (Trivandrum; p188) for a little sightseeing and shopping en route to nearby **Kovalam** (p189), where you have a night and a day to enjoy the beach, some fine dining and maybe a spot of surfing or diving.

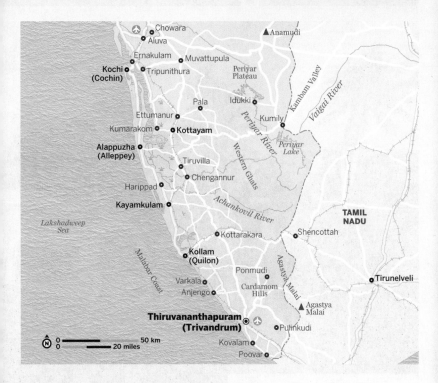

Arriving in Kerala

Kerala's major airports, Thiruvanan-thapuram (Trivandrum), Kochi and Kozhikode (Calicut) are served by international and domestic flights. A new international airport, 25km from Kannur, should be open by the time you read this.

Kerala is well served by trains, particularly along the west coast, and long-distance buses.

Sleeping

Kochi, Alleppey and to a lesser extent Trivandrum have some of India's most charming accommodation, including heritage guesthouses and family-run homestays. Kovalam is tightly packed with hotels and guesthouses; smaller places along the sandy paths behind Lighthouse Beach are usually better value than beachfront places. Book ahead for the December–January peak season; at other times you may well get discounts.

Backwater Boat Trips

Kerala's 900km of waterways spread watery tendrils through a lusciously green landscape where palm-shaded, winding canals are lined by back-in-time villages. It's an unforgettable South India experience.

Great For...

☑ **Don't Miss**

The experience of sleeping under a firmament of stars on a traditional houseboat.

To glide along the canals in a punted canoe, or sleep under the stars in a traditional houseboat, is pure enchantment. Backwater trips traverse palm-fringed lakes studded with cantilevered Chinese fishing nets, and wind their way along narrow, shady canals where coir (coconut fibre), copra (dried coconut kernels) and cashews are loaded onto boats. Along the way are isolated villages where farming life continues as it has for aeons.

Houseboats

The most popular way to explore the backwaters is to rent a houseboat for a night or two; these sleep anywhere from two to 14 or more people. This can be an expensive experience but for a couple on a romantic overnight jaunt or split between a group of travellers, it's usually worth every

Houseboat on Kerala backwaters

rupee. Houseboats vary wildly in luxury and amenities. The hire includes staff (at least a driver and cook), so catering is included, and you'll eat traditional Keralan meals of fish and vegetables cooked in coconut milk.

A one-night trip won't get you far through the backwaters.

Choosing a Houseboat

Houseboats can be chartered through private operators in Alleppey, Kollam and Kottayam. The choice of boats – especially at Alleppey – is mind-boggling and your selection of boat and operator can make or break the experience.

○ Try to avoid booking a houseboat until you arrive at the backwaters; visit the Alleppey houseboat dock (p191), talk to returning travellers or guesthouse owners, and search online to gauge costs and quality. Inspect boats before committing.

○ Ask to see the operator's certification: houseboat owners with a 'Green Palm' or 'Gold Star' certificate have met requirements such as solar panels, sanitary tanks and low-emission engines.

Canoes & Kayaks

Village tours by kayak or in a canoe or covered *kettuvallam* (rice barge) with a knowledgeable guide are a tranquil way to explore deeper into the waterways network and see village life in a way that's impossible on a houseboat or ferry. The tours (from Kochi, Kollam or Alleppey) last from 2½ to six hours and cost from around ₹400 to ₹1000 per person. The Munroe Island trip from Kollam is an excellent tour of this type.

Ferries

The cheapest means of seeing the waterways is to take a public ferry. One of the most popular trips is the scenic all-day tourist cruise between Kollam and Alleppey (₹400), departing from both ends of the route at 10.30am daily from July to March and every second day at other times.

DMYTRO GILITUKHA/SHUTTERSTOCK ©

Ayurvedic Resorts

Kerala is regarded as the home of ayurveda – Indian herbal medicine, aiming to restore balance in the body. Many specialist clinics, resorts and colleges provide ayurvedic treatments or teach ayurvedic techniques.

Great For...

☑ **Don't Miss**

A revitalising ayurvedic massage under swaying palms near the beach.

Ayurveda sees the world as having intrinsic order and balance. It argues that we possess three *doshas* (humours): *vata* (wind or air); *pitta* (fire); and *kapha* (water/earth). Deficiency or excess in any of them can result in disease.

Treatment aims to restore the balance, principally through two methods: panchakarma (internal purification), and herbal massage. Panchakarma, used to treat serious ailments, is an intense detox regime combining five types of therapy. These include *vaman,* therapeutic vomiting; *virechan*, purgation; *vasti*, enemas; *nasya*, elimination of toxins through the nose; and *raktamoksha*, detoxification of the blood. The body is first prepared over several days with a special diet, oil massages *(snehana)* and herbal steambaths *(swedana)*. Although it may sound

Having an ayurvedic treatment

pretty grim, panchakarma purification might only use a few of these treatments at a time. Still, this is no pampering spa holiday.

Ayurvedic Centres & Resorts

Pulinkudi & Chowara

There's a concentration of upmarket resorts amid the swaying palms around Pulinkudi and Chowara, a few kilometres southeast of Kovalam.

Niraamaya Surya Samudra
(☏8589982204, 0471-2229400; www.niraa maya.in; Pulinkudi; r incl breakfast ₹16,800-30,000; ❄🛜🏊) offers A-list-style seclusion. The 22 traditional Keralan homes, in a palm grove above sparkling seas, come with four-poster beds and open-air bathrooms. There's an infinity pool carved out of a single block of granite, a renowned spa, ayurvedic treatments and spectacular outdoor yoga platforms.

Dr Franklin's (☏0471-2480870; www. dr-franklin.com; Chowara; s/d hut €25/33, r from €30/40, with AC €45/66; @🛜🏊) is a reputable and less expensive alternative to the flashier resorts. Daily treatment with full meal plan costs €75. Accommodation is tidy and comfortable but not resort-style.

One of the original resorts, **Somath-eeram** (☏0471-2268101; www.somatheeram. org; Chowara Beach; s/d from €75/84; ❄🛜🏊) offers a full range of ayurvedic and panchakarma treatments, ayurvedic food, yoga and a high-standard accommodation, overlooking Chowara Beach.

Kochi

Run by third-generation ayurvedic practitioner Dr Subhash, this delightful waterside **treatment centre** (☏0484-2502362, 9447721041; www.ayurdara.com; Murikkumpad-am, Vypeen Island; ⊙9am-5.30pm) specialises in treatments of one to three weeks (₹1650 per day). By appointment only.

PIUS LEE/SHUTTERSTOCK ©

Best Keralan Beaches

Goa might pull in the package-holiday crowds, but Kerala's coastline – almost 600km of it – boasts a stunning string of golden-sand beaches, fringed by palms and washed by the Arabian Sea.

Great For...

☑ Don't Miss

In Kerala's beach towns it's hard to beat the beach shacks for fresh, inexpensive seafood.

The southern beaches are the busiest. Less-discovered, wilder choices await in the north.

Best Beach Towns

○ Varkala The beautiful cliff-edged coastline of Varkala is a Hindu holy place as well as a lively backpacker-focused resort. Good base for yoga, surfing or just chilling out.

○ Kovalam (p189) Kerala's most commercial beach resort is still fun and easily accessible with some good waves and a surf club. Resorts here and further south have a strong focus on ayurvedic treatments.

○ Kannur While Kannur itself is not particularly appealing, head 8km south to Thottada for gorgeous beaches and seafront homestays in local villages. Kannur town's

Varkala beach

4km-long Payyambalam Beach is popular with locals.

Southern Beaches

Most established of the resorts along the coast is Kovalam (p189), only a short hop from the capital, Trivandrum (p188). Once a quiet fishing village, Kovalam has two sheltered crescents of beach perfect for paddling or novice surfing, overlooked by a solid line of low-rise hotels and restaurants. If you're looking for something less busy, some lovely beaches and resorts cluster south of Kovalam in the area around Pulinkudi and Chowara, where ayurvedic treatments are popular.

North of Trivandrum is Varkala, which straggles along its dramatic, russet-and-gold-streaked cliffs. Although a holy town popular with Hindu pilgrims, Varkala has also developed into Kerala's backpacker bolthole and the cliffs are lined with guesthouses, open-front restaurants and bars all moving to a reggae, rock and trance soundtrack. For a quieter scene, travellers are drifting north to Odayam beach.

Even further north, Alleppey (p190) is best known for its backwaters, but also has a decent coastline up to Marari, while Kochi (p192) has Cherai Beach on Vypeen Island, a lovely stretch of white sand, with kilometres of lazy lagoons and backwaters only a few hundred metres from the seafront.

Far North & Islands

Fewer travellers make it to Kerala's far north, which means there are some beautifully deserted pockets of beach, where resorts are replaced by more traditional village life. Among the best are the peaceful white-sand beaches south of Kannur, or further north around the Valiyaparamba backwaters between Kannur and Bekal.

Even more far flung are the Lakshadweep Islands, a palm-fringed archipelago 300km west of Kerala. As well as pristine beaches, the islands boast some of India's best scuba diving and snorkelling.

Kathakali

Kerala has an intensely rich culture of performing arts, and the most celebrated Keralan art form is Kathakali, a colourful dance-drama usually based on stories from the great Hindu epics.

Great For...

☑ Don't Miss

Kochi's Kerala Kathakali Centre is one of the best venues for an introductory Kathakali performance.

Kathakali crystallised in its current form in the 16th century – around the same time as Shakespeare was penning his plays. The Kathakali performance is a dramatised presentation of a play, usually based on the Ramayana, the Mahabharata or the Puranas. All the great themes are covered – righteousness and evil, frailty and courage, poverty and prosperity, war and peace, love, lust and power struggles.

Drummers and singers accompany the actors, who tell the story through their precise movements, particularly *mudras* (hand gestures) and facial expressions.

Preparation for the performance is lengthy. Paint, fantastic costumes, ornamental headpieces and meditation transform the actors physically and mentally into the gods, heroes and demons they are about to play. Dancers even stain their eyes

Masked dancers at a Kathakali performance

Need to Know

Abbreviated introductory shows for tourists usually last about two hours, including make-up and costume sessions.

Take a Break

The Kochi cafe **Teapot** (Peter Celli St; tea ₹50-120, mains ₹200-300; ⊘8.30am-8.30pm) is perfect for 'high tea' before a performance at the Kerala Kathakali Centre.

★ Top Tip

Some Kathakali centres in Kochi and Kumily also give demonstrations of the Keralan ritual martial art *kalarippayat*.

Kalathiparambil Lane, Ernakulam; entry ₹300; ⊘make-up 6pm, show 7-8pm) and **Greenix Village** (☏9349372050, 0484-2217000; www.greenix.in; Kalvathy Rd, Fort Cochin; shows ₹350-500; ⊘10am-6pm, shows from 5pm) in Kochi; **Mudra Cultural Centre** (☏9061263381; www.mudraculturalcentre.com; Lake Rd; entry ₹200, video ₹200; ⊘Kathakali 5pm & 7pm, kalarippayat 6pm & 7.15pm) and **Navarasa Kathakali Centre** (☏9961740868; www.kalaripayattu.co.in; Thekkady Rd; ₹200; ⊘kalarippayat 6-7pm, Kathakali 7-8pm) in Kumily; and **Punarjani Traditional Village** (☏04865-216161; www.punarjanimunnar.org; 2nd Mile, Pallivasal; ₹200-300; ⊘shows 5pm & 6pm) in Munnar. Standard programs start with the intricate make-up application and costume-fitting, followed by a demonstration and commentary on the dance and then the performance – usually two hours in all. In Kovalam and Varkala there are short versions of the art in season.

Kerala Kalamandalam (☏0488-4262418; www.kalamandalam.org; courses per month ₹600; ⊘Jun-Mar) near Thrissur and **Margi Kathakali School** (☏0471-2478806; www.margitheatre.org; Fort) in Trivandrum offer courses for serious students, and you can attend these schools to see performances and practice sessions.

red with seeds from the *chundanga* plant to maximise the drama.

Where to See Kathakali

Traditionally performances start in temple grounds around 8pm and go on all night, but shorter versions are performed in tourist centres such as Kochi, Munnar and Kumily, to give visitors a taste of the art. Several spring festivals offer the chance to see full-night Kathakali performances, including Thirunakkara in Kottayam (March) and Kollam's Pooram festival (April). Otherwise the easiest places for travellers to see performances are at cultural centres such as **Kerala Kathakali Centre** (☏0484-2217552; www.kathakalicentre.com; KB Jacob Rd, Fort Cochin; shows ₹250-300; ⊘make-up from 5pm, show 6-7.30pm), **See India Foundation** (☏0484-2376471; devankathakali@yahoo.com;

Trivandrum

Thiruvananthapuram, Kerala's capital –
still usually known by its colonial name,
Trivandrum – is an easygoing introduction
to urban life down south, and the beach
resorts of Kovalam and Varkala are just a
short hop away.

◉ SIGHTS

Museum of History & Heritage
Museum

(☏9567019037; www.museumkeralam.org;
Park View; adult/child Indian ₹20/10, foreigner
₹200/50, camera ₹25; ◷10am-5.30pm Tue-Sun)
In a lovely heritage building within the
Kerala Tourism complex, this beautifully
presented museum traces Keralan history
and culture through superb static displays
and interactive audiovisual presentations.
Exhibits range from Iron Age implements to
bronze and terracotta sculptures, murals,
dhulichitra (floor paintings) and recreations
of traditional Keralan homes.

Napier Museum
Museum

(adult/child ₹10/5; ◷10am-5pm Tue & Thu-Sun,
1-5pm Wed) Housed in an 1880 wooden
building designed by British architect Robert Chisholm, this museum has an eclectic
display of bronzes, Buddhist sculptures,
temple carts and ivory carvings. The carnivalesque interior is stunning and worth a
look in its own right.

Zoological Gardens
Zoo

(☏0471-2115122; adult/child ₹20/5, camera/
video ₹50/75; ◷9am-5.15pm Tue-Sun) Yann
Martel famously based the animals in his
novel *Life of Pi* on those he observed here
in Trivandrum's zoological gardens. Shaded
paths meander through woodland, lakes
and native forest, where tigers, macaques
and hippos gather in reasonably large open
enclosures.

🔒 SHOPPING

Wander around **Connemara Market** (MG
Rd; ◷6am-9pm) to see vendors selling
vegetables, fish, live goats, fabric, clothes
and spices.

Napier Museum

TSCREATION27/SHUTTERSTOCK ©

EATING

Ariya Nivaas　　　South Indian **$**

(Manorama Rd; mains ₹40-150, thalis ₹100; ⊘6.45am-10pm, lunch 11.30am-3pm) Trivandrum's best all-you-can-eat South Indian veg thalis mean Ariya Nivaas is always busy at lunchtime, but service is snappy and the food fresh.

Azad Restaurant　　　Indian **$**

(MG Rd; dishes ₹60-200; ⊘11am-11.30pm) A busy family favourite serving up authentic Keralan seafood dishes such as fish *molee*, and excellent biryanis and tandoori. There's a takeaway barbecue on street level and the restaurant downstairs.

GETTING THERE & AWAY

AIR

Trivandrum International Airport (www.trivandrumairport.com), 5km west of the city, serves international destinations with direct flights to/from Colombo (Sri Lanka), Malé (Maldives) and several Gulf destinations. Domestic flights head to/from Mumbai (Bombay), Kochi, Bengaluru (Bangalore), Chennai (Madras) and Delhi.

BUS

State-run and private buses use the giant **KSRTC central bus stand** (☑0471-2462290; www.keralartc.com; Central Station Rd, Thampanoor), opposite the train station. Destinations include Alleppey (non-AC/AC ₹132/221, 3½ hours, every 15 minutes) and Ernakulam (Kochi; non-AC/AC ₹177/291, 5½ hours, every 15 to 30 minutes).

Buses leave for Kovalam beach (₹17, 30 minutes, every 20 minutes) between 6am and 9pm from the southern end of the East Fort bus stand on MG Rd.

TRAIN

Trains are often heavily booked, so it's worth visiting the **reservation office** (☑139; ⊘8am-8pm Mon-Sat, to 2pm Sun) at the main train station or booking online. There's a foreign tourist counter on the 1st floor. Most major trains arrive at Trivandrum Central Station. A good train for Bengaluru is the 16525 Bangalore Express

 Villa Maya

Trivandum's **Villa Maya** (☑0471-2578901; www.villamaya.in; 120 Airport Rd, Injakkal; starters ₹200-600, mains ₹400-1500; ⊘11am-11pm) is more an experience than a restaurant. Dining is either in the magnificent 18th-century Dutch mansion or in private curtained niches in the tranquil courtyard garden. The Keralan cuisine is expertly crafted, delicately spiced and beautifully presented. Seafood is a speciality, with dishes such as stuffed crab with lobster butter, but there are some tantalising veg dishes too.

(sleeper/3AC/2AC ₹415/1120/1620, 18 hours) at 12.45pm; for Mumbai the 16346 Netravathi Express (₹670/1795/2645, 31 hours) departs at 9.50am. There are frequent express trains to Kollam (₹55/140/490, 1¼ hours) and Ernakulam (₹90/165/490, 4½ hours), passing through Alleppey (₹80/140/490, three hours) or Kottayam.

GETTING AROUND

Prepaid taxi vouchers from the airport cost ₹350 to the city and ₹500 to Kovalam.

Kovalam

Once a calm fishing village clustered around its crescent beaches, Kovalam competes with Varkala as Kerala's most developed resort. Lighthouse Beach has hotels and restaurants built up along the shore, while Hawa Beach to the north is usually crowded with day trippers heading straight from the taxi stand to the sand.

SIGHTS & ACTIVITIES

Vizhinjam Lighthouse　　　Lighthouse

(Indian/foreigner ₹10/25, camera/video ₹20/25; ⊘10am-5pm) Kovalam's most distinguishing feature is the working

Fresh Seafood

Each evening a dozen or so restaurants lining Kovalam's Lighthouse Beach promenade display the catch of the day – just pick a fish or lobster, settle on a price and decide how you want it prepared. Market prices vary enormously depending on the day's catch, but at the time of research it was around ₹400 per fish fillet, tiger prawns were ₹900 per 500g, and lobster was ₹3500 per kilogram.

candy-striped lighthouse at the southern end of Lighthouse Beach. Climb the spiral staircase – or the brand-new elevator – for vertigo-inducing views up and down the coast.

Cool Divers & Bond Safari   Diving
(☏9946550073; www.bondsafarikovalam.com; introductory dive ₹6000, 3hr ocean safari ₹6000; ⊙9am-7pm) This new dive outfit offers state-of-the-art equipment, PADI courses and guided trips to local dive sites. It also has nifty Bond submarine scooters, where your head is enclosed in a helmet with an airhose to the surface – no diving experience required!

✖ EATING & DRINKING

For a romantic dining splurge, the restaurants at **Leela** (☏0471-2480101; www.theleela.com; ✳@☏✖) and **Vivanta by Taj Green Cove** (☏0471-6613000; http://vivanta.tajhotels.com; Samudra Beach) are pricey but top class. Just about all of Kovalam's restaurants will serve beer and wine discreetly.

Varsha Restaurant   South Indian $
(dishes ₹100-200; ⊙8am-10pm; ☏) This little restaurant just back from Lighthouse Beach serves some of Kovalam's best vegetarian food at budget prices. Dishes are fresh and carefully prepared. It's a great spot for breakfast and lunch in particular.

Bait   Seafood $$$
(Vivanta by Taj Green Cove; mains ₹300-800; ⊙12.30-3pm & 6-10.30pm) The seafood restaurant at the Vivanta fronts Samudra Beach, a golf-buggy ride from the hotel itself. It's designed as an upmarket alfresco beach shack, where you can watch the waves on one side and the chefs at work in the open kitchen on the other; the seafood and spicy preparations are top notch.

❶ INFORMATION

Tourist Facilitation Centre (☏0471-2480085; Kovalam Beach Rd; ⊙9.30am-5pm Mon-Sat) This helpful office is in the main entrance to Leela hotel near the bus stand.

❶ GETTING THERE & AROUND

Buses start and finish at an unofficial bus stand on the main road outside the entrance to Leela hotel, and all buses pass through Kovalam Junction, about 1.5km north of Lighthouse Beach. Buses connect Kovalam and Trivandrum every 20 minutes between 7am and 8pm (₹17, 30 minutes).

A taxi between Trivandrum and Kovalam beach is around ₹500; an autorickshaw should cost ₹350. From the bus stand to the north end of Lighthouse Beach costs around ₹50.

The main autorickshaw and taxi stand is at Hawa Beach.

Alleppey

Alappuzha – most still call it Alleppey – is the hub of Kerala's backwaters, home to a vast network of waterways and more than a thousand houseboats. In the small but chaotic city centre and bus-stand area, you'd be hard-pressed to agree with the 'Venice of the East' tag. But head west to the beach or in practically any other direction towards the backwaters and Alleppey becomes graceful and greenery-fringed, disappearing into a watery world of villages, punted canoes and, of course, houseboats.

SIGHTS & ACTIVITIES

Alleppey Lighthouse   Lighthouse

(Indian/foreigner ₹10/25, camera/video
₹20/25; ⊙9-11.45am & 2-5.30pm Tue-Sun) The
candy-striped lighthouse is a few blocks
back from the beach. There's a small museum containing on original oil lamp and you
can climb to the top via the spiralling staircase for 360-degree views of a surprisingly
green Alleppey.

Houseboat Dock   Boating

(dtpcaly@yahoo.com; ⊙prepaid counter 10am-
5pm) Where dozens of houseboat gather;
this is a good place to wander down and
compare a few. There's a government-run
prepaid counter where you can see the 'official' posted prices, starting at ₹7000 for
two people, up to ₹24,000 for a five-berth
boat. Even these prices fluctuate depending on demand.

Kerala Kayaking   Kayaking

(☎9846585674, 8547487701; www.
keralakayaking.com; per person 4/7/10hr
₹1500/3000/4500) The original and best

kayaking outfit in Alleppey. The young crew
here offer excellent guided kayaking trips
through narrow backwater canals. Paddles
in single or double kayaks include a support boat and motorboat transport to your
starting point. There are four-hour morning
and afternoon trips, seven- or 10-hour day
trips, and multiday village tours can also be
arranged.

✖ EATING

Homestays, resorts and houseboats all
offer home-style cooking.

Mushroom   Arabian, Indian $

(CCSB Rd; mains ₹70-150; ⊙noon-midnight) A
breezy open-air restaurant with wrought-iron
chairs, specialising in cheap, tasty and spicy
halal meals such as chicken *kali mirch*, fish
tandoori and chilli mushrooms. Lots of locals
and travellers give it a good vibe.

Chakara
Restaurant   Multicuisine $$$

(☎0477-2230767; Beach Rd; mini Kerala meal
₹500, mains from ₹450; ⊙12.30-3pm & 7-10pm)

An Alleppey waterway

Jew Town, Kochi

The restaurant at Raheem Residency is Alleppey's finest, with seating on a bijou open rooftop, reached via a spiral staircase, with views over to the beach. The menu creatively combines traditional Keralan and European cuisine, specialising in locally caught fish.

ℹ️ INFORMATION

DTPC Tourist Reception Centre (📞0477-2253308; www.dtpcalappuzha.com; Boat Jetty Rd; ⏰9am-5pm) Close to the bus stand and boat jetty. Staff are helpful and can advise on local tours.

ℹ️ GETTING THERE & AWAY

BOAT

Ferries run to Kottayam (₹15) and daily at 10am to Kollam (₹400) from the boat jetty on VCSB (Boat Jetty) Rd.

BUS

From the KSRTC bus stand, frequent buses head to Trivandrum (₹132, 3½ hours, every 20 minutes), Kollam (₹73, 2½ hours) and Ernakulam (Kochi, ₹55, 1½ hours).

TAXI

Taxis to Kochi cost ₹1800.

TRAIN

There are numerous daily trains to Ernakulam (2nd class/sleeper/3AC ₹50/140/490, 1½ hours) and to Trivandrum (₹80/140/490, three hours) via Kollam. The station is 4km southwest of town.

Kochi

Serene Kochi is a delightful place to spend some time and nap in some of India's finest homestays and heritage accommodation. Nowhere else in India will you find such an intriguing blend of medieval Portugal, Holland and an English village all grafted onto the tropical Malabar Coast.

Mainland Ernakulam is Kochi's hectic transport and cosmopolitan hub, while the historical towns of Fort Cochin and Mattancherry remain wonderfully atmospheric.

◉ SIGHTS
◉ Fort Cochin

Indo-Portuguese Museum   Museum
(🕾0484-2215400; Indian/foreigner ₹10/25; ⊙9am-1pm & 2-6pm Tue-Sun) This museum in the garden of the Bishop's House preserves the heritage of one of India's earliest Catholic communities, including vestments, silver processional crosses and altarpieces from the Cochin diocese. The basement contains remnants of the Portuguese Fort Immanuel, after which Fort Cochin is named.

◉ Mattancherry & Jew Town

About 3km southeast of Fort Cochin, Mattancherry is the old bazaar district and centre of the spice trade. These days it's packed with spice shops and pricey Kashmiri-run emporiums. In the midst of this, Jew Town is a bustling port area with a fine synagogue. Scores of small firms huddle together in dilapidated old buildings and the air is filled with the biting aromas of ginger, cardamom, cumin, turmeric and cloves, though the lanes around the Dutch Palace and synagogue are packed with antique and tourist-curio shops rather than spices.

Mattancherry Palace   Museum
(Dutch Palace; 🕾0484-2226085; Palace Rd; adult/child ₹5/free; ⊙9am-5pm Sat-Thu) Mattancherry Palace was a generous gift presented to the Raja of Kochi, Veera Kerala Varma (1537–61), as a gesture of goodwill by the Portuguese in 1555. The Dutch renovated the palace in 1663, hence its alternative name, the Dutch Palace. The star attractions here are the astonishingly preserved Hindu murals, depicting scenes from the Ramayana, Mahabharata and Puranic legends in intricate detail.

Pardesi Synagogue   Synagogue
(₹5; ⊙10am-1pm & 3-5pm Sun-Thu, closed Jewish holidays) Originally built in 1568, this synagogue was partially destroyed by the Portuguese in 1662, and rebuilt two years later when the Dutch took Kochi. It features an ornate gold pulpit and elaborate hand-painted, willow-pattern floor tiles from Canton, China, which were added in 1762. It's magnificently illuminated by Belgian chandeliers and coloured-glass lamps. The graceful clock tower was built in 1760. There's an upstairs balcony for women, who worshipped separately according to Orthodox rites.

⊕ TOURS

Art of Bicycle Trips   Cycling
(🕾08129945707; www.artofbicycletrips.com; Bastion St; 3hr/half-day tours ₹1450/2500; ⊙9am-6pm) Guided bicycle tours on quality mountain bikes include a morning tour of the historic Fort area and a half-day ride around the backwaters. A great way to see the area at a slow pace.

 Chinese Fishing Nets

The unofficial emblems of Kerala's backwaters are the half-dozen or so giant cantilevered Chinese fishing nets on Fort Kochi's northeastern shore. A legacy of traders from the AD 1400 court of Kublai Khan, these enormous, spiderlike, much photographed contraptions require at least four people to operate their counterweights at high tide.

Chinese fishing nets, Kochi
MADRUGADA VERDE/SHUTTERSTOCK ©

Tourist Desk   Tours
(📞0484-2371761, 9847044688; www.tourist
desk.in; Ernakulam Boat Jetty; ⏲8am-6pm) This
high-profile private tour agency runs the
popular full-day Water Valley Tour (₹1250,
departs 8am) by houseboat through local
backwater canals and lagoons. A canoe trip
through smaller canals and villages is included. It also offers a sunset dinner cruise
(₹850 per person) by canoe from Narakkal
Village on Vypeen Island, with the option of
an overnight stay at a beach bungalow.

🅐 SHOPPING

On Jew Town Rd in Mattancherry you'll find
Gujarati-run shops selling genuine antiques
mingled with knock-offs. Most shops in Fort
Cochin are identikit Kashmiri-run stores
selling North Indian crafts. Many shops
around Fort Cochin and Mattancherry
operate commission rackets, with autorickshaw drivers getting kick-backs (added to
your price) for bringing tourists.

Niraamaya   Clothing
(📞0484-3263465; www.ayurvastraonline.com;
Quiros St, Fort Cochin; ⏲10am-5.30pm Mon-Sat)
Popular throughout Kerala, Niraamaya sells
'ayurvedic' clothing and fabrics – all made
of organic cotton, coloured with natural
herb dyes, or infused with ayurvedic oils.
There's another branch in Mattancherry.

✖ EATING
Dal Roti   Indian $$
(📞9746459244; 1/293 Lily St; meals ₹150-250;
⏲noon-3pm & 6.30-10pm Wed-Mon) There's a
lot to like about busy Dal Roti. Friendly and
knowledgable owner Ramesh will hold your
hand through his expansive North Indian
menu, which even sports its own glossary,
and help you dive into his delicious range of
vegetarian, eggetarian and nonvegetarian
options. From *kati* rolls to seven types of
thali, you won't go hungry. No alcohol.

Kashi Art Cafe   Cafe $$
(Burgher St; breakfast & snacks ₹160-280;
⏲8.30am-10pm) An institution in Fort

Cochin, this natural-light-filled place has a
zen, casual vibe and solid wood tables that
spread out into a semi-courtyard space.
The coffee is strong and the daily Western
breakfast and lunch specials are excellent.
A small gallery shows off local artists.

Ginger House   Indian $$$
(📞8943493648; www.gingerhousecochin.com;
Jew Town Rd, Jew Town; mains ₹200-720; ⏲9am-
6.30pm, to 10pm Dec-May) Hidden behind a
massive antique-filled godown (warehouse)
is this weird and wonderful waterfront
restaurant, where you can feast on Indian
dishes and snacks – ginger prawns, ginger
ice cream, ginger lassi...you get the picture.
To get to the restaurant, walk through the
astonishing Heritage Arts showroom with
amazing sculptures and antiques – check
out the giant snake-boat canoe.

Malabar
Junction   International $$$
(📞0484-2216666; Parade Ground Rd; mains ₹420-
750, 5-course degustation ₹2000; ⏲12.30-3pm
& 7-11pm) Set in an open-sided pavilion, the
restaurant at Malabar House is movie-star
cool, with white-tableclothed tables in a
courtyard close to the small pool. There's a
seafood-based, European-style menu – the
signature dish is the impressive seafood
platter with grilled vegetables. Upstairs, the
wine bar serves upmarket tapas-style snacks
and fine wine by the glass.

🍷 DRINKING & ENTERTAINMENT

Kochi is a centre for Keralan arts and there
are several places where you can view
Kathakali. The bar at **XL Hotel** (Rose St;
⏲10am-11pm) is the most casual and salu-
brious of Fort Cochin's beer parlours.

GETTING THERE & AWAY

AIR

Cochin International Airport (📞0484-2610115;
http://cial.aero), at Nedumbassery, 30km
northeast of Ernakulam, has international flights
to/from the Gulf states, Sri Lanka, the Maldives,

Murals, Mattancherry Palace (p193)

Malaysia, Bangkok and Singapore. There are daily domestic flights to Chennai, Mumbai, Bengaluru, Delhi and Trivandrum.

BUS

Most government and private long-distance buses use the massive **Vyttila Mobility Hub terminal** (☎0484-2306611; www.vyttilamobility hub.com; ⊙24hr), about 2km east of Ernakulam Junction train station. Destinations include Alleppey (₹55, 1½ hours, every 10 minutes), Bengaluru (₹530 to ₹890, 14 hours, eight buses daily) and Trivandrum (₹177 to ₹290, five hours, every 30 minutes). Agents in Ernakulam and Fort Cochin sell tickets for private buses, including air-con and Volvo services.

A prepaid autorickshaw from Vyttila costs ₹86 to the boat jetty, ₹215 to Fort Cochin and ₹400 to the airport.

TRAIN

Ernakulam has two train stations, Ernakulam Town and Ernakulam Junction. Reservations for both are made at the **reservations office** (☎132; ⊙8am-8pm Mon-Sat, 8am-2pm Sun) at Ernakulam Junction.

A good train for Bengaluru is the 16525 Bangalore Express (sleeper/3AC/2AC ₹345/940/1345, 13 hours), departing Ernakulam Junction at 6pm. The 16346 Netravathi Express leaves Ernakulam Town at 2.10pm for Goa (Madgaon; ₹445/1175/1630, 15 hours) and Mumbai (₹615/1645/2465, 27 hours). Local and express trains head to Trivandrum (2nd class/sleeper/3AC ₹95/165/490, 4½ hours), via either Alleppey (₹50/140/490, 1½ hours) or Kottayam.

ⓘ GETTING AROUND

AC Volvo buses run between the airport and Fort Cochin (₹80, one hour, eight daily) via Ernakulam. Taxis cost around ₹1200.

Ferries are the fastest and most enjoyable transport between Fort Cochin and the mainland. There are services to both Fort Cochin jetties (Customs and Mattancherry) from Ernakulam's main jetty every 25 to 50 minutes between 4.40am and 9.10pm. One-way fares are ₹4 (₹6 between Ernakulam and Mattancherry).

KARNATAKA

In this Chapter

Mysuru..................................... 200
Hampi 204
Bengaluru................................206
Mysuru......................................209

Karnataka at a Glance...

A stunning introduction to southern India, Karnataka is a prosperous state with a winning blend of urban cool, glittering palaces, national parks, ancient ruins, beaches, yoga centres and legendary hang-outs.

At its nerve centre is the capital Bengaluru (Bangalore), a progressive city famous for its craft beer and restaurant scene. A few hours away you'll discover the regal splendour of enchanting Mysuru (Mysore).

If that all sounds too mainstream, head to the tranquil counter-cultural enclave of Hampi with hammocks, psychedelic sunsets and the boulder-strewn ruins of the old Vijayanagar capital.

Karnataka in Two Days

On day one enjoy the creature comforts of Bengaluru, with a spot of shopping, a visit to the **National Gallery of Modern Art** (p206), craft beer at **Arbor Brewing Company** (p207) and dining at **Karavalli** (p206). Day two head down to Mysuru, tour its splendid **palace** (p200), dive into **Devaraja Market** (p201) and enjoy a great Indian dinner at **Tiger Trail** (p209).

Karnataka in Five Days

Head back to Bengaluru to dive into the **Krishnarajendra Market** (p206) and experience hipster India at **Church Street Social** (p206). Travel overnight to **Hampi** (p204), which gives you two full days to soak up the unique atmosphere of the fascinating ruined Vijayanagar capital set in an other-worldly landscape.

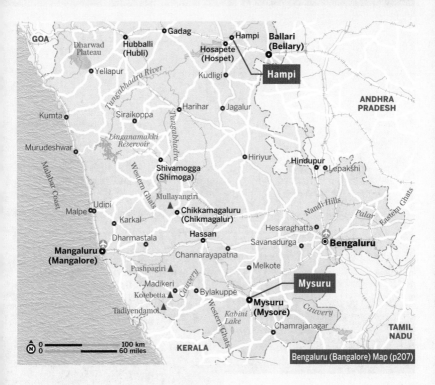

Bengaluru (Bangalore) Map (p207)

Arriving in Karnataka

Kempegowda International Airport, Bengaluru for international and domestic flights.

Bengaluru and **Mysuru** have good train and bus connections. Bengaluru City is Bengaluru's main station; Yeshvantpur station is the starting point for trains to Goa.

Hosapete (Hospet) is the gateway to Hampi, with daily trains and overnight sleeper bus services to/from Goa, Bengaluru and Mysuru.

Sleeping

Bengaluru and Mysuru have everything from sociable hostels to atmospheric boutique and heritage hotels and (especially in Bengaluru) glitzy five-star luxury. In Bengaluru, choosing a place near a metro station is a wise idea if you really want to explore the city. Hampi is great for budget travellers, with many inexpensive family-run guesthouses, plus a few more upscale guesthouses and lodges.

Mysuru

The historic settlement of Mysuru is one of South India's most enchanting cities, famed for its glittering royal heritage and magnificent monuments and buildings.

Great For...

☑ **Don't Miss**

Seeing how silk is made at the Government Silk Weaving Factory (p209).

Mysuru's World Heritage–listed palace is what brings most travellers here, but the city is also rich in tradition with a fascinating bazaar district thick with spices and incense stalls. Ashtanga yoga is another drawcard and there are several acclaimed schools that attract visitors from across the globe.

Mysuru isn't known as the City of Palaces for nothing, being home to a total of seven and an abundance of heritage architecture.

Mysuru Palace

Among the grandest of India's royal buildings, **Mysuru Palace** (Maharaja's Palace; www.mysorepalace.gov.in; Purandara Dasa Rd; Indian/foreigner/child under 10 incl audio guide ₹40/200/free; ⊙10am-5.30pm) was the seat of the Wodeyar maharajas. The original palace was gutted by fire in 1897; the one you see today was completed in 1912 by English

Mysuru Palace

ℹ Need to Know

Visit www.karnatakatourism.org/Mysore/en for a list of Mysuru's most notable buildings.

✕ Take a Break

Cafe Aramane (Sayyaji Rao Rd; mains ₹90-110; ☺8am-10pm) 🍴, between the Mysuru and Jaganmohan Palaces, is a great spot for dosas and thalis.

★ Top Tip

Mysuru is at its carnivalesque best during the 10-day Dussehra (locally spelled Dasara) festival in September/October.

---

architect Henry Irwin for ₹4.5 million. Entry to the palace grounds is by the **South Gate** (Purandara Dasa Rd).

Devaraja Market

Dating from Tipu Sultan's reign in the 18th century, this lively **bazaar** (Sayyaji Rao Rd; ☺6am-8.30pm) has local traders selling traditional items such as flower garlands, spices and conical piles of *kumkum* (coloured powder used for bindi dots), all of which make for some great photo ops. Refresh your bargaining skills before shopping.

Jaganmohan Palace

Built in 1861 as the royal auditorium, this stunning **palace** (Jaganmohan Palace Rd; adult/child ₹120/30; ☺8.30am-5pm) west of the Mysuru Palace now houses the **Jayachamarajendra Art Gallery**, with a huge collection of Indian paintings, traditional Japanese art and rare musical instruments. However, presentation is poor and the building neglected.

Chamundi Hill

This 1062m hill offers spectacular views of the city below, and is crowned with the striking **Sri Chamundeswari Temple** (http://chamundeshwaritemple.kar.nic.in; ☺7am-2pm, 3.30-6pm & 7.30-9pm). Queues are long at weekends, so visit during the week. From Central bus stand (p209) take bus 201 (₹28, AC); a return autorickshaw/Uber is around ₹450/700. Alternatively, you can take the foot trail comprising 1000-plus steps that Hindu pilgrims use to visit the temple.

Walking Tours

An excellent way to familiarise yourself with Mysuru's epic history, **Royal Mysore Walks** (📞9632044188; www.royalmysorewalks.com; from ₹500) offers a range of weekend walks as well as cycle and jeep tours.

Mysuru Palace

A HALF-DAY TOUR

The interior of Mysuru Palace houses opulent halls, royal paintings, intricate decorative details, as well as sculptures and ceremonial objects. There is a lot of hidden detail and much to take in, so be sure to allow yourself at least a few hours for the experience. A guide can also be invaluable.

After entering the palace the first exhibit is the ❶ **Doll's Pavilion**, which showcases the maharaja's fine collection of traditional dolls and sculptures acquired from around the world. Opposite the ❷ **Elephant Gate** you'll see the seven cannons that were used for special occasions, such as the birthdays of the maharajas. Today the cannons are still fired as part of Dasara festivities.

At the end of the Doll's Pavilion you'll find the ❸ **Golden Howdah**. Note the fly whisks on either side; the bristles are made from fine ivory.

Make sure you check out the paintings depicting the Dasara procession in the halls on your way to the ❹ **Marriage Pavilion** and look into the courtyard to see what was once the wrestling arena. It's now used during Dasara only. In the Marriage Pavilion, take a few minutes to scan the entire space. You can see the influence of three religions in the design of the hall: the glass ceiling represents Christianity, stone carvings along the hallway ceilings are Hindu design and the top-floor balcony roof (the traditional ladies' gallery) has Islamic-style arches.

When you move through to the ❺ **Private Durbar Hall**, take note of the intricate ivory inlay motifs depicting Krishna in the rosewood doors. The ❻ **Public Durbar Hall** is usually the last stop where you can admire the panoramic views of the gardens through the Islamic arches.

Private Durbar Hall
Rosewood doors lead into this hall, which is richly decorated with stained-glass ceilings, steel grill work and chandeliers. It houses the Golden Throne, only on display to the public during Dasara.

Entry to the Palace

Doll's Pavilion
The first exhibit, the Doll's Pavilion, displays the gift collection of 19th- and early-20th-century dolls, statues and Hindu idols that were given to the maharaja by dignitaries from around the world.

Public Durbar Hall
The open-air hall contains a priceless collection of paintings by Raja Ravi Varma and opens into an expansive balcony supported by massive pillars with an ornate painted ceiling of 10 incarnations of Vishnu.

Marriage Pavilion
This lavish hall used for royal weddings features themes of Christianity, Hindu and Islam in its design. The highlight is the octagonal painted glass ceiling featuring peacock motifs, the bronze chandelier and the colonnaded turquoise pillars.

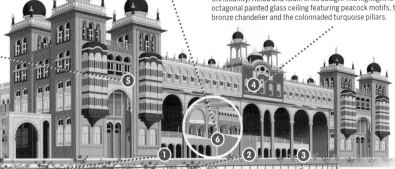

Elephant Gate
Next to the Doll's Pavilion, this brass gate has four bronze elephants inlaid at the bottom, an intricate double-headed eagle up the top and a hybrid lion-elephant creature (the state emblem of Karnataka) in the centre.

Golden Howdah
At the far end of the Doll's Pavilion, a wooden elephant howdah decorated with 80kg of gold was used to carry the maharaja in the Dasara festival. It now carries the idol of goddess Chamundeswari.

WAJ/SHUTTERSTOCK ©

Hampi

The magnificent ruins of Hampi, capital of the old Hindu Vijayanagar empire, dot an unearthly landscape where heaps of giant, rusty-hued boulders perch between jade-green palm groves, banana plantations and paddy fields.

Founded in 1336, the city of Vijayanagar grew into a thriving metropolis of about 500,000 people by the early 16th century, but was razed to the ground by the Muslim Deccan sultanates in 1565.

The Ruins

The 36-sq-km ruins have two main focal areas: the Sacred Centre, around Hampi Bazaar, and the Royal Centre, 2km south, where the Vijayanagar royalty lived and governed. You can rent bicycles (₹30 to ₹50 per day), mopeds (₹150 to ₹400) or an autorickshaw for the day (around ₹750) in Hampi Bazaar.

When visiting the Sacred Centre, don't miss the Virupaksha Temple, the Sule Bazaar, the Achyutaraya Temple and Lakshimi Narasmiha. Highlights of the Royal Centre include the Mahanavami-diiba, the Hazara-

---

Great For...

☑ Don't Miss

The ornate stone chariot, Vishnu's vehicle, in the Vittala Temple courtyard.

Virupaksha Temple

❶ Need to Know

The ₹500 ticket for Vittala Temple gives same-day admission to most of the paid sites here.

✕ Take a Break

The legendary **Mango Tree** (mains ₹140-310; ⊙7.30am-9.30pm) in Hampi Bazaar serves delicious Indian dishes.

★ Top Tip

It's possible to see Hampi in a day or two, but it's a fine place to linger longer.

ma Temple, the Zenana Enclosure, Elephant Stables and Queen's Bath.

The undisputed highlight of the Hampi ruins, the 16th-century **Vittala Temple** (Indian/foreigner/child under 15 ₹30/500/ free; ⊙8.30am-5.30pm) stands amid the boulders 2km northeast of Hampi Bazaar. Work possibly started on the temple during the reign of Krishnadevaraya (r 1509–29). It was never finished or consecrated, yet its incredible sculptural work remains the pinnacle of Vijayanagar art.

Hampi Demolitions

A long-time favourite budget travellers' hang-out, Hampi has become the scene of a bizarre struggle between local villagers and authorities bent on protecting Hampi's architectural heritage. In 2011 shops, hotels and homes in Hampi Bazaar were bulldozed overnight, with 1500 villagers evicted. Virupapur Gaddi village across the river became a new popular hang-out, only for many buildings there to be demolished in 2016. In 2017 Hampi Bazaar still had an enclave of guesthouses and restaurants, but the future of both villages remains unclear.

Getting There & Away

The town of Hosapete is the gateway to Hampi, with daily trains and overnight sleeper bus services to/from Goa, Bengaluru and Mysuru. Buses run between Hosapete's bus stand and Hampi (₹22, 30 minutes) every half-hour between about 6am and 7pm.

Bengaluru

Cosmopolitan Bengaluru is one of India's most progressive and developed cities, with a benevolent climate and a burgeoning drinking, dining and shopping scene.

⊙ SIGHTS

National Gallery of Modern Art   Gallery

(NGMA; ☑080-22342338; www.ngmaindia.gov. in/ngma_bangaluru.asp; 49 Palace Rd; Indian/ foreigner ₹20/500; ☺10am-5pm Tue-Sun) Housed in a century-year-old mansion – the former vacation home of the Raja of Mysuru – this art museum showcases an impressive permanent collection as well as changing exhibitions. The Old Wing exhibits works from pre-Independence, including paintings by Raja Ravi Varma and Abanindranath Tagore (founder of the avant-garde Bengal School art movement). Interconnected by a walk bridge, the sleek New Wing focuses on contemporary post-Independence works by artists including Sudhir Patwardhan and Vivan Sundaram.

Krishnarajendra Market   Market

(City Market; Silver Jubilee Park Rd; ☺6am-10pm) For a taste of traditional urban India, dive into the bustling Krishnarajendra Market and the dense grid of commercial streets that surround it. Weave your way around this lively colourful market past fresh produce, piles of vibrant dyes, spices and copperware. The colourful flower market in the centre is the highlight.

🔒 SHOPPING

Good areas include Commercial St, Vittal Mallya Rd and the MG Rd area.

Mysore Saree Udyog   Clothing

(www.mysoresareeudyog.com; 1st fl, 316 Kamaraj Rd; ☺10.30am-8.30pm) A great choice for top-quality silk saris, blouses, fabrics and men's shirts, this fine store has been in business for over 70 years and has something to suit all budgets. Most garments are made with Mysuru silk. Also stocks 100% *pashmina* (wool shawls).

Cauvery Arts & Crafts Emporium   Gifts & Souvenirs

(45 MG Rd; ☺10am-8pm; Ⓜ MG Rd) Government-run store famous for its expansive collection of quality sandal-wood and rosewood products as well as handmade weavings, silks and *bidriware* (metallic handicrafts). Fixed prices.

⊗ EATING

Bengaluru's adventurous dining scene keeps pace with the whims and rising standards of its hungry, moneyed locals and IT expats.

Mavalli Tiffin Rooms   South Indian $

(MTR; ☑080-22220022; www.mavallitiffinrooms. com; 14 Lalbagh Rd; snacks from ₹50, meals from ₹130; ☺6.30-11am & 12.30-9.30pm, closed Mon) A legendary name in South Indian comfort food, this super-popular eatery has had Bengaluru eating out of its hands since 1924. Head to the dining room upstairs, queue for a table, and then admire the images of southern beauties etched on smoky glass as waiters bring you delicious *idlis* (fermented rice cakes), dosas (savoury crepes) and frothing filter coffee served in silverware.

Church Street Social   Gastropub $$

(http://socialoffline.in; 46/1 Church St; mains ₹170-350; ☺9am-11pm Mon-Thu, to 1am Fri & Sat; 🔊; Ⓜ MG Rd) Bringing hipsterism to Bengaluru, this industrial warehouse-style space serves cocktails in beakers and its napkins are toilet paper–style (on a roll). The menu takes in fine breakfasts, meze platters, southern fried chicken burgers and 'gunpowder' calamari.

Karavalli   Seafood $$$

(☑080-66604545; Gateway Hotel, 66 Residency Rd; mains ₹500-1575; ☺12.30-3pm & 6.30-11.30pm; Ⓜ MG Rd) For the finest Indian seafood, look no further. The wonderfully atmospheric interior is perfect for a special meal, with subtle lighting, traditional

Bengaluru (Bangalore)

◉ Sights
1 National Gallery of Modern Art A1

🛍 Shopping
2 Cauvery Arts & Crafts Emporium............. D3
3 Mysore Saree Udyog.................................. D2

⊗ Eating
4 Church Street Social C3
5 Karavalli... D3

◎ Drinking & Nightlife
6 Lassi Shop.. C3

thatched roof, vintage woodwork and beaten brassware – though the garden seating is equally appealing. Choose from fiery Mangalorean fish dishes, spicy Kerala-style prawns, crab Milagu in a pepper masala and superb lobster *balchao* (₹1495).

🍷 DRINKING & ENTERTAINMENT

Bengaluru's wide choice of chic watering holes makes it the place to indulge in a spirited session of pub-hopping in what's the original beer town of India.

Lassi Shop   Cafe
(41 Church St; drinks ₹30-90; ⏲noon-midnight; 🛜) Kitsch-kool cafe on two levels run by

a couple of enthusiasts that's perfect for lassis, mocktails and cold-pressed juices: try the ABC (apple, beetroot and carrot). There's ample lounge seating so you can spread out, plus a few streetside tables too.

Arbor Brewing Company   Microbrewery
(www.arborbrewing.com/locations/india; 8 Magrath Rd; ⏲noon-12.30am Sun-Thu, to 1am Fri & Sat; 🛜) This classic brewpub was one of the first microbreweries to get the craft beer barrel rolling in Bengaluru. Choose from stout, porter, IPA, Belgian beers and spiced, sour and fruit beers.

Humming Tree
Live Music

(9945532828; www.facebook.com/thehum mingtree; 12th Main Rd, Indiranagar; ⏰11am-11.30pm Sun-Thu, to 1am Fri & Sat; Ⓜ Indiranagar) This popular warehouse-style venue has bands (starting around 9pm), DJs and a rooftop terrace. Cover charge is anything from free to ₹300. There's a good finger-food menu and happy hour until 7pm.

ⓘ GETTING THERE & AWAY

AIR

International and domestic flights arrive at Bengaluru's **Kempegowda International Airport** (☎1800 4254425; www.bengaluruairport.com), about 40km north from the central MG Rd area.

BUS

Bengaluru's huge, well-organised **Kempegowda bus stand** (Majestic; Gubbi Thotadappa Rd) is directly in front of City train station. It's wise to book long-distance journeys in advance. Destinations include Ernakulam (₹619 to ₹1139, 10 to 12 hours, seven buses between 4pm and 9.45pm), Hampi (₹629, 7½ hours, 11pm), Hosapete (₹334 to ₹696, eight hours, 17 buses between 4.30pm and 11.30pm), Mysuru (₹123 to ₹299, two to three hours, 51 buses daily from Mysuru Rd Satellite Bus Stand) and Panaji (₹919 to ₹1800, 11 to 13 hours, five buses between 6.30pm and 8.30pm).

TRAIN

City Station (www.bangalorecityrailwaystation. in; Gubbi Thotadappa Rd) is the main hub. **Cantonment Station** (Station Rd) is a sensible spot to disembark if you're arriving and headed for the MG Rd area. Major trains include the 16592 Hampi Express to Hosapete (sleeper/2AC ₹255/970, 9½ hours, 10pm); the 12007 Shatabdi to Mysuru (AC chair/AC executive ₹300/835, two hours, 11am except Wednesday); the 12614 Tippu Express to Mysuru (2nd-class/AC chair ₹90/310, 2½ hours, 3pm); and the 16256 Kanyakumari Express to Trivandrum (sleeper/2AC ₹410/1605, 16½ hours, 8pm).

ⓘ GETTING AROUND

Two metro lines (www.bmrc.co.in) are up and running. There was no interchange between the two, despite what the official maps indicate, at the time of research. Useful stops on the east–

Krishnarajendra Market (p206), Bengaluru

GOSEEFOTO/ALAMY ©

west Purple Line include Kempegowda (for the bus terminal), MG Rd (shopping and bars) and Indiranagar (restaurants and nightlife).

TO/FROM THE AIRPORT

Metered AC taxis to the centre cost between ₹750 and ₹1000; Uber and Ola cab rates are usually around ₹500 to ₹600; these rates include the ₹120 airport toll charge. Air-conditioned **Vayu Vajra** (☑1800 4251663; www.mybmtc.com) buses run regularly from the airport to destinations around the city, costing ₹170 to ₹260. The **Flybus** (www.ksrtc.in) runs from the airport to Mysuru (₹739, four hours) 10 times daily.

Mysuru

 ## SHOPPING

Mysuru is a great place to shop for sandalwood products, silk saris and wooden toys.

Government Silk Weaving Factory   Clothing
(☑8025586550; www.ksicsilk.com; Mananthody Rd, Ashokapuram; ⊙8.30am-4pm Mon-Sat, outlet 10.30am-7pm daily) Given that Mysuru's prized silk is made under its very sheds, this government-run outlet, set up in 1912, is the best and cheapest place to shop for the exclusive textile. Behind the showroom is the factory, where you can drop by to see how the fabric is made. It's around 2km south of town.

Sandalwood Oil Factory   Gifts & Souvenirs
(Mananthody Rd, Ashokapuram; ⊙outlet 9.30am-6.30pm, factory closed Sun) A quality place for sandalwood products including incense, soap, cosmetics and the expensive pure sandalwood oil (if in stock). Guided tours are available to show you around the factory.

EATING

Parklane Hotel   Multicuisine $$
(Parklane Hotel, 2720 Harsha Rd; mains ₹100-160; 🛜) Mysuru's most social restaurant with outdoor tables, lit up moodily by countless lanterns, and there's often live traditional music. The menu does delicious regional

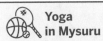 ## Yoga in Mysuru

This world-famous centre for yoga has over 20 established yoga schools and attracts thousands of international students each year to learn, practise or become certified in teaching ashtanga. For the most part students are required to be austerely committed to the art, and will need at least a month. A few schools have drop-in classes, including **Yoga Bharata** (☑0821-4242342; www.yogabharata.com; 1st Fl, 810 Contour Rd; 20-class pass ₹4500) and **Mystic School** (☑0821-4288490; www.mysoreyoga.in; 100 3rd A Main Rd, Gokulam; drop-in/1-month yoga classes ₹500/17,000).

dishes from across India as well as Chinese and Continental options and cold beers.

Tiger Trail   Indian $$$
(☑0821-4255566; Royal Orchid Metropole, 5 Jhansi Lakshmi Bai Rd; mains ₹200-650; ⊙7.30-10am, 12.30-3.30pm & 7.30-11pm; 🛜) This sophisticated hotel restaurant works up delectable Indian cuisine in a courtyard that twinkles with fairy lights at night. The North Indian dishes are particularly good; try a Lucknow chicken korma (₹300). Also has a fine lunch buffet.

GETTING THERE & AWAY

BUS

The **central bus stand** (Bengaluru-Nilgiri Rd) handles all KSRTC long-distance buses. Services include Bengaluru (₹123 to ₹299, two to three hours, every 30 minutes), Bengaluru Airport (₹739, 3½ to four hours, 12 daily), Ernakulam (₹739, eight to nine hours, three from 6pm) and Hosapete (₹381 to ₹608, nine to 12 hours, seven daily).

TRAIN

The 12613 Tippu Express to Bengaluru (2nd class/AC chair ₹90/305, 2½ hours) departs at 11.15am. The 16592 Hampi Express to Hosapete (3AC/2AC ₹840/1205, 12 hours) leaves at 7pm.

DARJEELING

In this Chapter
Singalila Ridge Trek 214
Tea Experience...............................218
Sights 220
Shopping.......................................223
Eating 223
Drinking & Nightlife 224

Darjeeling at a Glance...

Spread in ribbons over a steep mountain ridge, surrounded by emerald-green tea plantations and towered over by majestic Khangchendzonga (8598m), Darjeeling is the definitive Indian hill station. When you aren't gazing open-mouthed at Khangchendzonga, 80km to the north, you can explore colonial-era architecture, visit Buddhist monasteries, take an adventurous trek on Singalila Ridge or hire a mountain bike for a guided ride around the hilltops. Meanwhile the steep and winding bazaars below the town bustle with an array of faces and products from across the Himalayan region. And if energies start to flag, a good, steaming Darjeeling brew is never far away.

Darjeeling in Three Days

On day one see sights in town such as the **zoo** (p220), **mountaineering institute** (p218) and **Lloyd Botanical Gardens** (p220). Start day two off with the sunrise from **Tiger Hill** (p222), visit **Ghum** (p222) and be back in time for tea at the **Windamere Hotel** (p218). On day three visit **Makaibari tea estate** (p219) and take a joy ride on the **toy train** (p223).

Darjeeling in One Week

Try the challenging five-day **Singalila Ridge Trek** (p214) from Mane Bhanjhang to Phalut, through the scenic Singalila National Park (or there's a four-day version if you prefer more time sipping tea in Darjeeling).

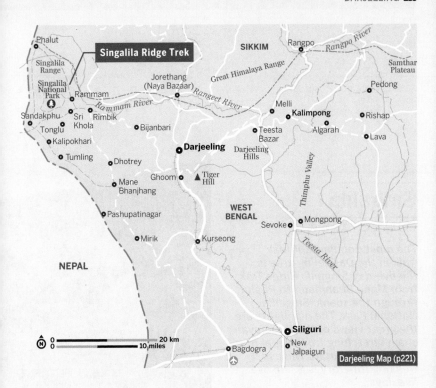

Singalila Ridge Trek

SIKKIM

Phalut

Singalila Range

Singalila National Park

Rammam

Jorethang (Naya Bazaar)

Great Himalaya Range

Rangpo

Rangpo River

Samthar Plateau

Pedong

Rangeet River

Rammam River

Sandakphu

Sri Rimbik

Melli

Kalimpong

Rishap

Tonglu

Khola

Bijanpari

Teesta Bazar

Algarah

Lava

Kalipokhari

Darjeeling

Darjeeling Hills

Tumling

Dhotrey

Ghoom

Tiger Hill

Thimphu Valley

Mane Bhanjhang

WEST BENGAL

Pashupatinagar

Sevoke

Mongpong

Mirik

Kurseong

Teesta River

NEPAL

0   20 km
0   10 miles

Siliguri

New Jalpaiguri

Bagdogra

Darjeeling Map (p221)

Arriving in Darjeeling

Bagdogra Airport Near Siliguri, 90km south of Darjeeling; daily flights from Delhi and Kolkata (Calcutta).

New Jalpaiguri (NJP) train station Located 6km from Siliguri; several daily services from Kolkata (10 to 13 hours), Delhi (21 to 33 hours) and Mughal Sarai Junction near Varanasi (12 to 18 hours).

Taxis To Darjeeling (three to four hours) from the airport or station: ₹1800 to ₹2200.

Sleeping

Darjeeling has a large selection of hotels, from elegant colonial-era heritage hotels on down the list. The main backpacker enclave is Dr Zakir Hussain Rd, on Darjeeling's highest ridge, so be prepared for a hike to the best budget places.

It's wise to book ahead for the high season (October to early December and mid-March to mid-May). In the low season prices can drop by 50%.

Singalila National Park

Singalila Ridge Trek

The most popular multiday walk in the Darjeeling area is the five-day Singalila Ridge Trek from Mane Bhanjhang to Phalut, through the scenic Singalila National Park. The highlights are the great views of the Himalayan chain stretching from Nepal to Sikkim and Bhutan. The usual trekking itinerary is 83km over five days.

Great For...

❶ Need to Know

Indian/foreigner ₹100/200, camera/video ₹100/500

Bring your passport, as you need to register at half a dozen army checkpoints.

★ **Top Tip**
Bottled and boiled water is available along the route, though it's cheaper to purify your own.

The ridge forms the India–Nepal border and the trail actually enters Nepal in several places. A shorter four-day option is possible by descending from Sandakhphu to Sri Khola on day three.

All-inclusive guided treks on this route are offered by Darjeeling agencies starting from about ₹3000 per person per day, though it's easy enough to arrange a DIY trek for less. Recommended agencies include **Himalayan Travels** (0354-2252254; kkguring@cal.vsnl.net.in; 18 Gandhi Rd, Darjeeling) and **Adventures Unlimited** (9933070013; www.adventuresunlimited.in; Dr Zakir Hussain Rd; 10am-6pm Mon-Sat).

Trek Stages

Day 1 (14km) Mane Bhanjhang (2130m) to Tonglu (3070m)/Tumling (2980m) via Meghma Gompa

Day 2 (17km) Tonglu to Sandakphu (3636m) via Kalipokhari and Garibas

Day 3 (17km) Sandakphu to Phalut (3600m) via Sabarkum

Day 4 (16km) Phalut to Rammam (2530m) via Gorkhey

Day 5 (19km) Rammam to Sri Khola or Rimbik (2290m)

Accommodation & Food

Private lodges, some with attached bathrooms, are available along the route for around ₹200 per dorm bed or ₹700 to ₹1400 per room. All offer food, normally a filling combo of rice, dhal and vegetables (₹200). Rooms have clean bedding and blankets so sleeping bags are not strictly necessary, but do bring a sleeping bag liner – and warm clothes for dawn peak viewing.

Hikers on Singalila Ridge

The only place where finding a bed can be a problem is Phalut where there is only one reliable place to stay. Trekkers' huts can be booked at Darjeeling's GTA Tourist Reception Centre (p224) but even they will tell you that you're better off at private lodges.

These are the main lodges for each overnight stop, in ascending order of price and quality:

Day 1 Trekkers' Hut, Mountain Lodge, Siddharta Lodge and Shikhar Lodge in Tumling; Trekkers' Hut in Tonglu.

★ Don't Miss

The superb panorama from Sandakhphu, which takes in, among other things, three of the world's four highest peaks – Lhotse, Everest and Khangchendzonga.

Day 2 Chewang Lodge in Kalipokhari; Trekkers' Hut, Namobuddha, Sunrise and Sherpa Chalet Lodge in Sandakphu.

Day 3 Trekkers' Hut and Forest Rest House in Phalut.

Day 4 Eden Lodge in Gorkhey; Trekkers' Hut, Namobuddha Lodge and Sherpa Lodge in Rammam.

When to Trek

October and November's clear skies and warm daytime temperatures make it an ideal time to trek, as do the long days and incredible rhododendron blooms of late April and May. Lodges can get booked out in October and early November, so consider a mid- to late November itinerary if you're planning the trek in autumn.

Guides

Local guides (₹1200 per day, including food and accommodation) are mandatory within the park. If you don't already have one, they must be arranged at the office of the **Highlander Trekking Guides Association** (☏9734056944; www.highlanderguidesandport ers.com; Mane Bhanjang), along with porters (₹700) if required.

Getting to/from the Trek

Mane Bhanjhang is 26km from Darjeeling and is served by frequent shared jeeps (₹70, 1½ hours), as well as a 7am bus from Chowk Bazaar bus and jeep station (p225). A chartered jeep costs ₹1200. From Rimbik, there are shared jeeps back to Darjeeling (₹150, five hours) at 7am and noon, and a bus at 6.30am (₹90). Book seats in advance.

✕ Take a Break

For a relaxing end to a trek, consider a stay at simple but comfortable and beautiful **Karmi Farm** (www.karmifarm. com; per person incl full board ₹2000), a two-hour drive from Rimbik near Bijanbari.

ANDREW WRIGHTING/ALAMY ©

Tea Experience

There's no better place than Darjeeling to enjoy the brew that has carried the town's name round the world. And while here you can learn all about tea by visiting or staying at tea estates.

Great For...

☑ **Don't Miss**

The true-blue afternoon-tea experience at the Windamere Hotel.

Darjeeling's aromatic muscatel tea is known for its amber colour, tannic astringency and a musky, spicy flavour. These days, other teas including green, oolong and premium white varieties are produced alongside the traditional black tea. Most of the produce is now organic, and the best grades fetch several hundred dollars per kilogram at auctions.

Top Brews

In Darjeeling, a pot of this fine brew is best enjoyed at **Sunset Lounge** (Chowrastra Sq; cup of tea ₹25-400; ⏰9.30am-9pm; 📶) or **House of Tea** (Nehru Rd; cup of tea ₹30-80; ⏰10am-8pm; 📶). Afternoon tea at the **Windamere Hotel** (afternoon tea ₹800; ⏰4-6pm) is a joy for aficionados of all things colonial, with shortcake, scones, cheese and pickle

Tea samples at Makaibara Tea Estate

❶ Need to Know

Purists say Darjeeling teas are best taken alone or with a lemon slice – never with milk!

✕ Take a Break

It's hard to beat Sunset Lounge (p218) for fine teas with a view.

★ Top Tip

To learn more, read Jeff Koehler's *Darjeeling: A History of the World's Greatest Tea* (2016).

sandwiches, and brews from the reputed Castleton Tea Estate; book in advance.

Visiting Tea Estates

For an absorbing and enlightening experience, several tea estates welcome visitors. The easiest places to learn about tea production are **Makaibari** (☏0353-2510071; www.makaibari.com; Pankhabari Rd; ⊙Tue-Sat mid-Mar–mid-Nov) **FREE** in Kurseong and Happy Valley (p220) at Darjeeling. Spring, monsoon and autumn are the busiest times, when the three respective 'flushes' are harvested. There's no plucking on Sunday, which means most of the machinery isn't working on Monday.

Staying Over

If you wish to spend a night amid the plantations, try a tea pickers' family at a **homestay**

(☏9832447774; www.volmakaibari.org; Makaibari tea estate; per person incl full board ₹800) at Makaibari, where you'll get to join your hosts for a morning's work in the tea bushes.

If you're in the mood for splurging, accommodation doesn't get any more exclusive than top-end **Glenburn** (☏9830070213; www.glenburnteaestate.com; Darjeeling; s/d incl full board ₹19,900/31,500), between Darjeeling and Kalimpong, a working tea estate and resort that boasts five members of staff for every guest.

How Darjeeling Got Started

In 1828, two British officers stumbled across the Dorje Ling monastery on a tranquil forested ridge, and passed word to Kolkata that it would be a perfect site for a sanatorium. The chogyal (king) of Sikkim agreed to lease the uninhabited land to the East India Company for £3000 a year. In 1835 the hill station of Darjeeling was born and the first tea bushes were planted. By 1857 Darjeeling's population had reached 10,000, mainly because of a massive influx of Gurkha tea labourers from Nepal.

⊙ SIGHTS

Darjeeling sprawls over a west-facing slope in a confusing web of interconnecting roads and steep flights of steps. The two main squares – Chowrasta, near the top of town, and Clubside junction – are linked by pedestrianised Nehru Rd (aka The Mall), which doubles as the main shopping street.

Padmaja Naidu Himalayan Zoological Park   Zoo

(☑0354-2254250; www.pnhzp.gov.in; Indian/foreigner incl Himalayan Mountaineering Institute ₹50/100; camera/video ₹10/25; ⊘8.30am-4pm Fri-Wed, ticket counter closes 3.30pm) This zoo, one of India's best, was established in 1958 to study, conserve and preserve Himalayan fauna. Housed within its rocky and forested environment are species such as Asiatic black bears, cloud leopards, red pandas and Tibetan wolves. The zoo, and its attached snow leopard–breeding centre (closed to the public), are home to the world's largest single captive population of snow leopards (currently 11). The zoo is a pleasant 20-minute downhill walk from Chowrasta along Jawahar Rd West. Alternatively, take a shared jeep (₹20, about 10 minutes) from Chowk Bazaar bus and jeep station, or hire a taxi (₹250).

Himalayan Mountaineering Institute   Museum

(HMI; ☑0354-2254087; www.hmi-darjeeling.com; Indian/foreigner incl zoo ₹50/100; ⊘8.30am-4.30pm Fri-Wed) Tucked away within the grounds of the zoo, this prestigious mountaineering institute was founded in 1954 and has provided training for some of India's leading mountaineers. Within the complex is the fascinating Mountaineering Museum. It houses sundry details and memorabilia from the 1922 and 1924 Everest expeditions, which set off from Darjeeling, as well as more recent summit attempts. Look for the Carl Zeiss telescope presented by Adolf Hitler to the head of the Nepali Army. Just beside the museum, near the spot where Tenzing Norgay was cremated, stands the Tenzing Statue. The intrepid Everest summiteer lived in Darjeeling for most of his life and was the director of the institute for many years.

Rangit Valley Ropeway   Cable Car

(return adult/child ₹175/90; ⊘10am-4pm, ticket office closes 2pm, closed 19th of every month) This scenic ropeway reopened in 2012, after a fatal accident halted operations in 2003. The 20-minute ride takes you from North Point down to the Takvar Valley tea estate, gliding over manicured tea bushes that look like giant broccoli growing on mountain slopes. Get here early if you want to explore the village and tea plantation. The last lift back is 5pm.

Happy Valley Tea Estate   Plantation

(☑8017700700; www.ambootia.com; Lebong Cart Rd; tour ₹100; ⊘8am-4pm Tue-Sun) This 1854 tea estate below Hill Cart Rd is worth visiting, especially when the plucking and processing are in progress (March to November). An employee will guide you through the aromatic factory and its withering, rolling, fermenting and drying processes, explaining how green, black and white teas all come from the same leaf. Take the marked turn-off about 1km northwest of town on Hill Cart Rd.

Lloyd Botanical Gardens   Gardens

(☑0354-2252358; ⊘8am-4.30pm) These pleasant gardens contain an impressive collection of Himalayan plants, most famously orchids and rhododendrons. Follow the signs along Lochnager Rd from the Chowk Bazaar bus and 4WD station, until the hum of cicadas replaces the honking of jeeps at the main entrance. A map is posted at the office at the top of the park.

Tibetan Refugee Self-Help Centre   Factory

(☑2255938; www.tibetancentredarjeeling.com; Lebong Cart Rd; ⊘9am-4.30pm Mon-Sat) Established in 1959, this refugee centre comprises a home for the aged, a school, an orphanage, a clinic, a gompa (Tibetan Buddhist monastery) and craft workshops that produce carpets, woodcarvings and

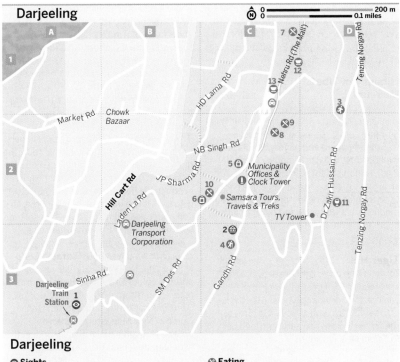

Darjeeling

◎ **Sights**
1 Darjeeling Himalayan Railway....................A3
2 Himalayan Tibet Museum.......................... C3

◆ **Activities, Courses & Tours**
3 Adventures Unlimited D1
4 Himalayan Travels C3

◎ **Shopping**
5 Hayden Hall C2
6 Nathmull's Tea Room................................ C2

✖ **Eating**
7 Glenary's C1
8 Kunga... C2
9 Lunar Restaurant C2
10 Park Restaurant C2

◯ **Drinking & Nightlife**
11 Gatty's Cafe D2
12 Himalayan Java C1
13 House of Tea...C1

woollen items. There's also an interesting, politically charged photographic exhibition portraying Tibetan history through B&W photos. Visitors are welcome to wander through the workshops. The handicrafts are for sale in the showroom and proceeds go straight back into the Tibetan community.

The quickest way to reach the centre is to walk steeply downhill from the north side of Bhanu Bhakta Sarani; take the alley down beside Hotel Dolphin. To return to Chowrasta Sq, take the steps to the left of the photo exhibition uphill (left at the gate)

for 10 minutes to the Bhutia Busty Gompa and continue uphill from there for another stiff 10 minutes. A chartered taxi via North Point costs around ₹250/500 one way/return.

Bhutia Busty Gompa
Buddhist Monastery

This temple originally stood on Observatory Hill, but was rebuilt in its present location by the chogyals of Sikkim in the 19th century. It houses fine murals depicting the life of Buddha, with Khangchendzonga providing a spectacular backdrop. Come for prayers at 4pm; it's often locked during the day. To get here, follow CR Das Rd downhill for five minutes from Chowrasta Sq, past a trinity of Buddhist rock carvings.

Himalayan Tibet Museum
Museum

(📞0354-2252977; www.himalayantibetmuseum. org; Gandhi Rd; ₹30; ⊙10am-6pm Thu-Tue) This new museum gives a good introduction to Tibetan culture and history. Displays include fine *thangkas* (Tibetan cloth paintings), Buddhist Tantric implements, musical instruments and even an eagle bone used for bloodletting in traditional Tibetan medicine. It's well done and never politically dogmatic. A photo exhibit is planned for downstairs.

Tiger Hill
Viewpoint

To watch the dawn light break over a spectacular 250km stretch of Himalayan horizon, including Everest (8848m), Lhotse (8501m) and Makalu (8475m) to the far northwest, rise early and jeep out to Tiger Hill, 11km south of Darjeeling,

above Ghum. The skyline is dominated by Khangchendzonga ('great five-peaked snow fortress'), India's highest peak and the world's third-highest. On either side of the main massif are Kabru (7338m), Jannu (7710m) and Pandim (6691m), all serious peaks in their own right.

This daily morning spectacle (views are best in autumn and spring) is a major tourist attraction, and you'll find hundreds of 4WDs leaving Darjeeling for Tiger Hill every morning at 4am – traffic snarls en route are quite common. At the summit you can pay to stand in the pavilion grounds or warm up in one of the heated lounges (₹30 to ₹100 with tea). It can be a real bunfight here, so if you prefer your Himalayan views in solitude you might want to try somewhere else.

Organised sunrise trips – usually returning via the famous **Batasia Loop** (₹10) on the Darjeeling Himalayan Railway and the colourful Tibetan Buddhist monasteries in Ghum – Yiga Choling Gompa, Guru Sakya Gompa and Samten Choling Gompa (New Monastery) – can be booked through a travel agency or directly with jeep drivers at the Clubside taxi

View from Tiger Hill to the Himalaya

stand (p225). Return trips cost ₹1300 per vehicle, or ₹250 per seat.

Observatory Hill
Religious Site

Sacred to both Buddhists and Hindus, this hill was the site of the original Dorje Ling monastery that lent Darjeeling its name. Today, devotees come to a temple in a small cave to honour Mahakala, a Buddhist protector deity also worshipped in Hinduism as a wrathful avatar of Shiva the destroyer. The summit is marked by several shrines, a flurry of colourful prayer flags and the ringing notes from numerous devotional bells, but sadly no mountain views.

A path leading up to the hill through giant Japanese cedars starts about 300m along Bhanu Bhakta Sarani from Chowrasta; watch out for marauding monkeys. Before you reach the summit a side path to the left leads down to the Mahakala Cave (ask for the *gufa*). The summit temple is staffed by a Hindu priest and a Tibetan Buddhist lama sitting side by side in an admirable display of religious coexistence.

🅐 SHOPPING

Nathmull's Tea Room
Tea

(www.nathmulltea.com; Laden La Rd; ⊗9am-8pm Mon-Sat, daily Mar-May, Oct & Nov) Darjeeling produces some of the world's finest teas and Nathmull's is the best place to pick up some, with more than 50 varieties. Expect to pay ₹200 to ₹400 per 100g for a decent tea, and up to ₹5000 per 100g for the finest flushes. There are also attractive teapots, strainers and cosies as souvenirs. To taste the teas for sale here head to Sunset Lounge (p218).

Hayden Hall
Arts & Crafts

(www.haydenhalldarjeeling.org; Laden La Rd; ⊗10am-5pm) 🖋 Sells Tibetan-style yak wool carpets as part of its charitable work (₹10,800 for a 0.9m by 1.8m carpet) and offers shipping. You can see the carpets being made out the back. There are also good jumpers, caps, gloves, shrugs and bags made by local women.

 Riding the Toy Train

The World Heritage–listed **Darjeeling Himalayan Railway** (steam/diesel joy ride ₹1100/630), known affectionately as the toy train, is one of the few hill railways still operating in India. The train made its first journey along its precipice-topping, 2ft-wide tracks in September 1881.

Services on the section of line between Kurseong and New Jalpaiguri (NJP) mainline station are constantly in flux, and monsoon rains seem to block sections of track as fast as engineers can repair them. At the time of research the only daily passenger service leaving Darjeeling was train 52588 at 4pm, stopping in Ghum (1st/2nd class ₹145/30) at 4.30pm and arriving in Kurseong (₹210/60) at 6.50pm. The return train leaves Kurseong at 7am.

Steam-powered joy rides (₹1100) leave Darjeeling at 10.40am, 1.20pm and 4.05pm for a two-hour return trip. The same trips on a diesel service (₹630) leave at 8am, 11am and 1.30pm. All joy rides pause for 10 minutes at the scenic Batasia Loop and then stop for 20 minutes in Ghum, India's highest train station, to visit the small **railway museum** (₹20; ⊗10am-1pm & 2-4pm).

Book joy rides at least a day or two ahead at Darjeeling train station (p225) or online at www.irctc.co.in.

🅧 EATING

Tax will add on 14.5% to most bills, with service on top of that.

Kunga
Tibetan $

(51 Gandhi Rd; mains ₹120-190; ⊗7.30am-8.30pm) Kunga is a cosy wood-panelled place run by a friendly Tibetan family, strong on noodles and *momos,* and with excellent juice, fruit muesli curd and *shabhaley* (Tibetan pies). The clientele includes locals, which is a mark of its culinary authenticity. You'll find it at street level below Dekeling Hotel.

Glenary's
Multicuisine $$

(Nehru Rd; mains ₹235-300; ⊙noon-9pm; 🛜)
This elegant restaurant sits atop the famous bakery and cafe of the same name and is a Darjeeling staple. Of note are the Continental and Chinese dishes and the tandoori specials; try the beef steak and potato or the delicious-smelling baked-cheese macaroni. The wooden floors, linen tablecloths and recently expanded window seating add to the classy atmosphere.

Lunar Restaurant
Indian $$

(51 Gandhi Rd; mains ₹160-200; ⊙7.30am-9pm)
This bright and clean space just below Dekeling Hotel is perhaps the best vegetarian Indian restaurant in town, with good service and great views from the large windows. The *masala dosas* (curried vegetables inside crisp pancakes) come with delicious dried fruit, nuts and cheese. Access to this 1st-floor joint is via the same staircase as Hotel Dekeling.

 When to Visit

Most tourists visit Darjeeling in autumn (October and November) and spring (mid-March to mid-May) when skies are dry, panoramas are clear and temperatures are pleasant. Bring an extra jumper if visiting from December to February. The rainy months (June to September) are best avoided.

Singalila National Park (p214)
GNOMEANDI/ALAMY ©

Park Restaurant
Indian, Thai $$

(☎0354-2255270; 41 Laden La Rd; mains ₹200-350; ⊙noon-9pm) The intimate Park is deservedly very popular for its tasty North Indian curries (great chicken tikka masala) and surprisingly authentic Thai dishes, including the tasty *tom kha gai* (coconut chicken soup) and spicy green papaya salad. Renovations plan to move the Thai dishes to a separate pan-Asian dining area; look for the ornate Thai-style entrance.

DRINKING & NIGHTLIFE

The top-end hotels all have classy bars; the **Windamere** (☎0354-2254041; www.windamerehotel.com; Jawahar Rd West; @🛜) is the most atmospheric place to kick back with an early evening gin and tonic.

Himalayan Java
Cafe

(Nehru Rd; coffee ₹100; ⊙7am-8.30pm; 🛜)
Branch of the Nepal cafe chain, serving up good coffee and cakes, plus breakfast pancakes, waffles and sandwiches (snacks ₹150 to ₹250), in a stylish industrial interior.

Gatty's Cafe
Bar

(Dr Zakir Hussain Rd; beer ₹170; ⊙6-11pm; 🛜)
Backpacker-friendly Gatty's is the only place in town that has a pulse after 9pm, with live music on the weekend and open-mic and movie nights during the week. The food (mains ₹170 to ₹200) includes house-made lasagne, and pitta with hummus and falafel, plus good espresso and cold Kingfisher and Tuborg.

INFORMATION

GTA Tourist Reception Centre (☎9434247927; Silver Fir Bldg, Jawahar Rd West; ⊙9am-6pm Mon-Sat, to 1pm every other Sat) The staff are friendly, well organised and the best source of information on Darjeeling.

Windamere Hotel

ℹ️ GETTING THERE & AWAY

AIR

The nearest airport is 90km away at Bagdogra, about 12km from Siliguri. A chartered taxi from Darjeeling costs ₹2200. Allow four hours for the drive, to be safe.

BUS

Samsara Tours, Travels & Treks (0354-2252874; www.samsaratourstravelsandtreks. com; Laden La Rd) can book 'luxury' air-con buses from Siliguri to Kolkata (₹1300 to ₹1700, 12 hours).

JEEP & TAXI

Numerous shared jeeps leave the crowded **Chowk Bazaar Bus & Jeep Station** (Old Super Market Complex) for Siliguri (₹130, three hours) and Kurseong (₹70, 1½ hours), departing between 7am and 3.30pm. **Darjeeling Transport Corporation** (Laden La Rd) offers chartered jeeps to Kurseong (₹1500).

To New Jalpaiguri or Bagdogra, get a connection in Siliguri, or charter a jeep or taxi from Darjeeling for ₹2200.

TRAIN

The nearest major train station is at New Jalpaiguri (NJP), near Siliguri. Tickets can be bought for major services out of NJP at **Darjeeling train station** (0354-2252555; www.irctc.co.in; Hill Cart Rd; ⊗8am-5pm Mon-Sat, to 2pm Sun).

ℹ️ GETTING AROUND

There are several taxi stands around town, including at Clubside and on Hill Cart Rd near the train station, but rates are absurdly high for short hops. You can hire a porter to carry your bags up to Chowrasta Sq from Chowk Bazaar for around ₹100.

Shared minivans to anywhere north of the town centre (eg North Point) leave from the northern end of the Chowk Bazaar Bus and Jeep Station. For Ghum, get a shared jeep (₹20) from along Hill Cart Rd.

VARANASI

In this Chapter
The Ghats.................................230
Sights 234
Tours.....................................235
Shopping...............................236
Eating 236
Drinking & Entertainment...........239

Varanasi at a Glance...

Varanasi is the India of your imagination, one of Hinduism's holiest cities and one of the most colourful and fascinating places on earth. Pilgrims come to the ghats lining the Ganges to wash away sins in the sacred waters or to cremate their loved ones. Intimate rituals of life and death take place in public, and the sights, sounds and smells on the ghats – not to mention almost constant attention from touts – can be intense. Most visitors agree Varanasi is magical – but not for the faint-hearted. Still, the so-called City of Light may turn out to be your favourite stop of all.

Varanasi in Two Days

Rise early on day one to explore the ghats, preferably starting at sunrise. In the evening witness the *ganga aarti* (river worship ceremony) at **Dashash-wamedh Ghat** (p232).

On day two enjoy a sunrise boat trip on the Ganges, browse some shops and cafes, visit the **Vishwanath Temple** (p234) and treat yourself to dinner at **Darbangha** (p238).

Varanasi in Four Days

On day three dig deeper into Varanasi life (and death) on a **Varanasi Walks** (p235) tour. Enjoy a great meal and some Indian classical music at **Brown Bread Bakery** (p236). On day four revisit the ghats, make a trip to **Benares Hindu University** (p235), and don't miss India's best lassi at **Blue Lassi** (p239).

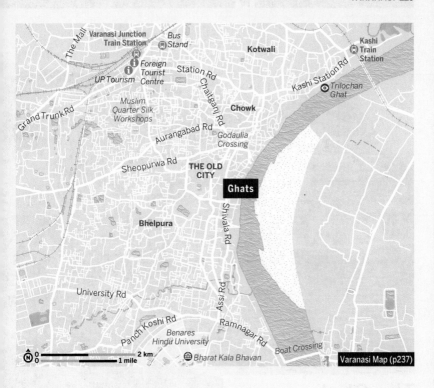

Varanasi Map (p237)

Arriving in Varanasi

Lal Bahadur Shashtri Airport In Babatpur, 24km northwest of Varanasi; flights from Delhi, Mumbai, Bengaluru (Bangalore) and other Indian cities, and Bangkok.

Varanasi Junction station Trains from Delhi, Agra and Kolkata (Calcutta).

Mughal Sarai Junction station Located 18km east of Varanasi; more Agra trains.

Bus stand AC buses to/from Delhi.

Sleeping

Most budget hotels, and some midrange gems, are tucked among the narrow streets off the ghats. To experience local life, ask UP Tourism (p240) about the many family homes offering guesthouse accommodation for under ₹500. For five-star luxury, there are some great choices in neighbourhoods west of the river such as Bhelpura, Aurangabad Rd and Cantonment.

LOUISA COOK/STOCKIMO/ALAMY ©

The Ghats

Spiritually enlightening and fantastically photogenic, Varanasi is at its brilliant best by the ghats, the long stretch of steps leading down to the water on the western bank of the Ganges.

Great For...

☑ Don't Miss

The 7pm *ganga aarti* (river worship ceremony), with prayers, fire and dance, at Dashashwamedh Ghat.

About 80 ghats border the river, but the main group extends about 5km from Assi Ghat, near the university, northwards to Raj Ghat, located near the road and rail bridge.

Most ghats are used for bathing but there are also several 'burning ghats' where bodies are cremated in public. The main one is Manikarnika (p232): you'll often see funeral processions threading their way through the backstreets to this ghat.

The best times to visit the ghats are dawn, when the river is bathed in a mellow light as pilgrims come to perform *puja* (prayers) to the rising sun, and sunset when the main *ganga aarti* (river worship ceremony) takes place at Dashashwamedh Ghat (p232).

A boat trip (p240) along the river provides the perfect introduction, although for most of the year the water level is low

'Burning' ghats, River Ganges

Manikarnika Ghat
Man Mandir Ghat
Dashashwamedh Ghat
Munshi Ghat
Pandhey Ghat
Harishchandra Ghat
Kedar Ghat
Hanuman Ghat
Assi Ghat

❶ Need to Know

Tourists can, respectfully, watch cremations at the 'burning' ghats – but don't take photos.

✕ Take a Break

Brown Bread Bakery (p236) is a fabulous stop any time from breakfast buffet onwards.

★ Top Tip

Resist offers to 'follow me for a better view': you'll be pressured for money.

enough for you to walk freely along the whole length of the ghats. It's a world-class 'people-watching' stroll as you mingle with the fascinating mixture of people who come to the Ganges not only for a ritual bath but also to wash clothes, do yoga, offer blessings, sell flowers, get a massage, play cricket, wash their buffaloes, improve their karma by giving to beggars or simply hang around.

Major Ghats

Listed below from south to north.

Assi Ghat

The furthest south of the main ghats and one of the biggest, Assi Ghat is particularly important as the River Assi meets the Ganges near here and pilgrims come to worship a Shiva lingam (phallic image of Shiva)

beneath a peepul tree. Evenings are particularly lively, as the ghat's vast concreted area fills up with hawkers and entertainers. There's also music and yoga at sunrise. It's a popular starting point for boat trips.

Hanuman Ghat

Hanuman Ghat is popular with Rama devotees (Hanuman was Rama's stalwart ally in his quest to rescue Sita from the demon Ravana).

Harishchandra Ghat

Harishchandra Ghat is a cremation ghat – smaller and secondary in importance to Manikarnika, but one of the oldest ghats in Varanasi.

Kedar Ghat

A colourful ghat with many steps and a small pool, where a fire *aarti* is held every evening at 6.30pm.

Munshi Ghat

Munshi Ghat (Darbhanga Ghat) is one of the more photogenic ghats along the Old City stretch of the Ganges.

Pandhey Ghat

Lots of laundry is spread to dry at this ghat.

Dashashwamedh Ghat

Varanasi's liveliest and most colourful ghat. The name indicates that Brahma sacrificed *(medh)* 10 *(das)* horses *(aswa)* here. In spite of the oppressive boat owners, flower sellers, massage practitioners and touts trying to drag you off to a silk shop, it's a wonderful place to linger and people-watch while soaking up the atmosphere. Every evening at 7pm an elaborate *ganga aarti* (river worship) ceremony with *puja* (prayers), fire and dance is staged here.

Man Mandir Ghat

Man Mandir Ghat was built in 1600 by Raja Man Singh, but was poorly restored in the 19th century. Its northern corner has a fine stone balcony.

Manikarnika Ghat

Manikarnika Ghat, the main burning ghat, is the most auspicious place for a Hindu to be cremated. Dead bodies are handled by outcasts known as *doms*, and are carried through the alleyways of the Old City to the holy Ganges on a bamboo stretcher, swathed in cloth. The corpse is doused in the Ganges prior to cremation.

Huge piles of firewood are stacked along the top of the ghat; every log is carefully weighed on giant scales so that the price of

Pilgrims at the ghats

cremation can be calculated. Each type of wood has its own price, sandalwood being the most expensive. There is an art to using just enough wood to completely incinerate a corpse.

You can watch cremations but always show reverence by behaving respectfully. Photography is strictly prohibited. You're almost guaranteed to be led by a priest, or more likely a guide, to the upper floor of a nearby building where you can watch cremations taking place, and then asked for a donation (in dollars) towards the cost of wood. If you don't want to make a donation, don't follow them.

Above the steps here is a tank known as the **Manikarnika Well**. Parvati is said to have dropped her earring here and Shiva dug the tank to recover it, filling the depression with his sweat. The **Charanpaduka**, a slab of stone between the well and the ghat, bears footprints made by Vishnu. Privileged VIPs are cremated at the Charanpaduka, which also has a temple dedicated to Ganesh.

Scindhia Ghat

Scindhia Ghat was originally built in 1830, but was so huge and magnificent that it collapsed into the river and had to be rebuilt.

Trilochan Ghat

At Trilochan, two turrets emerge from the river, and the water between them is especially holy.

Touts & Guides

The attention from touts in Varanasi, particularly around the ghats and the Old City, is incredible: you will have to put up with persistent offers from touts and rickshaw drivers for 'cheapest and best' boat trips, guides, tour operators, travel agents, silk shops and money changers (to name a few). Take it all in good humour but politely refuse.

Do not book unofficial guides, which are whom most guesthouses hire. If you want a guide, go through UP Tourism (p240) to avoid most of the hassles above. If not, have fun shopping!

Vehicle Access

Taxis and autorickshaws cannot access the Dashashwamedh Ghat area between 9am and 9pm due to high pedestrian traffic. You'll be dropped at Godaulia Crossing and will need to walk the remaining 400m or so to the entrance to the Old City, or 700m or so all the way to Dashashwamedh Ghat. During banned hours, autorickshaws line up near Godaulia Crossing at a stand on Luxa Rd.

PRADEEP SOMAN/ALAMY ©

Vishwanath Temple

GOUR SHANKER GUPTA/ALAMY ©

◉ SIGHTS

The 'Old City' of Varanasi is situated along the western bank of the Ganges and extends back from the riverbank ghats in a labyrinth of alleys called *galis* that are too narrow for traffic – which is a blessing, because it means the most interesting part of the city is free of exhaust fumes, honking horns and automotive near-death experiences. Watch out, however, for the cows – and their slippery dung!

Vishwanath Temple   Hindu Temple
(Golden Temple; ⊘3am-11am, 12.30-8pm & 9-11pm) There are temples at almost every turn in Varanasi, but this is the most famous of the lot. It is dedicated to Vishveswara – Shiva as lord of the universe. The current temple was built in 1776 by Ahalya Bai of Indore; the 800kg of gold plating on the tower and dome was supplied by Maharaja Ranjit Singh of Lahore 50 years later.

The area is full of soldiers because of security issues and communal tensions. Bags, cameras, mobile phones, pens and any electronic device must be deposited in lockers (₹20) before you enter the alleyway it's in – or just leave your stuff at your hotel. Though accounts vary as to whether or not foreigners can go in the temple itself, we found it to be fairly straightforward: Head to Gate 2, where security will instruct you to walk past the long lines of Indians waiting in the queue, then go through a metal detector and security check. Walk past another line of Indians until you are pointed to a desk, where you must show your passport (not a copy) and leave your shoes. Then enter the temple through a door across the alley.

Once inside, things can be quite intense, with people pushing and tripping over each other for a chance to give an offering and touch the lingam, which absolves one of all sins. At other times, it's much more peaceful. Hindus routinely wait in lines for 48 hours to enter on particularly holy days.

On the northern side of Vishwanath Temple is the **Gyan Kupor Well** (Well of Knowledge). The faithful believe drinking its water leads to a higher spiritual plane, though they are prevented from doing so by a strong security screen. Non-Hindus are not allowed to enter here, and the rule is strictly enforced.

Benares Hindu
University   University, Historic Site
(BHU; www.bhu.ac.in) Long regarded as a centre of learning, Varanasi's tradition of top-quality education continues today at Benares Hindu University, established in 1916. The wide, tree-lined streets and parkland of the 5-sq-km campus offer a peaceful atmosphere a world away from the city outside. On campus is **Bharat Kala Bhavan** (Indian/foreigner ₹10/150; ⊙10am-5.30pm Mon-Fri), a roomy museum with a wonderful collection of miniature paintings, as well as 12th-century palm-leaf manuscripts, sculptures and local history displays.

 TOURS

If time is short, UP Tourism (p240) can arrange guided tours by taxi of the major sites, including a 5.30am boat ride.

 **Varanasi
Shopping Tips**

Do not go to any shop with a guide or autorickshaw driver. Be firm and don't do it. Ever. You will pay 40% to 60% more for your item due to insane commissions, and you'll also be passively encouraging this practice. Do yourself a favour and walk there, or have your ride drop you a block away.

Impostor stores are rife in Varanasi, usually spelled one letter off or sometimes exactly the same. Ask for a business card – if the info doesn't match, you've been had.

Varanasi Walks   Walking
(☏9793714111; www.varanasiwalks.com; tours ₹1000-1600) ✎ The cultural walks on offer from this agency specialising in themed walks explore beyond the most popular ghats and temples, giving eye-opening insight into this holy city. The American

Cow wandering a Varanasi street

founder, Jai, has lived in Varanasi for years, and most of the guides were born and raised here. Walks are available by reservation, booking online or by phone.

SHOPPING

Varanasi is justifiably famous for silk brocades and beautiful Benares saris, but don't believe much of what the silk salesmen tell you about the relative quality of products, even in government emporiums. Instead, shop around and judge for yourself.

There are loads of musical instrument shops on Bengali Tola (near Rana Ghat), many of which offer lessons.

Baba
Blacksheep Fashion & Accessories

(B12/120 A-9, Bhelpura; ⊙9am-8pm) If the deluge of traveller enthusiasm is anything to go by, this is the most trustworthy, non-pushy shop in India. Indeed it is one of the best places you'll find for silks (scarves/saris from ₹500/4000) and *pashmina* (shawls from ₹1700).

Mehrotra
Silk Factory Fashion & Accessories

(www.mehrotrasilk.in; 4/8A Lal Ghat; ⊙10am-8pm) In a labyrinth of alleys behind Lal Ghat, this fixed-price shop, its floor cushioned for seating, offers fine silks for fair prices. Grab something as small as a scarf or as big as a bedcover. There's

another **branch** (21/72 Englishia Line; ⊙10am-8pm) near the railway station.

✖ EATING

Many eateries in the Old City shut in summer due to unbearable humidity and water levels that often flood the ghats and around.

Brown Bread
Bakery Multicuisine $$

(☎9792420450; www.brownbreadbakery.com; Bengali Tola, near Pandey Ghat; mains ₹125-400; ⊙7am-10pm; 🛜) 🌿 This restaurant's fabulous menu includes more than 40 varieties of European-quality cheese and more than 30 types of bread, cookies and cakes – along with excellent pastas, sandwiches, pizzas and more. Sit downstairs at street level (AC in summer) or upstairs at the casual rooftop cafe, with seating on cushions around low tables and glimpses of the Ganges.

Pop in for the shockingly European breakfast buffet (from 7am to noon; ₹300) or the free, nightly live classical-music performances (at 7.30pm) by the **Learn for Life** (☎0542-2390040; www.learn-for-life.net; D55/147 Aurangabad) school. Warning: don't be fooled by impostors who pretend to be the BBB. Note this new location (on Bengali Tola, near Pandey Ghat), and remember: the real BBB will never accept cash donations for Learn for Life.

Varanasi

◎ Sights
1 Assi Ghat.....................................C6
2 Dashashwamedh Ghat.............................C2
3 Gate 2.......................................C1
  Gyan Kupor Well ....(see 12)
4 Hanuman Ghat.................................C4
5 Harishchandra Ghat...........................C4
6 Kedar Ghat...................................C4
7 Man Mandir Ghat..............................C2
8 Manikarnika Ghat.............................D1
9 Munshi Ghat..................................C2
10 Pandhey Ghat................................C3
11 Scindhia Ghat...............................D1
12 Vishwanath Temple...........................C1

✦ Activities, Courses & Tours
13 Learn for Life Society......................A1

⬡ Shopping
14 Baba Blacksheep.............................B4
15 Organic by Brown Bread Bakery...............B6

✖ Eating
16 Brown Bread Bakery..........................C3
17 Darbangha...................................C2
18 Open Hand...................................B6
19 Vegan & Raw.................................B5

⬡ Drinking & Nightlife
20 Blue Lassi..................................C1

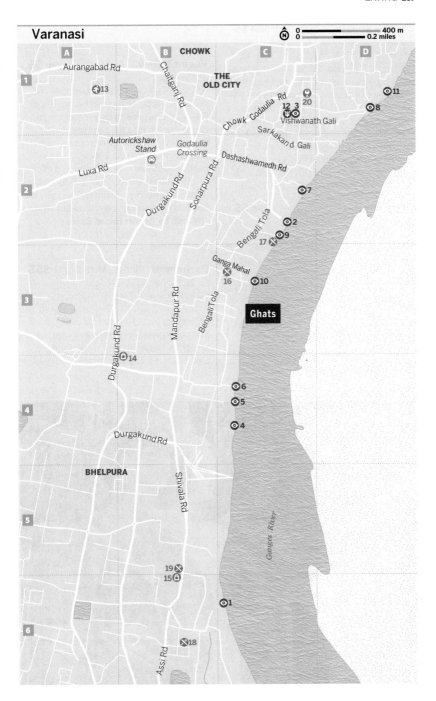

Varanasi

N 0 — 400 m
0 — 0.2 miles

A **B** CHOWK **C** **D**

Aurangabad Rd

THE
OLD CITY

☸13

Chaitganj Rd

⊙11

Godaulia Rd

⌖20

Chowk

12 3

Vishwanath Gali

⊙8

Autorickshaw
Stand

Godaulia
Crossing

Sarkakand Gali

Luxa Rd

Durgakund Rd

Sonarpura Rd

Dashashwamedh Rd

⊙7

Bengali Tola

⊙2

17 ✕9

Ganga Mahal

✕16

⊙10

Mandapur Rd

Bengali Tola

Ghats

Durgakund Rd

🔒14

⊙6

⊙5

⊙4

Durgakund Rd

BHELPURA

Shivala Rd

Ganges River

19 ✕
15 🔒

⊙1

18 ✕

Assi Rd

Canton Royale   Indian $$

(www.hotelsuryavns.com; S-20/51A-5 The Mall
Rd; mains ₹200-390; ⏰11am-11pm) Housed
in a nearly 200-year-old heritage building,
Hotel Surya's excellent main restaurant
has a colonial elegance; on warm evenings
you can eat on the large lawn. It's one of
Varanasi's best top-end choices, offering a
great-value, global hodgepodge, from Mexican and Thai to Chinese and Continental.
But really, it's the Indian that's excellent,
including a wonderful thali (traditional 'all-
you-can-eat' plate meal; ₹500 to ₹750).

Open Hand   Cafe $$

(www.openhand.in; 1/128-3 Dumraub Bagh; mains
₹160-280; ⏰8am-8pm; 🛜) 🌿 This shoes-off
cafe and gift shop serves real espresso and
French-press coffee alongside breakfast
platters featuring pancakes, omelettes
and muesli. There's also a range of salads,
sandwiches, pastas and baked goods,
which are excellent. Sit on the narrow
balcony or lounge around the former home
all day on the free wi-fi.

There's also a large selection of gorgeous
handicrafts (jewellery, toys, clothing) made
in the local community. Couldn't be more
pleasant.

Vegan & Raw   Vegan $$

(Shivala Rd, near Tulsi Ghat; mains ₹170-220;
⏰9am-9.30pm; 🛜) This casual courtyard
restaurant is an offshoot of Brown Bread
Bakery (p236), featuring excellent vegan
dishes, including a full page of salads
from spinach-radish-walnut to papaya-
pomegranate-linseed. Entrées lean towards
pastas, but there's also tofu, *momo* (Tibetan dumplings) and couscous. Eclectic live
music is performed Tuesday, Thursday and
Saturday at around 7pm. It's behind the
Organic by Brown Bread Bakery (www.
brownbreadbakery.com; 2/225 Shivali; ⏰7am-
8pm; 🛜) shop.

Darbangha   Indian, Multicuisine $$$

(📞9129414141; Brijrama Palace Hotel, Munshi/
Darbhanga Ghat; mains ₹750-1100, thalis ₹1750;
⏰noon-3pm & 7.30-10.30pm) Seriously some
of the best Indian food we've ever had.
The *palak chaman* (paneer in spinach and
spices) is heaven in your mouth and the
aloo chaat is a gourmet street-food revela-

Saris for sale

Blue Lassi

tion. There's also a good list of Continental and Thai options. For nonguests there's a minimum charge of ₹1000 per person. It's worth it.

🍸 DRINKING & ENTERTAINMENT

Wine and beer shops are dotted discreetly around the city, usually away from the river. (Note that it is frowned upon to drink alcohol on or near the holy Ganges.) Liquor laws regarding proximity of temples ensure nobody is licensed, but rooftops here can usually discreetly fashion up a beer. For bars, head to midrange and top-end hotels away from the ghats.

There's nightly live **Indian classical music** at Brown Bread Bakery (p236).

Prinsep Bar   Bar
(www.tajhotels.com; Gateway Hotel Ganges, Raja Bazaar Rd; ⊙noon-11pm Mon-Sat, to midnight Sun) For a quiet drink with a dash of history, try this tiny bar named after James Prinsep, who drew wonderful illustrations of

Varanasi's ghats and temples (but stick to beer as the 25mL cocktail pour is weak).

Blue Lassi   Lassi
(lassi ₹40-90; ⊙9am-10pm; 🛜) Your long, thirsty search for the best lassi in India is over. Look no further than Blue Lassi, a tiny, hole-in-the-wall yoghurt shop that has been churning out the freshest, creamiest, fruit-filled lassis since 1925. The grandson of the original owner still works here, sitting by his lassi-mixing cauldron in front of a small room with wooden benches for customers to sit on and walls plastered with messages from happy drinkers.

There are more than 80 delicious flavour combos, divided by section – plain, banana, apple, pomegranate, mango, papaya, strawberry, blueberry, coconut and saffron. We think banana and apple, the latter flecked with fresh apple shreds, just about top the long list. (What the hell, make it banana-apple!)

The whole scene here is surreal: the lassi takes ages to arrive while a UN-rivalling group of thirsty nationalities chats away; when it does, it's handed to you with the

River Trips

A dawn rowing-boat ride along the Ganges is a quintessential Varanasi experience. The early-morning light is particularly inspiring, and all the colour and clamour of pilgrims bathing and performing *puja* (offerings or prayers) unfold before you. The hour-long trip south from Dashashwamedh Ghat to Harishchandra Ghat (a cremation ghat) and back is a popular option.

Early evening is also a good time on the river. You can light a lotus flower candle (₹10) and set it adrift on the water.

The official government price of boats is ₹250 per hour for two to four people, but you'll be lucky to manage ₹300 per person per hour, even after hard bargaining. Try to arrange a boat the day before. If you arrive just before sunrise, you'll find yourself in a Varanasi Stand-off: a battle of wills between yourself, a boatman and the unforgiving rising sun – to the tune of ₹1000 per person. And make sure to specify that the price you agree is in rupees! Many boatmen love to say '100!' and later claim they meant dollars or euros.

Brown Bread Bakery (p236) can arrange hassle-free rides in its own boats for ₹150 per hour per person, with coffee and cakes to boot.

---

care of a priceless work of art as the deceased are carried by the front of the shop on the way to Burning Ghat (Manikarnika). *Namaste!*

INFORMATION

UP Tourism (☎0542-2506670; www.uptourism.gov.in; Varanasi Junction Train Station;

10am-6pm) The patient Mr Umashankar at the office inside the train station has been dishing out reasonably impartial information to arriving travellers for years; he's a mine of knowledge, so this is a requisite first stop if you arrive here by train. Get the heads-up on autorickshaw prices, the best trains for your travels, the lie of the land or details on Varanasi's paying-guesthouse program, or arrange a guided tour.

GETTING THERE & AWAY

AIR

Lal Bahadur Shashtri Airport, 24km northwest of town in Babatpur, is served by several airlines with nonstop flights to selected cities in India, including Delhi, Mumbai and Bengaluru. Thai Airways flies direct to Bangkok. Autorickshaws from the city to the airport cost ₹350. A taxi is about ₹800.

BUS

The main bus stand is opposite Varanasi Junction train station. AC buses to Delhi (₹1227, 16 hours) leave at 10am and 2.30pm.

TRAIN

Varanasi Junction, also known as Varanasi Cantonment (Cantt), is the main station. A few daily trains leave for New Delhi and Agra. For Agra, there are more trains from Mughal Sarai Junction, 18km from Varanasi, to Tundla, 24km from Agra.

Luggage theft has been reported on trains to and from Varanasi, so take extra care. Reports of drugged food and drink aren't unheard of, so it's probably best to politely decline any offers from strangers.

Go to the **Foreign Tourist Centre** (◯8am-1.50pm & 2-8pm Mon-Sat, 8am-2pm Sun) to purchase foreign-tourist quota tickets: it's in the white-and-orange PRS building, about 200m to the right of the train station as you exit.

Sadhu (holy man) meditating

Handy Trains from Varanasi Junction

Destination	Train No & Name	Fare (₹)	Duration (hr)	Departures
Agra Fort	14853 Marudhar Exp	350/950/1365	13	5.25pm
New Delhi	12561 Swatantra S Exp	415/1100/1565	12	12.40am

Fares: sleeper/3AC/2AC

❶ GETTING AROUND

CYCLE-RICKSHAW

A small ride – up to 2km – costs ₹50. Rough prices from Godaulia Crossing include Assi Ghat (₹50), Benares Hindu University (₹60) and Varanasi Junction train station (₹60). Be prepared for hard bargaining.

TAXI & AUTORICKSHAW

Prepaid booths for autorickshaws and taxis are directly outside Varanasi Junction train station and give you a good benchmark for prices around town – though it doesn't work as well as some other cities as there are usually no officials policing it, so you'll have to haggle here, too.

If the drivers are playing by the system, you'll pay an administration charge (₹5 for autorickshaws, ₹10 for taxis) at the booth then take a ticket which you give to your driver, along with the fare, once you've reached your destination.

Sample fares:

Airport auto/taxi ₹225/650

Assi Ghat auto/taxi ₹90/300

Godaulia Crossing auto/taxi ₹95/250

Half-day tour (four hours) taxi ₹500

Full-day tour (eight hours) taxi ₹900

HIMACHAL
PRADESH

In this Chapter
Tibetan Culture in
McLeod Ganj 246
Manali Adventure Activities 250
McLeod Ganj 254
Manali 257

Himachal Pradesh at a Glance...

With spectacular snowy peaks and plunging river valleys, beautiful Himachal is India's outdoor adventure playground. From trekking and climbing to rafting, paragliding and skiing, if it can be done in the mountains, it can be done here. Villages perched on staggering slopes enchant with fairy-tale architecture and their people's easygoing warmth. The valley town Manali lures adventurers, backpackers and families alike. Hill stations such as the state capital Shimla appeal with a holiday atmosphere and colonial echoes, and such is the richness of the Himachali jigsaw that in McLeod Ganj, the Dalai Lama's home-away-from-home, you might even think you've stumbled into Tibet.

Himachal Pradesh in Three Days

Make McLeod Ganj your base and spend day one exploring the centres of Tibetan life here, the **Tsuglagkhang Complex** (p247) and **Central Tibetan Secretariat** (p248). Next day take the beautiful hike up to **Triund** (p118). On day three visit the **Norbulingka Institute** (p257) and **Tibetan Children's Village** (p249). You'll have time to enjoy the cafes and shopping too.

Himachal Pradesh in One Week

Head over to Manali (travelling overnight will give you more time there - but less sleep!). Take your first day relatively easy with a visit to **Hadimba Temple** (p258) and a walk to **Jogini waterfalls** (p251). Devote your remaining two or thee days to the mountains with a **trek** (p251) to Bhrigu Lake or Beas Kund, or over the Chandrakani Pass.

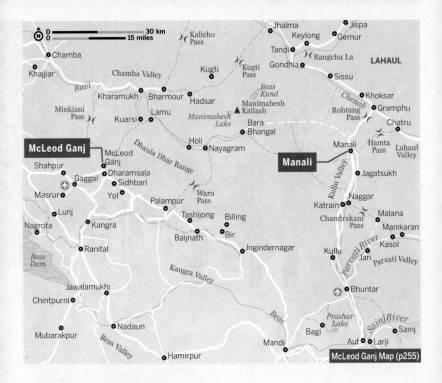

McLeod Ganj Map (p255)

Arriving in Himachal Pradesh

Airports Gaggal (for Dharamsala and nearby McLeod Ganj) and Bhuntar (for Manali) airports have daily flights from Delhi when not interrupted by weather. A picturesque narrow-gauge 'toy train' runs up to Shimla from Kalka (near Chandigarh), with connections to/from Delhi.

Bus Plentiful bus services connect Dharamsala and Shimla to the outside world. Manali also has bus services from Delhi and Chandigarh.

Sleeping

McLeod Ganj has many budget guest-houses, some good-value midrangers and a couple of boutiquey, Tibetan-styled hotels. Advance bookings advisable in April, May, June and October.

Manali is overstocked with mediocre midrangers. The best budget places are in Old Manali; some good upmarket hotels lie between the town centre and Old Manali. Many places slash prices in July and August and October to March (except Christmas–New Year).

LUCAS VALLECILLOS/ALAMY ©

Tibetan Culture in McLeod Ganj

The residence of His Holiness the 14th Dalai Lama and home to a large Tibetan population, the small mountain town of McLeod Ganj has a strong spiritual/ alternative vibe and attracts thousands of international visitors each year.

Great For...

☑ Don't Miss

The monks' lively debating sessions in the Tsuglagkhang courtyard from 2pm to 3pm (except Sunday).

Some visitors come to McLeod for courses in Buddhism, meditation or yoga, or to volunteer with the Tibetan community, or to trek in the Dhauladhar mountains. On a short visit, there's plenty to absorb and fascinate in the main Tibetan religious and cultural centres, as well as good shopping and eating.

McLeod's Tibetan community took off when the Dalai Lama established his base here in 1960. China had invaded Tibet, then a de facto independent state, in 1950. The Dalai Lama fled to India in 1959. Many other Tibetans have risked similar dangerous crossings, and today there are 100,000 or more of them in India. Many new arrivals come first to the McLeod Ganj area, where they find support from their community (over 10,000 strong) and a legion of NGOs.

Young monks in Tsuglagkhang Complex

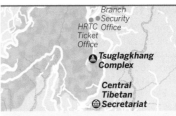

Branch
● ●Security
HRTC Office
Ticket
Office

▲ **Tsuglagkhang
Complex**

**Central
Tibetan**
🏛 **Secretariat**

❶ Need to Know

The monsoon (late June to early September) is exceptionally heavy here, and best avoided.

✕ Take a Break

Moonpeak (p256) is a great cafe just uphill from the Tsuglagkhang Complex.

★ Top Tip

For the Dalai Lama's schedules and just about everything you need to know about His Holiness, visit www.dalailama.com.

Tsuglagkhang Complex

The main focus of visiting pilgrims, monks and many tourists, the **Tsuglagkhang Complex** (Temple Rd; ⊙5am-8pm Apr-Oct, 6am-6pm Nov-Mar) includes the main Tibetan temple and other dependencies.

Tsuglagkhang

The revered Tsuglagkhang, built in 1969, is the Tibetan exiles' concrete equivalent of the Jokhang temple in Lhasa which was destroyed in 1966 during the Cultural Revolution. Its central image is a gilded statue of the Sakyamuni Buddha (the name refers to the Buddha's birthplace Sakya). To its left is a gilded replica of the 7th-century statue of Avalokitesvara (the bodhisattva of compassion, Tibet's patron deity) that stood in the Jokhang temple, containing relics that were rescued from the destruction and smuggled

out of Tibet. Beside the Avalokitesvara is a gilded statue of Padmasambhava, the Indian sage believed to have helped spread Buddhism in 8th-century Tibet.

Kalachakra Temple

Before visiting the Tsuglagkhang itself, pilgrims first visit the Kalachakra Temple on its west side. Mesmerising murals here depict the Kalachakra (Wheel of Time) mandala, specifically linked to Avalokitesvara, of whom the Dalai Lama is a manifestation.

Tibet Museum

This absorbing **museum** (http://tibet museum.org; ⊙9am-1pm & 2-6pm Sun, Tue-Fri & 1st Sat of the month, to 5pm Oct-Mar) FREE tells the story of Tibetan history, the Chinese occupation and the Tibetan resistance and exodus, through photographs, video and clear English-language display panels. It also covers the Dalai Lama and his life's work.

Meeting the Dalai Lama

Put simply, the Dalai Lama is too busy with spiritual duties to give private audiences to everyone who comes to McLeod Ganj. Tibetan refugees are automatically guaranteed an audience, but travellers must make do with the occasional public teachings held at the Tsuglagkhang. These are typically given in September or October and after Losar (Tibetan New Year) in February or March, and on other occasions depending on his schedule.

To attend a teaching, register with your passport at the **Branch Security Office** (☏221560; Bhagsu Rd, McLeod Ganj; ⊗9am-1pm & 2-5pm Mon-Fri & 1st Sat of the month) in the days leading up to the teaching (registration is also usually possible at the temple in the early morning before the teaching starts). Bring a cushion and an FM radio with headset (around ₹450 in local shops) for simultaneous translation.

Central Tibetan Secretariat

Inside the government-in-exile compound at Gangchen Kyishong, 2km downhill from the Tsuglagkhang, the **Library of Tibetan Works & Archives** (☏9218422467; www.ltwa. net; Gangchen Kyishong; ⊗9am-1pm & 2-5pm Mon-Sat, closed 2nd & 4th Sat of the month) began life as a collection of sacred manuscripts saved from the Cultural Revolution. Today it has more than 120,000 manuscripts and books in Tibetan, and more than 15,000 books on Tibet, Buddhism and the Himalayan region in English and other languages.

Upstairs is a fascinating **cultural museum** (₹20) with statues, old Tibetan artefacts and books, and some astonishing three-dimensional mandalas in wood and sand.

His Holiness, the 14th Dalai Lama, at Tsuglagkhang Complex

Also worth a visit is the colourful **Nechung Gompa** below the library building, seat of the Tibetan state oracle.

Men-Tsee Khang

Established to preserve the traditional arts of Tibetan medicine and astrology, **Men-Tsee-Khang** (Tibetan Medical & Astrological Institute; ☑01892-223113; www.men-tsee-khang.org; Gangchen Kyishong; ⏱9am-1pm & 2-5pm Mon-Sat, closed 2nd & 4th Sat of the month) is a college, clinic, museum, research centre and astrological institute rolled into one. The astrological folk can do you a 45-minute oral consultation (₹2000; reg-

ister in person half a day ahead with your birth date, time and place), or a detailed life-horoscope online (US$85 plus US$20 taxes).

The **Men-Tsee-Khang Museum** (₹20) has three floors of fascinating displays on the sophisticated sciences of Tibetan astrology and medicine, told via illustrative *thangkas* (Tibetan cloth paintings) as well as samples of medicines, their plant and mineral sources, and instruments that have been used for treatments – such as the brass hammer for treating tumours, insanity and body aches.

Up in McLeod Ganj, the **Men-Tsee-Khang Therapy Centre** (☑01892-221484; www.men-tsee-khang.org; TIPA Rd; ⏱9am-1pm & 2-5pm Mon-Sat, closed 2nd & 4th Sat of the month) offers traditional Tibetan medical treatments including massages, compresses, herbal baths and steam therapies.

Tibetan Children's Village

Three kilometres northwest of McLeod, near Dal Lake, the **Tibetan Children's Village** (☑01892-221348; www.tcv.org.in; ⏱office 9am-12.30pm & 1.30-5pm Mon-Fri) provides free education and lodging for nearly 2000 refugee children. It's now one of 12 such schools around India, and welcomes visitors. You can get there by autorickshaw (₹100) or taxi (₹150) from McLeod.

Tibetan Institute of Performing Arts

This flourishing **arts school** (TIPA; ☑9418087998; http://tipa.asia; TIPA Rd; ⏱9am-5pm Mon-Sat, closed 2nd & 4th Sat of the month) keeps traditional Tibetan dance, music and colourful folk opera *(lhamo)* very much alive among the exile community. You can visit its folk museum and ask at the office for a tour (donations welcome for both).

TIPA stages irregular Tibetan cultural performances including a 1½-hour show of folk and ritual dance and song, *Dances from the Roof of the World*. Check the websites for upcoming events.

★ Top Tip
Photos are normally allowed inside the Tsuglagkhang Complex, except in the Kalachakra Temple.

ANAND PUROHIT/GETTY IMAGES ©

Manali Adventure Activities

Manali is the adventure-sports capital of Himachal Pradesh, arguably of all India, and it's easy to organise anything from hiking to skiing to rafting or paragliding through operators here.

Great For...

☑ **Don't Miss**

Getting up into the hills outside Manali – the scenery is magnificent!

Walking & Trekking

Most agencies offer multiday mountain treks for ₹1600 to ₹3000 per person per day including guides, transport, porters or pack animals, food and camping equipment. Generally the larger the group, the lower the price per person. June, September and October are overall the best months.

Popular shorter trekking options include the following:

Hamta Pass To Chatru in Lahaul (four days).

Chandrakani Pass (3650m) From Naggar to Malana, accessible late May to October (two or three days).

Beas Kund Mountain lake (three days, with the option of extra days hiking up surrounding mountains).

Bhrigu Lake Altitude 4250m (three days).

Paragliding, Solang Nullah

ⓘ Need to Know

Different activities have different seasons; June, September and October are the best months overall.

✕ Take a Break

Drifters' Inn (p259) in Old Manali is a top spot for food and all manner of drinks.

★ Top Tip

It's best to avoid the monsoon (essentially July and August) for any outdoor activities.

Plenty of shorter walks are possible from Manali. The usual rules on safe trekking apply – tell someone where you're going and don't walk alone. If you want a guide, they typically cost ₹1500 for day hikes.

One good, quite strenuous, day hike (about five hours up, four hours down) is up to Lama Dugh meadow at 3380m, west of town (1500m higher than Manali). A good short walk (about an hour each way) goes from Vashisht village, 2km north of central Manali, to the pretty Jogini waterfalls.

Hamta Pass Trek

Easily accessible from Manali, this camping trek crosses from the Hamta Valley (an offshoot of the Kullu Valley where Manali lies) to Lahaul's Chandra Valley. Most treks start by driving up to the spot known as Jobri, where the Hamta Nullah and Jobri Nullah streams meet. Two easy days to start off, with a combined ascent of around 800m, are good for acclimatisation. The climb to the pass (4270m) from Balu Ka Gera is steep and tiring but there are sublime snow-peak views from the top. Best times: the second half of September and October, after the monsoon.

Day 1 Jobri to Chika (5km, two hours).

Day 2 Chika to Balu Ka Gera (9km, four hours).

Day 3 Balu Ka Gera to Shiagouru via Hamta Pass (15km, eight hours).

Day 4 Shiagouru to Chatru (10km, four hours).

Mountain Biking

Agencies offer bike hire for ₹400 to ₹800 per day (and can give current info on routes) or will take you on guided rides. **Himalayan Bike Bar** (www.facebook.com/himalayanbikebar; Mission Rd; ⊙10am-8pm Mon-Sat) is an enthusiastic mountain-biking specialist renting and selling bikes.

Rafting

There is 14km of Grade II and III white water between Pirdi, on the Beas River 43km south of Manali, and the take-out point at Jhiri; trips with Manali agencies cost anywhere between ₹650 and ₹1150 per person, plus transport (around ₹2000 to ₹2500 per van). May, June, late September and October are the best times (it's banned from 15 July to 15 August because of the monsoon).

Skiing & Snowboarding

From January to mid-March, Solang Nullah, 13km north of Manali, transforms into Himachal's main ski and snowboarding resort. Equipment can be hired from Manali agencies or at Solang Nullah from ₹500 per day. The piste offers limited options for experienced skiers, but there is off-piste powder and backcountry skiing for the experienced from the top of the cable car. In April and May there's snowshoe ski touring in areas like the Hamta valley, upper Solang valley and around Gulaba. Agencies such as Himalayan Caravan, **Himalayan Adventurers** (☏01902-252750; www.himalayan adventurers.com; 44 The Mall; ⊗9am-9pm) and Himalayan Extreme Centre offer ski touring packages.

Rock Climbing

Cliffs in the Manali area at Solang, Aleo and Vashisht have a good range of bolted and traditional routes ranging from French 5a to 7b (British 4a to 6b). A day's climbing for beginners or experienced climbers costs ₹1500 to ₹2000 with Manali agencies, including transport. Solang and the Chatru

Cyclists on Rohtang Pass

area in Lahaul are tops for bouldering. Sunny, dry November is a good month.

Paragliding

Paragliding is popular at Solang Nullah and at less crowded Gulaba and Marhi (on the way up to the Rohtang La north of Manali) from April to October (except during the monsoon). September and October generally have the best thermals, though May and June can be good at Gulaba and Marhi. Tandem flights at Solang Nullah

> ★ **Top Tip**
>
> You can go canyoning in several places around Manali. Himalayan Extreme Centre charges ₹1650 to ₹1850 per person for a day of descending four different waterfalls above Vashisht.

cost around ₹900 for a one- to two-minute flight, or ₹2000 to ₹3000 for five to 10 minutes from the top of the cable car. Pilots should have a licence issued by the Himachal Pradesh Department of Tourism. Adventure-tour operators can organise tandem flights at Gulaba and Marhi for ₹1000 to ₹4000 depending on duration.

Fishing

The rivers of the Kullu Valley, in which Manali lies, and some of its side valleys, are rich in brown and rainbow trout. The season runs from March to June and October to November, and rods and tackle can be hired from agencies in Manali; daily fishing licences, available at the **Hotel Kunzam** (The Mall), cost ₹100. Himalayan Extreme Centre can fix you up with a rod, spoon, hook and permit for ₹500 for a day's fishing on Manalsu Nala, which flows through Old Manali, and offers three-day Sainj River packages.

Agencies

Himalayan Extreme Centre (☑9816174164; www.himalayan-extreme-centre.com; Old Manali; ⊙9am-8pm) This long-running, professional and friendly outfit can arrange almost any activity you fancy. Drop into their shop/office and browse the catalogue.

Himalayan Trails (☑9816828583; www.himalayantrails.in; Dragon Market, Old Manali; ⊙9.30am-10pm) Energetic young company doing trekking, day hikes, mountain biking, rock climbing and more; runs open-group treks that individuals can join, and has mountain bikes for rent.

Himalayan Caravan (☑9816316348; www.himalayancaravan.com; Old Manali; ⊙office 9am-10pm mid-Mar–mid-Dec) Professional operator good for trekking, rock climbing, mountaineering, snowboarding and skiing.

CHLOE HALL/ALAMY ©

McLeod Ganj

 **ACTIVITIES**

Triund Hike
Hiking

You can enjoy several glorious hours on the moderately strenuous hike up to the panoramic mountain meadow of Triund, about 1150m higher than McLeod at 2900m. Start by walking 1km up Dharamkot Rd through pine woods to the **Himalayan Tea Shop** (items ₹30-80; ⏱6am-8.30pm) at Dharamkot village. Head along the left side of the water tank opposite the tea shop, and after 50m turn up a path to the right. This winds up through the forest to emerge on a jeep track after 1km: go 500m to the right to reach the little Gallu Devi temple on a panoramic ridge. From here a scenic path climbs east through rhododendron woods, gaining 800m altitude in a fairly strenuous 2½ to three hours to Triund. You pass a couple of tea shops, and Triund has a few *dhabas* (simple eateries) – which also offer tents, sleeping bags and beds if you want to stay.

🔒 SHOPPING

Dozens of shops and stalls sell Tibetan artefacts, including *thangkas,* turquoise necklaces, yak-wool shawls and 'singing' bowls. Some are Tibetan-run, but others are run by Kashmiri traders who apply a degree of sales pressure. Several local cooperatives offer the same goods without the hassle.

Tibetan Handicraft Center
Arts & Crafts

(☎01892-221415; www.tibetan-handicrafts.com; Jogiwara Rd; ⏱9am-5pm Mon-Sat) 🍃 This cooperative employs refugees for the weaving of Tibetan carpets. You'll pay around ₹13,500 for a 0.9m by 1.8m traditional wool carpet, and they'll ship it if you like (₹2500 to ₹3500 to Europe, ₹4500 to the USA). Visitors are welcome to watch the weavers in action. There's also a shop with other attractive goods, including quality *thangkas* (₹20,000 plus).

Green Shop
Arts & Crafts

(Bhagsu Rd; ⏱9.30am-7pm Mon-Sat) 🍃 Sells appealing handmade recycled paper products, organic peanut butter, tahini and more.

Village Boutique
Arts & Crafts

(Temple Rd; ⏱9am-6pm Tue-Sun) Sells rugs, purses, bags, singing bowls, deity figurines and wall hangings, many of them Tibetan-made; profits go to the Tibetan Children's Village (p249).

🍴 EATING & DRINKING

McLeod Ganj is crammed with traveller-oriented restaurants serving omelettes, pancakes, Indian, Tibetan and Chinese staples, pizzas, pasta and assorted other European food. Also here are some of North India's best cafes, with good coffee and English-style tea.

McLeod Ganj

◉ Sights
1	Central Tibetan Secretariat	C6
2	Cultural Museum	C6
3	Kalachakra Temple	C4
4	Library of Tibetan Works & Archives	C6
5	Men-Tsee-Khang	C6
6	Men-Tsee-Khang Museum	C6
7	Nechung Gompa	C6
8	Tibet Museum	C4
9	Tibetan Children's Village	A1
10	Tibetan Institute of Performing Arts	D2
11	Tsuglagkhang	C4
12	Tsuglagkhang Complex	C4

🔒 Shopping
13	Green Shop	C3
14	Tibetan Handicraft Center	C3
15	Village Boutique	C3

🍴 Eating
16	Green Hotel Restaurant	D3
17	Himalayan Tea Shop	D1
18	McLlo Restaurant	C3
19	Moonpeak	C3
20	Nick's Italian Kitchen	C3
21	Shangrila Vegetarian Restaurant	C3

McLeod Ganj

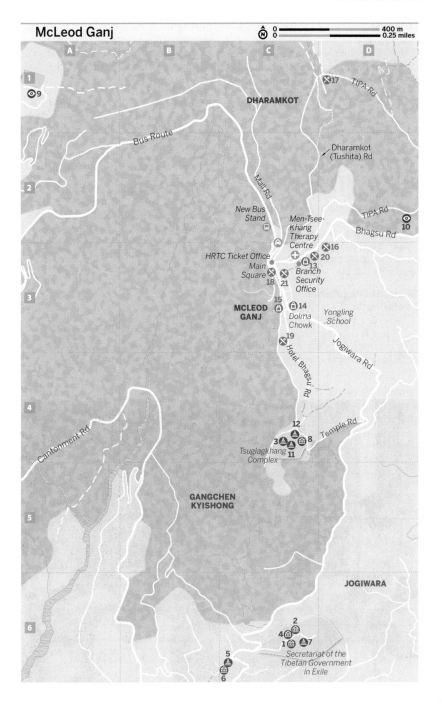

0 400 m
0 0.25 miles

DHARAMKOT

Bus Route

Mall Rd

Dharamkot
(Tushita) Rd

New Bus
Stand

Men-Tsee-
Khang
Therapy
Centre

TIPA Rd

Bhagsu Rd

HRTC Ticket Office
Main
Square

Branch
Security
Office

MCLEOD
GANJ

Dolma
Chowk

Yongling
School

Jogiwara Rd

Hotel Bhagsu Rd

Cantonment Rd

Temple Rd

Tsuglagkhang
Complex

GANGCHEN
KYISHONG

JOGIWARA

Secretariat of the
Tibetan Government
in Exile

Moonpeak   Multicuisine $$

(www.moonpeak.org; Temple Rd; mains ₹150-300; ⊘7am-9pm; 🛜) A little chunk of Seattle, transported to India. Come for excellent coffee, breakfasts, cakes, imaginative brown-bread open sandwiches (like poached chicken with mango, lime and coriander sauce), soups, salads and plenty of well-prepared veg and non-veg main dishes.

It's also a gallery and has a great laid-back bluesy taste in music.

Nick's Italian Kitchen   Italian $

(Bhagsu Rd; mains ₹80-190; ⊘7am-9pm; 🛜) Unpretentious, well-run Nick's has been serving up tasty vegetarian pizzas, lasagne, ravioli, gnocchi and quiches for years. Follow up a ground coffee with one of their desserts – apple pie or a heavenly slice of lemon cheesecake.

Shangrila Vegetarian Restaurant   Tibetan, Indian $

(Jogiwara Rd; mains ₹70-90; ⊘7.30am-8.30pm; 🛜) Shangrila is run by monks of the Gyudmed monastery, some of whom wait on tables and help to engender a notably friendly atmosphere. It serves up tasty, well-priced Tibetan staples including *momos* (Tibetan dumplings) in soup and *baglebs* (large fried *momos*).

Green Hotel Restaurant   Multicuisine $$

(Bhagsu Rd; mains ₹110-180; ⊘6.30am-9.30pm; 🛜) This traveller-oriented hotel restaurant, with a sunny terrace and comfy couches inside, serves very good vegetarian food and the earliest breakfasts in town.

McLlo Restaurant   Multicuisine $$

(Main Sq; mains ₹200-400; ⊘9.30am-11.30pm) Crowded nightly and justifiably popular, this large, four-floor place serves a mind-boggling menu of Indian, Chinese and international fare, including pizzas and pasta. The semi-open-air top floor is one of McLeod's best places to enjoy a cold beer (₹220 plus).

🛈 GETTING THERE & AWAY

Dharamsala airport is at Gaggal, 22km southwest of McLeod Ganj. Air India and SpiceJet

Chai stall, McLeod Ganj

BLOOMBERG/GETTY IMAGES ©

both fly daily to/from Delhi, though flights are sometimes cancelled in bad weather.

BUS

McLeod's new bus stand is 150m north of the main square. Some long-distance buses come here but there are more frequent arrivals and departures at Dharamsala bus station, 3km down the hill (10km via the looping bus route). Buses run from Dharamsala bus station to McLeod Ganj (₹15, 35 minutes) about every half-hour from 6am to 9pm. Buses and overcrowded jeeps (₹15) run down the hill from McLeod to Dharamsala from 4am to 8pm.

You can book government-run Himachal Road Transport Corporation (HRTC) buses from both McLeod and Dharamsala at McLeod's **HRTC ticket office** (Main Sq; ⊙9am-7pm). Travel agencies sell seats on private buses to various destinations.

Delhi The HRTC has eight daily buses from McLeod Ganj (₹580 to ₹1275, 12 to 13 hours) including comfortable Volvo AC coaches at 5.30pm and 7pm, plus 10 buses daily from Dharamsala (₹542 to ₹1240, 12 hours). Private buses (₹900 to ₹1100, 12 hours) leave McLeod Ganj between 6pm and 7pm.

Manali The HRTC has a Volvo AC (₹815, 10 hours) from Dharamsala at 9.30pm, plus ordinary buses from Dharamsala (₹360) at 7am and 6pm and from McLeod Ganj (₹400, 11 hours) at 4.30pm. Private buses (₹400 to ₹600, 11 hours) leave McLeod between 8.30pm and 9.30pm.

TAXI

McLeod's **taxi stand** (☎01892-221034; Mall Rd) is just north of the main square. Fares include ₹100 to Gangchen Kyishong, ₹200 to Dharamsala bus station, ₹800 to Dharamsala airport and ₹4500 to Manali.

Manali

Surrounded by high peaks in the beautiful green Kullu Valley, with mountain adventures beckoning from all directions, Manali is a year-round magnet for backpackers, adventurers and Indian families and honeymooners.

 Norbulingka Institute

The wonderful **Norbulingka Institute** (☎9418436410; www.norbulingka.org; local & Tibetan ₹20, tourist ₹50; ⊙9am-5.30pm), 11km southeast of McLeod Ganj, was established in 1988 to teach and preserve traditional Tibetan art forms and is a fascinating place to visit.

You can see artisans at work on woodcarving, metal statue–making, *thangka* painting and embroidery, on free tours. Also set among the institute's Japanese-influenced gardens are the **Deden Tsuglakhang temple**, with a 4m-high gilded Sakyamuni statue, and the **Losel Doll Museum** (local & Tibetan ₹5, tourist ₹20), which uses traditionally dressed dolls to illustrate aspects of Tibetan culture in charming dioramas. The workshops are closed on Sundays and the second Saturday each month, but the rest of the complex is open. The institute's shop sells some of the expensive but beautiful crafts made here, including jewellery, painted boxes and embroidered clothes and cushions. Vegetarian meals and snacks, and good coffee, are available at the **Hummingbird Cafe** (mains ₹150-200; ⊙7am-9pm; 🛜).

A taxi to or from McLeod Ganj costs ₹350. Or catch a Palampur-bound bus from Dharamsala and get off at Sacred Heart School, Sidhpur (₹7, 15 minutes), from where it's a 1km gentle uphill walk.

In busy seasons (mid-April to mid-July, mid-September to mid-October, Christmas–New Year) the main town can get almost overrun. Old Manali, about 2km northwest of the main town, is the backpacker headquarters and still has some of the feel of an Indian mountain village.

Hadimba Temple

This much-revered wood-and-stone temple, constructed in 1553, stands in a clearing in the cedar forest about 2km west of central Manali. Pilgrims come from across India to honour Hadimba, the demon wife of the Pandava Bhima from the Mahabharata. The temple's wooden doorway, under a three-tier pagoda-style roof, is richly carved with figures of gods, animals and dancers; antlers and ibex horns adorn the outside walls. Inside is a large sacrificial stone where grisly animal slaughterings used to take place.

Hadimba Temple
GRANT DIXON/GETTY IMAGES ©

🔒 SHOPPING

Manali is crammed with shops selling souvenirs from Himachal, Tibet and Ladakh, including turquoise jewellery and lots of brass Buddhas. The local speciality is traditional wool Kullu shawls – lightweight but wonderfully warm and attractively patterned – for which a good place to start is **Bhuttico** (☏01902-252196; The Mall; ⊙9am-7pm Mon-Sat), which charges fair, fixed prices and has several shops around town.

✖ EATING

Manali has some good Indian and international restaurants, and lots of inexpensive travellers' cafes (mostly in Old Manali).

Dylan's Toasted & Roasted   Cafe $

(www.dylanscoffee.com; Manu Temple Rd; coffees & breakfasts ₹50-170; ⊙9am-10pm Mon-Sat; 🛜) This ever popular hole-in-the-wall cafe serves the best coffee in town, plus cinnamon tea, hearty breakfasts, pancakes and wicked desserts including 'Hello to the Queen' – ice cream, melted chocolate and fried banana chunks on a bed of broken biscuits.

Chopsticks   Asian $$

(The Mall; mains ₹120-300; ⊙9am-11pm; 🛜) The most popular traveller choice in central Manali, tightly packed Chopsticks serves a big range of Tibetan, Chinese and Japanese dishes with professional efficiency. Amid Tibetan lutes and Chinese lanterns, it does good *momos*, *gyoza* (their Japanese equivalent), *thenthuk* (a Tibetan soup with short, flat noodles) and Sichuan chicken and lamb.

La Plage   French $$$

(☏9805340977; www.facebook.com/la.plage. manali; mains ₹400-700; ⊙noon-11pm late May–late Aug, closed Mon Aug) Dinner at this outpost of a chic Goan eatery is like being invited to the hip Paris apartment of your much, much cooler friend. French standards such as onion soup or mushroom quiche are joined by specialities such as overnight-cooked lamb, smoked trout, broccoli-and-courgette lasagne and a decadent chocolate thali dessert. Decent Indian and international wines too.

It's 1km from Old Manali bridge in an apple orchard, and will provide free transport from/to the bridge if you call.

Lazy Dog Lounge   Multicuisine $$$

(Manu Temple Rd; mains ₹180-600; ⊙11am-1am; 🛜) This slick restaurant-bar features big plates of fresh, flavourful international food – from pumpkin-and-coconut soup to oven-baked trout and Thai rice bowls, as well as good Indian dishes – that's well above typical backpacker fare. Sit on chairs, benches or cushions in a space that's classy yet earthy, or relax in the riverside garden.

Kullu shawls

RICHARD I'ANSON/GETTY IMAGES ©

🍷 DRINKING & NIGHTLIFE

Restaurants doubling as bars provide the bulk of Manali's nightlife. A particularly popular spot is the **Hangout** (Manu Temple Rd; mains ₹150-500; ⊙noon-midnight, from 5pm Thu), with its outdoor firepits and jam sessions (and also good food). Check out music evenings at **Rendez-Vous** (Manu Temple Rd; mains ₹120-590; ⊙8am-11pm; 🛜), **Drifters' Inn** (Manu Temple Rd; mains ₹230-380; ⊙9.30am-11pm; 🛜) and **Johnson Lodge** (📞01902-251523; www.johnsonlodge. com; Circuit House Rd; ❄🛜).

ℹ️ GETTING THERE & AWAY

Manali's closest airport is 50km south at Bhuntar, with daily Air India flights to/from Delhi (weather permitting). Taxis between the airport and Manali cost ₹1400 to ₹1500 – or you can flag down a Manali-bound bus (₹70, two hours) on the road outside.

BUS & TAXI

Government-run HRTC buses go from the **bus station** (The Mall). Himachal Tourism (HPTDC)

runs a few services to Delhi and Shimla and these are generally the most comfortable on their routes. They leave from the bus station but tickets are sold at the **HPTDC office** (📞01902-252116; The Mall; ⊙8am-8pm mid-April–mid-Jul & mid-Sep–mid-Nov, 9am-7pm rest of year). Private buses start from the **private bus stand** (Hwy 3), 1.2km south of the bus station; tickets are sold at travel agencies along the Mall.

Delhi The HPTDC's comfortable AC Volvo coaches (₹1300, 14 hours) go at 5.30pm and, in busy seasons, 5pm and/or 6pm. Private bus companies run similar overnight services for ₹900 to ₹1800 depending on season. The HRTC runs five AC Volvos (₹1412) each afternoon, plus an AC deluxe (₹1122) at 5.50pm, and seven ordinary or 'semi-deluxe' services.

Dharamsala The HRTC operates a Volvo AC (₹820, 10 hours) at 8pm, and ordinary buses (₹360) at 8.20am and 7pm. There are usually a couple of evening-departure private buses for around ₹550. **Him-aanchal Taxi Operators Union** (📞01902-252205; The Mall) charges ₹5000 to Dharamsala.

In Focus

India Today   262
India struggles with poverty, population and gender-based issues, but is emerging as a superpower.

History   264
Mughal majesty, the British Raj, the world's biggest democracy – it's all here.

The Way of Life   275
The threads that bind the multifarious fabric of Indian society.

Hindu India   278
Deities and beliefs of the country's major religion.

Delicious India   280
Delectable, delightful and downright irresistible, Indian cuisine will have your taste buds dancing for joy.

Architecture & the Arts   283
Indian creativity is everywhere, from the strains of the sitar to sculpted temples to Bollywood dance numbers.

Landscape & Wildlife   286
Vast and varied landscapes are home to a fabulous family of creatures large and small.

Gateway of India (p130), Mumbai

India Today

*With so many states, languages, religions, traditions,
opinions and people jostling for space and attention,
what is striking about India is not its problems, but
how well things work considering these many obstacles.
Despite challenges ranging from poverty and religious
tensions to violence against women, India continues to
thrive as the most successful nation in South Asia and
the largest democracy in the world.*

The Political Landscape

India's politics continues to be shaped by the leadership of prime minister Narendra Modi, who surged to power in 2014, as the Bharatiya Janata Party scored a landslide victory over the ruling Indian National Congress. Modi was painted as a religious fundamentalist and hawk by opponents, but his tenure has been more conciliatory than many feared.

Modi's focus on neoliberal economics has brought solid support from many sectors of the Indian population. Modi decreased welfare spending but lowered taxes, reduced red tape, and increased investment by foreign companies, leading to growing opportunities for India's middle classes.

Perhaps Modi's bravest manoeuvre came on 8 November 2016, when the government, without warning, demonetised the nation's ₹500 and ₹1000 banknotes, in a shock move intended

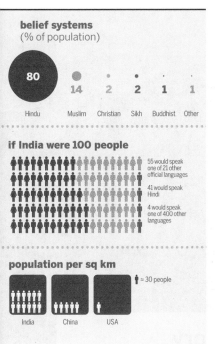

belief systems
(% of population)

80 — Hindu
14 — Muslim
2 — Christian
2 — Sikh
1 — Buddhist
1 — Other

if India were 100 people

55 would speak one of 21 other official languages
41 would speak Hindi
4 would speak one of 400 other languages

population per sq km

♦ ≈ 30 people

India   China   USA

to drive tax-avoiders, corrupt officials and terrorism-funders out into the open.

Progress on social issues has been less dynamic. Violence against women continues to tarnish India's reputation, following a string of high-profile rapes and murders. Nevertheless, there is some progress; the government is debating a 33% quota for women workers in the public sector.

Plentiful People & Problem Neighbours

India is fast emerging as a global superpower, but its greatest resource – its 1.27 billion people – is also perhaps its greatest challenge. India regularly ranks as the world's fastest growing economy, but nearly a quarter of its people live below the official poverty line. With the population continuing to grow by 1.2% (12.7 million people) per year, India faces a struggle to ensure that economic growth filters down to ordinary people.

Growing power has also placed India into conflict with its neighbours. The traditional divide between China and India – the Himalaya – is becoming increasingly porous as China expands its influence in Nepal and Pakistan. China's supply of military equipment to Pakistan is one bone of contention. The Pakistan China Economic Corridor, a network of road and rail links and gas and oil pipelines, reinforces the impression that India is being hemmed in by its neighbour to the north.

India–Chinese relations are further complicated by the status of the Dalai Lama, the spiritual leader of Tibetan Buddhism, who lives in exile in McLeod Ganj near Dharamsala. India's acceptance of Tibetan refugees is an ongoing source of tension with China, which disputes Indian ownership of parts of Arunachal Pradesh and Aksai Chin in Kashmir. An incursion by Chinese forces into Arunachal Pradesh in 2016 has revived fears that China nurtures ambitions to claim the region it refers to as South Tibet.

The Kashmir Impasse

Decades of border skirmishes between India and Pakistan over the disputed territory of Kashmir show no signs of letting up, with a further upsurge in violence in 2016 following the killing of the Kashmiri militant commander Burhan Wani by Indian troops. In the subsequent protests, 85 people were killed and 13,000 injured. The dispute over Kashmir has plagued India–Pakistan relations ever since Partition in 1947, and the predominantly Muslim Kashmir Valley is still claimed in its entirety by both countries.

The dispute has led to three India–Pakistan wars – in 1947, 1965 and 1971 – and a string of incursions and firing incidents across the Line of Control has killed tens of thousands of civilians on both sides of the divide.

History

Through invasions and empires, through the birth of religions and the collapse of civilisations, India has proved itself to be, in the words of its first prime minister, Jawaharlal Nehru, 'a bundle of contradictions held together by strong but invisible threads'. The nation is a marvellous patchwork, stitched together from a legion of communities and cultures who have found greater strength bonded together than apart.

1500 BC

Indo-Aryan civilisation takes root in the fertile Indo-Gangetic basin, speaking early Sanskrit, from which Hindi later evolves.

1500–1200 BC

The Rig-Veda, the first of Hinduism's canonical Vedas, is written; earliest forms of priestly Brahmanical Hinduism emerge.

563–483 BC

The life of Siddhartha Gautama, who attains enlightenment in Bodhgaya, transforming into the Buddha (Awakened One).

Kailasa Temple (p151), Ellora Caves

Indus Valley Civilisation

Urban culture on the subcontinent first emerged in the Indus Valley, straddling the modern India–Pakistan border, where the Harappan culture flourished for over 1000 years from around 2500 BC. Its greatest cities were Moenjodaro and Harappa in Pakistan; Lothal near Ahmedabad is a major site in India. Many elements of Harappan culture later became assimilated into Hinduism: Harappan clay figurines suggest worship of a mother goddess (later personified as Kali) and a male three-faced god in yogi pose (believed to be the historic Shiva).

The Aryans & the Rise of Religions

A traditional explanation for the decline of Harappan civilisation is that from around 1500 BC Aryan tribes from Afghanistan and Central Asia began to filter into northwest India, eventually controlling northern India as far as the Vindhya Hills, with many of the original inhabitants, the Dravidians, being pushed south. A rival theory claims that the Aryans (from a Sanskrit word

| **321–185 BC** | **c 300 BC** | **AD 319–510** |
| Rule of the Maurya kings. This pan-Indian empire briefly adopts Buddhism during the reign of emperor Ashoka. | Buddhism spreads across subcontinent and to Sri Lanka and Southeast Asia via Ashoka's monastic ambassadors. | The golden era of the Gupta dynasty is marked by a creative surge in literature and the arts. |

Amber Fort interior (p104), Jaipur

★ **History Reads**

A Traveller's History of India, Sinharaja Tammita-Delgoda

Empires of the Indus, Alice Albinia

India: a History, John Keay

Indian Summer, Alex von Tunzelmann

for 'noble') were the original inhabitants of India. It's questionable whether the Aryans were a distinct race, so any 'invasion' could simply have been an arrival of new ideas from neighbouring cultures.

What is certain is that the Aryans were responsible for the great Sanskrit literary tradition. The Hindu sacred scriptures, the Vedas, were written between 1500 and 1200 BC, and the caste system became formalised.

Two of India's most significant religions, Buddhism and Jainism, arose in the northern plains around 500 BC. Both the Buddha and Jainism's Mahavir questioned the Vedas and were critical of the caste system, attracting many lower-caste followers.

The Mauryan Empire

Chandragupta Maurya, who came to power in 321 BC, was the founder of the first great Indian empire. With its capital at Pataliputra (modern-day Patna), the Mauryan empire eventually stretched from Bengal to Afghanistan and south into modern-day Karnataka. It reached its peak under emperor Ashoka, who converted to Buddhism in 262 BC and spread the faith across the subcontinent.

Ashoka's rule was characterised by flourishing art and sculpture, while his reputation as a philosopher-king was enhanced by the expressive rock-hewn 'Ashokan edicts' that he used to instruct his people, express remorse at the suffering resulting from his battles, and delineate his enormous territory. Most of these mention and define the concept of *dhamma*, variously as good behaviour, obedience, generosity and goodness.

But after Ashoka's death in 232 BC, the disparate Mauryan empire rapidly disintegrated, collapsing altogether in 185 BC. One of his many legacies is the Indian national flag: its central design is the Ashoka Chakra, a wheel with 24 spokes.

The Golden Age of the Guptas

North India's next major empire didn't arise till the 4th century AD, when Chandragupta I, king of a minor tribe called the Guptas, came to prominence by marrying a princess of one

500–600	1192	1206
Emergence of the Rajputs in Rajasthan: 36 clans spread across the region to secure their own kingdoms.	Forces of the Muslim Mohammed of Ghur (from present-day Afghanistan) take Delhi, ending Hindu supremacy in North India.	Mohammed of Ghur is murdered; in the absence of an heir, his kingdom is usurped by his generals. The Delhi Sultanate is born.

of the most powerful tribes, the Liccavis. The Gupta empire grew rapidly and under Chandragupta II (r 375–413) achieved its greatest extent. The Chinese pilgrim Fa-hsien, visiting India at the time, described a people 'rich and contented', ruled over by enlightened and just kings.

Astronomy, medicine and the arts flourished, with some of the finest work done at Ajanta, Ellora, Sanchi and Sarnath. The Guptas were tolerant of Buddhism but towards the end of their period, Hinduism became the dominant religious force, eclipsing Jainism and Buddhism.

The invasions of the Huns at the beginning of the 6th century signalled the end of Gupta power, and power in North India again devolved to a number of separate Hindu kingdoms.

Mahavir & the Buddha

Mahavir, the 24th and last *tirthankar* (enlightened teacher) of Jainism, and the religion's founder, and the Buddha were contemporaries, and their teachings overlapped. The Buddha laid out the discrepancies (and his critiques) in the *Sankha Sutta* and *Devadaha Sutta*, referring to Mahavir as Nigantha ('free from bonds') NatHe putta. Read them at the Theravada resource, www.access toinsight.com.

The Hindu South

Southern India has always laid claim to its own unique history, insulated by distance from the political developments in the north. It was from the fertile coastal plains that the greatest southern empires – the Cholas, Pandyas, Chalukyas, Cheras and Pallavas – came into their own.

The Chalukyas ruled mainly over the Deccan region of south-central India, although their power occasionally extended further north. In the far south, the Pallavas ruled from the 4th to 9th centuries and pioneered Dravidian architecture, with its exuberant, almost baroque, style.

The south's prosperity was based on trading links with other civilisations, among them Egypt and Rome. In return for spices, pearls, ivory and silk, the Indians received Roman gold. Indian merchants also extended their influence to Southeast Asia. The Cholas, based in modern-day Tamil Nadu, set about turning trade influence into territorial conquest. Under Rajaraja Chola I (985–1014) they controlled almost the whole of South India, the Deccan plateau, Sri Lanka, parts of the Malay peninsula and the Sumatran-based Srivijaya kingdom.

Throughout this period, Hinduism remained the bedrock of South Indian culture.

The Muslim North

Small, pioneering Arabian forces first reached North India in 663, but it wasn't until more than three centuries later that land assaults seriously began to convulse the north.

At the vanguard of Islamic expansion was Mahmud of Ghazni, who turned Ghazni (in today's Afghanistan) into one of the world's most glorious capital cities. From 1001 to 1025, Mahmud conducted 17 raids into India, most notably on the famous Shiva temple

1325–51	1336	1398
Mohammed bin Tughlaq expands the Delhi Sultanate southwards but has to abandon the new capital at Daulatabad.	Foundation of the mighty Hindu Vijayanagar empire, the ruins of whose capital can be seen today around Hampi (Karnataka).	Timur (Tamerlane) mercilessly sacks Delhi, on the pretext that the sultans are too tolerant with their Hindu subjects.

★ **Mughal Marvels**

Taj Mahal (p68)
Red Fort (p38)
Agra Fort (p80)
Fatehpur Sikri (p76)
Humayun's Tomb (p46)

Taj Mahal (p68), Agra

at Somnath in Gujarat. A Hindu force of 70,000 died trying to defend this temple, which fell in early 1026. Mahmud transported a massive haul of gold and other booty back to his capital. These raids shattered the balance of power in North India, allowing subsequent invaders to claim territory for themselves.

In 1191, Mohammed of Ghur advanced into India in brutal fashion, before being defeated in a major battle against a confederacy of Hindu rulers. He returned the following year and routed his enemies. One of his generals, Qutb-ud-din Aibak, captured Delhi and was appointed governor; it was during his reign that the great Delhi landmark, the Qutb Minar Complex, containing India's first mosque, was built. Within a short time almost all of North India was under Muslim control.

Qutb-ud-din Aibak became the first sultan of Delhi. Ala-ud-din Khilji, who came to power in 1296, pushed the borders of the Delhi sultanate inexorably south.

North Meets South

Mohammed bin Tughlaq ascended the Delhi throne in 1324. With dreams of controlling South India directly as part of his empire, Tughlaq decided to move his capital 1100km south to Daulatabad, near Aurangabad in Maharashtra. Tughlaq forcefully marched the entire population of Delhi south to his new city – but soon realised this left the north undefended, so the entire capital was moved north again. The superb Daulatabad fortress remains as a monument to his megalomanic vision.

The last great sultan of Delhi, Firoz Shah, died in 1388, and the sultanate's fate was sealed when Timur (Tamerlane) made a devastating raid from Samarkand in 1398. Timur's sacking of Delhi was truly merciless; some accounts say his soldiers slaughtered every Hindu inhabitant.

After Tughlaq's withdrawal from the south, several splinter kingdoms arose. The two most significant were the Islamic Bahmani sultanate, which emerged in 1345 with its capital at Gulbarga, and later Bidar, and the Hindu Vijayanagar empire, founded in 1336 with its capital at Hampi. The battles between the two were among the bloodiest commu-

1469	1510	1526
Guru Nanak, founder of the Sikh faith, is born in a village near Lahore (in modern-day Pakistan).	Portuguese forces capture Goa under the command of Alfonso de Albuquerque.	Babur becomes the first Mughal emperor after conquering Delhi and stuns Rajasthan by routing its confederate force.

nal violence in Indian history and ultimately resolved nothing in the two centuries before the Mughals ushered in a more enlightened age.

The Mughals

At its height the Mughal empire covered almost the entire subcontinent. Its significance, however, lay not only in its size. Mughal emperors presided over an artistic golden age and had a passion for building that resulted in some of the finest architecture in India, including Shah Jahan's sublime Taj Mahal.

The founder of the Mughal line, Babur, marched into Punjab from his capital at Kabul in 1525. With technological superiority brought by firearms, Babur defeated the larger armies of the sultan of Delhi at the Battle of Panipat in 1526.

Babur's son, Humayun (r 1530–56) was defeated by a powerful ruler of eastern India, Sher Shah, in 1539 and forced to withdraw to Iran – a fact reflected in the Iranian style of his tomb in Delhi. Humayun eventually conquered Delhi in 1555, dying the following year to be succeeded by his son Akbar (r 1556–1605), who managed to extend the empire over a mammoth area.

Akbar, whose name means 'great' in Arabic, was indeed probably the greatest of the Mughals: he not only had military ability but was also a man of culture and a wise leader, skilfully integrating Hindus into his empire, using them as advisers, generals and administrators.

Akbar's son Jehangir (r 1605–27) kept his father's empire intact, despite challenges to his authority. His son Shah Jahan (r 1627–58) secured his position by executing all male relatives who stood in his way. He also built the Taj Mahal (the mausoleum of his wife Mumtaz Mahal) as well as the mighty Red Fort in Delhi, and converted Agra Fort into a palace that would later become his own prison.

The last of the great Mughals, Aurangzeb (r 1658–1707), imprisoned his father (Shah Jahan) and gained the throne after a two-year struggle against his brothers. Aurangzeb devoted his resources to extending the empire's boundaries, and thus fell into much the same trap as Mohammed Tughlaq three centuries earlier. He faced serious challenges

The Rajputs

Throughout the Mughal period, there remained strong Hindu powers, most notably the Rajputs, a proud warrior caste with a passionate belief in the dictates of chivalry, both in battle and state affairs. Hereditary rulers of many princedoms in Rajasthan, the Rajputs opposed every foreign incursion into their territory, but they were never united. When they weren't battling outside oppressors, they squandered their energies fighting one another. This eventually led to their territories becoming vassal states of the Mughal empire. Their prowess in battle, however, was acknowledged, and some of the best military men in the Mughal armies were Rajputs – among them Maharaja Man Singh, founder of the mighty Amber Fort near Jaipur, who was a leading general of emperor Akbar.

1601	**1631**	**1707**
Sir James Lancaster commands the maiden trading voyage of the British East India Company.	Construction of the Taj Mahal begins after Shah Jahan vows to build the world's most beautiful mausoleum for wife Mumtaz Mahal.	The death of Aurangzeb, the last great Mughal emperor, triggers the gradual collapse of the Mughal empire into rebellion and anarchy.

★ **Colonial-Era Architecture**

Colaba and Kala Ghoda, Mumbai (p128)

Old Goa (162) and Panaji (p170), Goa

Shimla, Himachal Pradesh

Mysuru Palace (p200), Mysuru (Mysore)

Mysuru Palace (p200), Mysuru

from the Hindu Marathas under their great leader Shivaji, in central India, and from the British in Bengal. Dissatisfaction among the Hindu population at taxes and religious intolerance also weakened the Mughal grip. After Aurangzeb's death, Delhi was sacked by Persia's Nadir Shah in 1739. Mughal 'emperors' continued to rule until the First War of Independence (Indian Uprising) in 1857, but they were emperors without an empire.

The Rise of European Power

During the 15th century, the Portuguese sought a sea route to the Far East so they could trade directly in spices. En route, they found lucrative trading opportunities on the Indian coast, when Vasco da Gama arrived on the Kerala coast in 1498, having sailed around Africa. In 1510, the Portuguese captured Goa and in its heyday, the trade flowing through 'Golden Goa' was said to rival that passing through Lisbon. The Portuguese enjoyed a century-long monopoly over Indian and Far Eastern trade with Europe, but they lacked the resources to maintain a worldwide empire, and were quickly eclipsed after the arrival of the British and French.

In 1600, Queen Elizabeth I granted a London trading company a monopoly on British trade with India. In 1613, the East India Company established its first trading post at Surat in Gujarat. Further posts governed by the company were established at Madras (Chennai) in 1639, Bombay (Mumbai) in 1661 and Calcutta (Kolkata) in 1690.

The French, who established themselves at Pondicherry (Puducherry) by 1672, vied with the British for control of Indian trade. At one stage, they appeared to hold the upper hand, even taking Madras in 1746. But they were outmanoeuvred by the British, and by the 1750s were no longer a serious influence on the subcontinent.

Britain's Surge to Power

Following the establishment of the British trading post at Calcutta in 1690, business expanded rapidly. Under the apprehensive gaze of the nawab (local ruler), the 'factories' took on an increasingly permanent (and fortified) appearance. In June 1756, the nawab

1757	1857	1858
Battle of Plassey: Robert Clive defeats nawab of Bengal in East India Company's first military victory in India.	The First War of Independence (Indian Uprising) against the British.	Power is officially transferred from the East India Company to the British Crown, beginning the period known as the British Raj.

attacked Calcutta and locked his British prisoners in a tiny cell. The space was so cramped and airless that many were dead by the following morning.

Six months later, Robert Clive, an employee in the military service of the East India Company, led an expedition to retake Calcutta and made an agreement with one of the nawab's generals to overthrow the nawab himself. He did this in June 1757, at the Battle of Plassey (now called Palashi). The company's agents embarked on a period of unbridled profiteering, and when a subsequent nawab was defeated at the Battle of Baksar in 1764, the British were confirmed as the paramount power in east India.

In 1771, Warren Hastings was made governor in Bengal. During his tenure, the company greatly expanded its control and concluded a series of treaties with local rulers in the power vacuum following the disintegration of the Mughal empire.

In the south, a local ruler, Hyder Ali, and his son Tipu Sultan, waged a brave and determined campaign against the British. But in the Fourth Mysore War (1789–99), Tipu Sultan was killed at Srirangapatnam, and British power took another step forward. The long-running struggle with the Marathas in central India was concluded a few years later.

By the early 19th century, India was effectively under British control, although there remained a patchwork of nominally independent 'princely states' governed by maharajas (or similarly titled princes) and nawabs. Trade and profit remained the main focus of British rule in India: iron and coal mining were developed, tea, coffee and cotton became key crops, and a start was made on the vast rail network that's still in use today. The Mughal-era zamindar (landowner) system was encouraged, further entrenching the growth of an impoverished, landless peasantry.

The First War of Independence (Indian Uprising)

In 1857, half a century after establishing firm control of India, the British suffered a serious setback. To this day, the causes of the Indian Uprising are the subject of debate. The key factors included the influx of cheap goods, such as textiles, from Britain that destroyed many livelihoods; the dispossession of territories from many rulers; and taxes on landowners.

The incident popularly held to have sparked the uprising took place at an army barracks in Meerut in Uttar Pradesh on 10 May 1857. A rumour leaked out that a new type of bullet was greased with what Hindus claimed was cow fat, while Muslims maintained that it came from pigs; pigs are considered unclean to Muslims, and cows are sacred to Hindus.

In Meerut, the commanding officer lined up his soldiers and ordered them to bite off the ends of their bullets. Those who refused were immediately marched off to prison. The following morning, the soldiers of the garrison rebelled, shot their officers and marched to Delhi. Of the 74 Indian battalions of the Bengal army, 47 mutinied. The soldiers and peasants rallied around the ageing Mughal emperor in Delhi. They held Delhi for some months and besieged the British residency in Lucknow for five months before they were finally suppressed.

1885	**1919**	**1940**
The Indian National Congress, a key player in the future freedom struggle, is set up.	Protesters massacred by British troops at Jallianwala Bagh, Amritsar. Gandhi responds with program of civil disobedience.	The Muslim League adopts its Lahore Resolution, championing greater Muslim autonomy.

Almost immediately, the East India Company was wound up and direct control of India was assumed by the British government.

The Road to Independence

Opposition to the British increased at the turn of the 20th century, spearheaded by the Indian National Congress, the country's oldest political party, which first met in 1885 and soon began to push for participation in government.

India contributed hugely to Britain's WWI war effort, with more than one million Indian volunteers enlisted and sent overseas, suffering more than 100,000 casualties. The contribution was sanctioned by Congress leaders, but no rewards for it resulted after the war, and disillusion followed. Disturbances were particularly persistent in Punjab, and in April 1919 a British army contingent was sent to quell the unrest in Amritsar, where it ruthlessly fired into a crowd of unarmed protesters at Jallianwala Bagh. News of the massacre quickly turned huge numbers of otherwise apolitical Indians into Congress supporters.

Mahatma Gandhi

One of the great figures of the 20th century, Mohandas Karamchand Gandhi was born in 1869 in Porbandar, Gujarat. After studying in London (1888–91), he worked as a barrister in South Africa, where he became politicised, railing against the discrimination he encountered.

Gandhi returned to India in 1915 with the doctrine of *ahimsa* – nonviolence – central to his political plans, and committed to a simple and disciplined lifestyle. Within a year, Gandhi had won his first victory, defending farmers in Bihar from exploitation. This was when it's said he first received the title 'Mahatma' (Great Soul).

Gandhi came to the forefront in the Congress movement after the Jallianwala Bagh massacre, coordinating a national campaign of *satyagraha* (nonviolent protest) against British rule. Not everyone involved in the struggle agreed with Gandhi's policy of nonviolence, yet the Congress Party and Gandhi remained at the forefront of the push for independence.

In early 1930, Gandhi captured the imagination of the country by leading a march of several thousand followers to Dandi on the Gujarat coast, where he ceremoniously made salt by evaporating sea water, thus publicly defying the much-hated salt tax. Released from jail in 1931 to represent the Indian National Congress at the second Round Table Conference in London, he won the hearts of many British people but failed to gain any real concessions from the government.

As political power-sharing began to look more likely, India's large Muslim minority realised that an independent India would be dominated by Hindus and that, while Gandhi's approach was fair-minded, others in the Congress Party might not be so willing to share power. By the 1930s Muslims were raising the possibility of a separate Islamic state.

Disillusioned with politics, Gandhi resigned his parliamentary seat in 1934. He returned spectacularly to the fray in 1942 with the Quit India campaign, urging the British to leave

1942	**1947**	**1947–48**
Mahatma Gandhi launches the Quit India campaign, demanding that the British leave India without delay.	India gains independence on 15 August, a day after Pakistan. Mass cross-border migration of Hindus and Muslims follows Partition.	First India-Pakistan War, after the maharaja of Kashmir signs the Instrument of Accession ceding his state to India.

India immediately. His actions were deemed subversive, and he and most of the Congress leadership were imprisoned.

In the frantic independence bargaining that followed the end of WWII, Gandhi stood almost alone in urging the preservation of a single India, and his work on behalf of all communities drew resentment from some Hindu hardliners. He was assassinated at Birla House in Delhi on 30 January 1948 by a Hindu zealot, Nathuram Godse.

The Persian Language

Persian was the official language of several Indian empires, from Mahmud of Ghazni to the Delhi Sultanate to the Mughals. Urdu, which combines Persian, Arabic and indigenous languages, evolved over hundreds of years and came into its own during Mughal times.

Independence & Partition

The Labour Party victory in the British elections in July 1945 dramatically altered the political landscape. For the first time, Indian independence was accepted as a legitimate goal. The two major Indian parties, however, had deeply divergent ideas of what form independence would take. Mohammed Ali Jinnah, the leader of the Muslim League, championed a separate Islamic state, while the Congress Party, led by Jawaharlal Nehru, campaigned for an independent greater India.

In early 1946, a British mission failed to bring the two sides together and the country slid closer towards civil war. In February 1947, the nervous British government made the momentous decision that Independence would come by June 1948. A new viceroy, Lord Louis Mountbatten, encouraged the rival factions to agree upon a united India, but to no avail. A decision was made to divide the country and, faced with increasing civil violence, Mountbatten made the precipitous decision to bring forward Independence to 15 August 1947.

Dividing the country into separate Hindu and Muslim territories was immensely tricky; some areas were clearly Hindu or Muslim, but others were evenly mixed, and there were 'islands' of communities in areas predominantly settled by other religions. An independent British referee was given the odious task of drawing the borders, well aware that the effects would be catastrophic for countless people. The problem was worst in Punjab, one of the most fertile and affluent regions of the country, which had large Muslim, Hindu and Sikh communities, with antagonisms already running at fever pitch. The Sikhs saw their homeland divided down the middle.

Huge population exchanges took place and the resulting bloodshed was even worse than anticipated. Trains full of Muslims, fleeing westward, were held up and slaughtered by Hindu and Sikh mobs. Hindus and Sikhs fleeing to the east suffered the same fate at Muslim hands. The army sent to maintain order proved totally inadequate. By the time the Punjab chaos had run its course, more than 10 million people had changed sides and at least 500,000 had been killed.

1948	1965	1966
Mahatma Gandhi is assassinated in New Delhi by Nathuram Godse, who is later convicted and hanged.	Skirmishes in Kashmir and the Rann of Kutch flare into the Second India-Pakistan War, with the biggest tank battles since WWII.	Indira Gandhi, daughter of Jawaharlal Nehru, becomes prime minister of India, remembered today for her heavy-handed rule.

India and Pakistan became sovereign nations in August 1947 as planned, but the violence and migrations continued and the integration of a few states, especially Kashmir, was yet to be completed. The Constitution of India went into effect on 26 January 1950, and, after untold struggles, independent India officially became a Republic.

Independent India

Jawaharlal Nehru tried to steer India towards a policy of nonalignment, balancing cordial relations with Britain with moves towards the USSR.

The 1960s and 1970s were tumultuous times for India. A border war with China resulted in the loss of parts of Aksai Chin (Ladakh) and smaller areas in the northeast. Wars with Pakistan in 1965 (over Kashmir) and 1971 (over Bangladesh) also contributed to a sense among many Indians of having enemies on all sides.

The hugely popular Nehru died in 1964 and his daughter Indira Gandhi (no relation to Mahatma Gandhi) was elected prime minister in 1966. Unlike Nehru, however, Indira Gandhi was always a profoundly controversial figure whose historical legacy remains hotly disputed.

In 1975, facing serious opposition and unrest, she declared a state of emergency (which later became known as the Emergency). Freed of parliamentary constraints, Gandhi was able to boost the economy, control inflation remarkably well and decisively increase efficiency. On the negative side, political opponents often found themselves in prison, India's judicial system was turned into a puppet theatre and the press was fettered.

Gandhi was bundled out of office in the 1977 elections, but the 1980 election brought her back to power with a larger majority than ever before, firmly laying the foundation for a family dynasty that would continue to dominate Indian politics for decades. Indira Gandhi was assassinated in 1984 by one of her Sikh bodyguards after her decision to attack the Golden Temple in Amritsar, which was being occupied by a fundamentalist Sikh preacher. Her son Rajiv took over and was subsequently killed in a suicide bomb attack in 1991. His widow, Sonia, later became president, with Manmohan Singh as prime minister. However, the Congress party lost popularity as the economy slowed, and has been accused of cronyism and corruption.

The 2014 federal elections saw the Congress party suffer a humiliating defeat under the shaky leadership of Rahul Gandhi, Indira's grandson. The BJP, headed by Narendra Modi, swept to power in a landslide victory, promising to shake up Indian politics and usher in a new era of neoliberal economics. Modi was formerly chief minister of Gujarat, which had been transformed into an economic powerhouse during his tenure. Some continue to ask questions about Modi's role in riots in Gujarat in 2002, which killed nearly 1000 people, mostly Muslims, but an official inquiry in 2014 cleared him of any wrong-doing. His forceful, charismatic style has made him hugely popular with business leaders and the BJP's Hindu-nationalist traditionalists, as well as with the ordinary man on the street, and as prime minister, Modi has thus far offered vision and hope, and a broadly inclusive agenda, focusing on the economic situation rather than religious rivalries.

1971	1984	2014
Third India-Pakistan War: India gets involved in the campaign of East Pakistan (now Bangladesh) for independence from West Pakistan.	Indira Gandhi orders assault on Sikh separatists occupying Amriitsar's Golden Temple; four months later, she is assassinated.	Narendra Modi, born into a Gujarati grocery family, achieves a historic landslide victory for the BJP, routing the Congress Party.

Street market, Varanasi (p227)

The Way of Life

*Spirituality and family lie at the heart of Indian society,
intertwining in ceremonies to celebrate auspicious
occasions and life's milestones. Despite a growing number
of nuclear families (primarily in the more cosmopolitan
cities such as Mumbai, Bengaluru and Delhi), the extended
family remains a cornerstone in both urban and rural
India, with men usually the main breadwinners and
generally considered household heads.*

Marriage, Birth & Death

For all Indian communities, marriage, birth and death are important and marked with ceremonies according to religion. Hindus are in the majority in India. Around 15% of the population is Muslim.

Marriage is an exceptionally auspicious event for Indians – for most Indians, the idea of being unmarried by their mid-30s is unpalatable. Although 'love marriages' have spiralled upwards in recent times (mainly in urban hubs), most Indian marriages are still arranged, be the family Hindu, Muslim, Sikh, Jain or Buddhist.

Dowry, although illegal, is still a key issue in many arranged marriages (mostly in conservative communities), with some families plunging into debt to raise the required cash and merchandise (from cars and computers to refrigerators and televisions). Health workers claim that India's high rate of abortion of female foetuses is predominantly due to the financial burden of providing a daughter's dowry. (Sex identification tests are banned in India, but they are still clandestinely carried out in some clinics.)

Divorce and remarriage is becoming more common (primarily in bigger cities), but divorce is still not granted by courts as a matter of routine and is not looked upon very favourably by society.

The birth of a child is another momentous occasion, with its own set of special ceremonies at various auspicious times during early childhood. For Hindus these include the casting of the child's first horoscope, name-giving, feeding the first solid food, and the first hair cutting.

Hindus and Sikhs cremate their dead, and funeral ceremonies are designed to purify and console both the living and the deceased. Muslims bury their dead.

The Caste System

Although the Indian constitution does not recognise the caste system, caste still wields considerable influence, especially in rural India, where the caste you are born into largely determines your social standing in the community. It can also influence your vocational and marriage prospects.

Traditionally, caste is the basic social structure of Hindu society. Living a righteous life and fulfilling your dharma (moral duty) raises your chances of being reborn into a higher caste and thus into better circumstances. Hindus are born into one of four varnas (castes): Brahmin (priests and scholars), Kshatriya (soldiers and administrators), Vaishya (merchants) and Shudra (labourers). Castes are further divided into thousands of *jati*, groups of 'families' or social communities, which are sometimes but not always linked to occupation.

Beneath the four main castes are the Dalits (formerly known as Untouchables), who hold menial jobs such as sweepers and latrine cleaners. To improve the Dalits' position, the government reserves a number of parliamentary seats and almost 25% of government jobs and university student places for them.

Women in India

According to the most recent census (2011), India's 586 million women accounted for some 48.5% of the total population, with an estimated 68% of those working (mostly as labourers) in the agricultural sector.

Women in India are entitled to vote and own property. Although the professions are male dominated, women are steadily making inroads. They still only account for around 11% of national parliamentary members, however.

Hijras

India's most visible non-heterosexual group is the *hijras,* a caste of transvestites and eunuchs who dress in women's clothing. Some are gay, some are hermaphrodites and some were unfortunate enough to have been kidnapped and castrated. *Hijras* have long had a place in Indian culture, and in 2014 the Indian Supreme Court recognised *hijras* as a third gender and as a class entitled to reservation in education and jobs. Conversely, in 2013, homosexuality was ruled to be unlawful. Section 377 of the Indian Penal Code, which harks back to 1861, makes homosexual sex legally punishable.

Hijras work mainly as uninvited entertainers at weddings and celebrations of the birth of male children. In 2014, Padmini Prakash became India's first transgender daily TV news-show anchor, indicating a new level of acceptance.

In low-income families, especially, girls can be regarded as a serious financial liability because at marriage a dowry might be demanded. Urban middle-class women are far more likely to receive a tertiary education, but once married they are still often expected to 'fit in' with their in-laws and be a homemaker above all else.

India remains a conservative society, and many traditionally minded people still consider that a woman is somehow wanton if she goes out after dark or does not dress modestly.

According to India's National Crime Records Bureau (NCRB), reported incidences of rape have gone up over 50% in the last 10 years, but it's believed that only a small percentage of sexual assaults are reported.

Following the highly publicised gang-rape and murder of a 23-year-old student in Delhi in 2012, tens of thousands of people protested in the capital and beyond. It took a year before laws were amended to address the problem of sexual assault, including harsher punishments such as life imprisonment and the death penalty. Despite this, sexual violence against women is still a major problem. In 2015 the NCRB reported that there were 34,651 cases of rape across India, a decline of 5.7% from 2014. The NCRB reported a slight increase of 2.5% in other sexual offences, with 84,222 cases in 2015 (up from 82,235 in 2014).

In a bid to address the sexual assault problem, the government has made it mandatory for all mobile phones sold in India from 2017 to have a panic button. In addition, there will be an increase in female police officers and the opening of centres for women victims of violence. Public awareness programs have also been launched. Although these moves are steps in the right direction, India still has a very long way to go.

Indian Attire

The elegant sari comes in a single piece (between 5m and 9m long and 1m wide) and is ingeniously tucked and pleated into place without pins or buttons. Worn with the sari are the choli (tight-fitting blouse) and a drawstring petticoat. Also common is the *salwar kameez*, a tunic-and-trouser combination accompanied by a dupatta (long scarf).

Traditional men's attire includes the dhoti (a long loincloth pulled up between the legs) and in the south, the sarong-like lungi and *mundu*. A kurta is a long, usually collarless, tunic or shirt; *churidar* are close-fitting trousers often worn under a kurta.

Sport

Cricket has long been engraved on the nation's heart, with the first recorded match in 1721, and India's first test-match victory in 1952 in Chennai against England. It's not only a national sporting obsession, but a matter of enormous patriotism, especially evident whenever India plays against Pakistan. Cricket – especially the Twenty20 format (www.cricket20.com) – is big business in India, attracting lucrative sponsorship deals and celebrity status for its players. International games are played at various centres – see Indian newspapers or check online (www.espncricinfo.com is excellent) for details about upcoming matches.

The launch of the Indian Super League (ISL; www.indiansuperleague.com) in 2013 has achieved its aim of promoting football as a big-time, big-money sport.

Some say it was the Mughal emperor Akbar who first introduced rules to the sport of polo, but that the sport as it's played today was largely influenced by a British cavalry regiment stationed in India during the 1870s. Today there's a renewed interest in polo and, although it remains an elite sport, it's attracting more attention from the country's burgeoning upper middle class. Polo is played during the cooler winter months in major cities, including Delhi, Jaipur and Mumbai.

Temple sculpture of Shiva

Hindu India

Hinduism, India's major faith, is practised by around 80% of the population. It has no central authority and is not a proselytising religion. Essentially, Hindus believe in Brahman, who is eternal, uncreated and infinite. Everything that exists emanates from Brahman and will ultimately return to Brahman. The multitude of gods and goddesses are merely manifestations – knowable aspects of this formless phenomenon.

Brahman

The One; the ultimate reality. Brahman is formless, eternal and the source of all existence. Brahman is *nirguna* (without attributes) and is often described as having three main representations, the Trimurti: Brahma, Vishnu and Shiva.

Brahma

Only during the creation of the universe does Brahma play an active role. At other times he is in meditation. India has few Brahma temples today. His consort is Saraswati, the goddess of learning, and his vehicle is a swan. Brahma is generally depicted with four (crowned and bearded) heads.

Vishnu

The preserver or sustainer, Vishnu is asso-ciated with 'right action'. He protects and sustains all that is good in the world. He is usually depicted with four arms, holding a lotus, a conch shell (which can be blown like a trumpet, so symbolises the cosmic vibration from which existence emanates), a discus and a mace. His consort is Laksh-mi, the goddess of wealth, and his vehicle is Garuda, the man-bird creature. The Ganges is said to flow from his feet.

> ### Fascinating Hindu Temples
> **Vittala Temple (p205), Hampi**
> **Kailasa Temple (p151), Ellora**
> **Vishwanath Temple (p234), Varanasi**
> **Hadimba Temple (p258), Manali**
> **Shiva Temple, Elephanta Island (p136), Mumbai**

Shiva

Shiva is the destroyer – to deliver salvation – without whom creation couldn't occur. Shiva's creative role is phallically symbolised as the frequently worshipped lingam. With 1008 names, Shiva takes many forms, including Nataraja, lord of the *tandava* (cosmic victory dance), who paces out the creation and destruction of the cosmos.

Sometimes Shiva has snakes draped around his neck and is shown holding a trident (representing the Trimurti) while riding Nandi, his bull. Nandi symbolises power and potency, justice and moral order. Shiva's consort, Parvati, is capable of taking many forms.

Other Prominent Deities

The Hindu pantheon is said to have a staggering 330 million deities. Elephant-headed Ga-nesh, son of Parvati and Shiva, is the god of good fortune, remover of obstacles, and patron of scribes (the broken tusk he holds was used to write sections of the Mahabharata). His animal vehicle is the ratlike Mooshak.

Krishna is an incarnation of Vishnu sent to earth to fight for good and combat evil. His dalliances with the gopis (milkmaids) and his love for Radha have inspired countless paintings and songs. Hero of the Mahabharata epic, Krishna is depicted with blue skin, and is often seen playing the flute.

Hanuman, king of the monkeys, is a hero of the Ramayana epic and loyal ally of its pro-tagonist Rama. He embodies the concept of bhakti (devotion).

Among Shaivites (followers of the Shiva movement), shakti, the divine creative power of women, is worshipped as a force in its own right. It is embodied in the ancient goddess Devi (divine mother), who is also manifested as Durga and, in a fiercer evil-destroying incarnation, Kali.

Reincarnation

Hindus believe that earthly life is cyclical: you are born again and again (a process known as samsara). Living a righteous life and fulfilling your dharma (moral code of behaviour; social duty) will enhance your chances of being reborn into a higher caste and better cir-cumstances. Alternatively, if enough bad karma has accumulated, rebirth may take animal form. But it's only as a human that you can gain sufficient self-knowledge to escape the cycle of reincarnation and achieve moksha (liberation).

Curries and *roti* (bread)

SANTHOSH VARGHESE/SHUTTERSTOCK ©

Delicious India

*From contemporary fusion dishes to traditional snacks,
it's the sheer variety that makes eating your way round
India so rewarding. India has an impressive array of
vegetarian food, but carnivores won't be disappointed either, with plenty on offer from hearty curries to
succulent tandoori platters. Adding flair to the national
smorgasbord are regional variations making the most of
local ingredients, be it native spices or fresh herbs.*

Land of Spices

Christopher Columbus was actually searching for the black pepper of Kerala's Malabar Coast when he stumbled upon America. The region still grows the finest quality of the world's favourite spice, and it's integral to most savoury Indian dishes.

Indian 'wet' dishes – commonly known as curries in the West – usually begin with the crackle of cumin seeds in hot oil and have turmeric as an essential spice, but coriander seeds are the most widely used spice and lend flavour and body to just about every dish.

Rice Paradise

Rice is a staple, especially in South India. Long-grain white rice varieties are the most popular, served hot with just about any 'wet' cooked dish. You'll find countless regional varieties that locals will claim to be the best in India, though this honour is usually conceded to basmati, a fragrant long-grain variety that's widely exported around the world. Rice is often accompanied by curd to enrich the mix, and is usually served after you have finished with the rotis (breads).

Flippin' Fantastic Bread

While rice is paramount in the south, wheat is the mainstay in the north. Roti is the generic term for Indian-style bread, and is also used interchangeably with chapati to describe the most common variety, an unleavened round bread made with whole-wheat flour and cooked on a *tawa* (hotplate). *Paratha* is a layered pan-fried flat bread, which may be stuffed, and makes for a hearty breakfast. *Puri* – puffy, fried bread pillows – are another popular sauce soaker-upper. Naan is a larger, thicker bread, baked in a tandoor and usually eaten with meaty sauces or kebabs.

Dhal-icious!

The whole of India is united in its love for dhal (curried lentils or pulses). You may encounter up to 60 different pulses: the most common are *channa* (chickpeas); tiny yellow or green ovals called *moong* (mung beans); salmon-coloured *masoor* (red lentils); the ochre-coloured southern favourite, *tuvar* (yellow lentils; also known as *arhar*); *rajma* (kidney beans); *urad* (black gram or lentils); and *lobhia* (black-eyed peas).

Meaty Matters

Although India probably has more vegetarians than the rest of the world combined, it still has an extensive repertoire of carnivorous fare. Chicken, lamb and mutton (which is sometimes actually goat) are the mainstays; religious taboos make beef forbidden to devout Hindus and pork to Muslims.

In northern India, you'll come across meat-dominated, spicy Mughlai cuisine, which includes rich curries, kebabs, koftas (meatballs) and biryanis, and traces its history back to the Mughal empire.

Tandoori meat dishes are another North Indian favourite. The name is derived from the clay oven, or tandoor, in which the marinated meat is cooked.

Deep-Sea Delights

Seafood is particularly prominent on the west coast, from Mumbai down to Kerala, which is the biggest fishing state. Goa boasts particularly succulent prawns and fiery fish curries, and the fishing communities of the Konkan Coast – between Goa and Mumbai – are renowned for their seafood recipes. Fish is also king in West Bengal, puddled with ponds and lakes.

Fruit & Veg

Sabzi (vegetables) is a word recognised in every Indian vernacular. They're generally cooked *sukhi* (dry) or *tari* (in a sauce).

Potatoes are ubiquitous and popularly cooked with various masalas (spice mixes) or other vegetables, or mashed and fried for the street snack *aloo tikki* (mashed-potato patties), or cooked with cauliflower to make *aloo gobi* (potato-and-cauliflower curry). Fresh green peas turn up stir-fried with other vegetables in pilaus and biryanis and in one of North India's signature dishes, *mattar paneer* (unfermented cheese and pea curry). Also popular is *saag* (a generic term for leafy greens), which can include mustard, spinach and fenugreek.

India's fruit basket is bountiful. Luscious tropical fruits such as pineapples and papayas abound along the southern coast. Peak mango season is April and May, with India offering more than 500 juicy varieties.

Vegetarians & Vegans

India is king when it comes to vegetarian fare. There's little understanding of veganism (the term 'pure vegetarian' means without eggs), and animal products such as milk, butter, ghee (clarified butter) and curd are included in most dishes. If you are vegan, your first problem is likely to be getting the cook to understand your requirements, though big hotels and larger cities are getting better at this. For further information, try Indian Vegan (www.indianvegan.com).

Dear Dairy

Milk and milk products make a staggering contribution to Indian cuisine: *dahi* (curd/yoghurt) is commonly served with meals and is great for subduing heat; paneer is a godsend for the vegetarian majority; lassi is one in a host of nourishing sweet and savoury beverages; ghee is the traditional and pure cooking medium.

Sweet at Heart

India has a colourful kaleidoscope of *mithai* (Indian sweets), often sticky and sinfully sugary. The main categories are *barfi* (a fudgelike milk-based sweet), soft *halwa* (made with vegetables, cereals, lentils, nuts or fruit), *ladoos* (sweet balls made with gram flour and semolina), and sweets made from *chhana* (unpressed paneer), such as *rasgullas*. An equally scrumptious offering is crunchy *jalebis* (coils of deep-fried batter dunked in sugar syrup; served hot).

Street Food

Tucking into street eats is a highlight of travelling in India. Whatever the time of day, vendors are frying, boiling, roasting, peeling, simmering or baking different foods to lure peckish passers-by. The fare can be as simple as peanuts roasted in hot sand, or a cavalcade of taste such as *chole bhature* (puffed bread served with spicy chickpeas and dipped in fragrant sauce).
To avoid tummy troubles:

- Avoid unclean-looking stalls or ones that locals are avoiding (places popular with families are probably your safest bets).

- Unless a place is reputable (and busy), it's best to avoid eating meat from the street.

- Don't be tempted by glistening pre-sliced fruit, whose luscious veneer comes from regular dousing of (often dubious) water.

Wall painting, City Palace (p106), Jaipur

Architecture & the Arts

India's magnificent artistic heritage is a reflection of its richly diverse ethnic groups and traditions. From the exquisite body art of mehndi *(henna) to the soulful chants in ancient temples and the vividly decorated trucks rumbling along dusty roads, the wealth of creative expression is a highlight of India travel. Many artists today fuse ancient and contemporary techniques to produce work that is as edgy as it is evocative.*

Music

Indian classical music traces its roots back to Vedic times, when religious poems chanted by priests were first collated in an anthology called the Rig-Veda. Over the millennia classical music has been shaped by many influences, and the legacy today divides into Carnatic (characteristic of South India) and Hindustani (the classical style of North India, influenced by Persian conventions from Mughal times) music. With common origins, they share a number of features. Both use the *raga* (the melodic shape of the music) and *tala* (the rhythmic meter characterised by the number of beats) as a basis for composition and improvisation; *tintal,* for example, has a *tala* of 16 beats. The audience follows the *tala* by clapping at the appropriate beat, which in *tintal* is at beats one, five and 13. There's no clap at the beat of nine; that's the *khali* (empty section), which is indicated by a wave of the hand.

Carnatic and Hindustani music are performed by small ensembles, generally of three to six musicians, and have many instruments in common. The most striking difference, at least for those unfamiliar with them, is Carnatic's greater use of voice.

Dance

The ancient Indian art of dance is traditionally linked to mythology and classical literature. Classical dance is based on well-defined traditional disciplines. Some classical styles:

o **Bharatanatyam** Originated in Tamil Nadu, and has been embraced throughout India.

o **Kathak** With Hindu and Islamic influences, Kathak suffered a period of notoriety when it moved from the courts into houses where *nautch* (dancing) girls tantalised audiences with renditions of the Krishna-and-Radha love story. It was restored as a serious art form in the 20th century.

o **Kathakali** Has its roots in Kerala; is essentially a kind of drama based on mythological subjects.

India folk dance ranges from the high-spirited bhangra of Punjab to the theatrical dummy-horse dances of Karnataka and Tamil Nadu.

Cinema

India's film industry is the biggest in the world – twice as big as Hollywood, with around 2000 feature films produced in the country annually. Mumbai (Bombay), the Hindi-language film capital, aka Bollywood, is the biggest, but India's other major film-producing cities – Chennai (Kollywood), Hyderabad (Tollywood) and Bengaluru (Sandalwood) – also have considerable output.

Mainstream 'masala' movies – named for their 'spice mix' of elements – are designed to have something for everyone, blending romance, action, slapstick humour and moral themes. They are often tear-jerkers, packed with dramatic twists and interspersed with numerous song-and-dance performances. Indian films made for the local market eschew explicit sex, and admit very little kissing; but lack of overt eroticism is often compensated for by heroines dressed in skimpy attire, and plenty of intense flirting and innuendo.

Some Indian art-house films, usually more socially and politically relevant than their commercial cousins, and made on infinitely smaller budgets, win kudos at global film festivals. In 2013 *Dabba* (Lunchbox), a non-Bollywood romantic comedy written and directed by Ritesh Batra, won the Grand Rail d'Or at Cannes International Critics' Week.

Painting

The Indo-Persian style – characterised by geometric design coupled with flowing form – arose in Islamic royal courts, with the Persian influence blossoming after artisans fled to India following the 1507 Uzbek attack on Herat (in present-day Afghanistan).

The development of the characteristic Mughal style of painting is generally credited to the third Mughal emperor, Akbar (r 1556–1605), who recruited artists from far and wide. Often in colourful miniature form, Mughal painting depicts court life, architecture, nature and battle and hunting scenes, and also embraced detailed portraits. As Mughal power and wealth declined, many artists moved to Rajasthan where the Rajasthani school of miniature painting developed from the late 17th century.

In the 21st century, paintings by modern Indian artists have been selling at record numbers (and prices) around the world. One very successful online art auction house is Saffronart (www.saffronart.com). The larger cities, especially Delhi and Mumbai, are India's contemporary art centres, with a range of galleries.

Literature

India has a long tradition of literature in Sanskrit (today used mainly as a ceremonial language in religious contexts) such as the Vedas, scriptures that began to be compiled over 3000 years ago, and the epic tales of the Ramayana, Mahabharata and the Puranas.

> ### Indian Instruments
>
> One of the best-known Indian instruments is the large, stringed sitar, with which the soloist plays the raga of classical music. Other stringed instruments include the sarod (which is plucked) and the *sarangi* (played with a bow). Also popular is the tabla (twin drums), which provides the *tala*. The drone, which runs on two basic notes, is provided by the oboelike *shehnai* or the stringed *tampura* (also spelt tamboura).

The writer mostly credited with first propelling India's cultural richness onto the world stage is the Nobel Prize winner Bengali Rabindranath Tagore (1861–1941), with works such as *Gitanjali* (Song Offerings), *Gora* (Fair-Faced) and *Ghare-Baire* (The Home and the World).

India has an ever-growing list of internationally acclaimed contemporary authors. Several India-born authors have won the prestigious Man Booker Prize, the most recent being Aravind Adiga, who won in 2008 for his debut novel, *The White Tiger*. The prize went to Kiran Desai in 2006 for *The Inheritance of Loss;* Kiran Desai's mother, novelist Anita Desai, has thrice been a Booker Prize nominee. Arundhati Roy won the 1997 Booker for *The God of Small Things,* while Salman Rushdie took this coveted award in 1981 for *Midnight's Children*.

Religious Architecture

For Hindus, the square is a perfect shape, and complex rules govern the location, design and building of each temple, based on numerology, astrology, astronomy and religious principles. Essentially, a temple represents a map of the universe. At the centre is an unadorned space, the *garbhagriha* (inner sanctum), providing a residence for the temple's deity and symbolising the 'womb-cave' of the universe's origin. Above a Hindu temple's shrine rises a tower superstructure – a stepped *vimana* in South India, a curvilinear *sikhara* in North India.

Jain temples can resemble Hindu ones from the outside, but inside they're often a riot of sculptural ornamentation, the very opposite of ascetic austerity.

Buddhist shrines have their own unique features. Stupas, composed of a solid hemisphere topped by a spire, essentially evolved from burial mounds. They served as repositories for relics of the Buddha and, later, other venerated souls. Some have a *chaitya* (assembly hall) leading up to the stupa itself.

India has a rich collection of Islamic sacred sites. The Mughals uniquely melded Persian, Indian and provincial styles. Renowned examples include Humayun's Tomb in Delhi, Agra Fort, and the ancient fortified city of Fatehpur Sikri. Emperor Shah Jahan was responsible for some of India's most spectacular architectural creations, most notably the Taj Mahal.

Indian roller

TEEKAYU/SHUTTERSTOCK ©

Landscape & Wildlife

At 3,287,263 sq km, India is the world's seventh largest country and encompasses everything from tropical jungles to arid deserts to icy mountain peaks. India is celebrated for its big, bold species – tigers, elephants, rhinos, leopards and bears. But there's much more, including a mesmerising collection of colourful birds and some of the world's most endangered and intriguing wildlife, such as the Ganges river dolphin and the Asiatic lion.

The Land

Three major features shape India's topography: the Himalaya, along the northern borders; the alluvial plains of the sacred River Ganges, across the north of the country; and the Deccan, an elevated plateau that forms the core of India's triangular southern peninsula.

The Big Beasts

Asian elephants are revered in Hindu custom and were able to be domesticated and put to work. Many still survive in the wild. Because they migrate long distances in search of food, these 3000kg animals require huge parks; some of the best for elephant viewing are Corbett Tiger Reserve in Uttarakhand and Nagarhole National Park in Karnataka.

There are far fewer one-horned rhinos left, and two-thirds of the world's total population can be found in Kaziranga National Park in Assam, where over 2000 wander the lush grasslands.

Then there's the tiger. This awesome, iconic animal is critically endangered but can be seen, if you're lucky, at tiger reserves around the country – your best chances are in Ranthambhore National Park (p116) and some tiger reserves in Madhya Pradesh, Maharashtra and Karnataka.

Other Mammals

Tigers apart, India is home to 14 other cat species. An estimated 12,000 to 14,000 leopards are scattered among forests throughout the country. Up to 750 highly elusive snow leopards (a separate species) inhabit Himalayan regions. The Asiatic lion, on the brink of extinction a century ago, now seems to be doing quite well in Gujarat's Sasan Gir National Park, with a population of over 500.

The most abundant animals you'll see in India are deer (nine species), antelope (six species), goats and sheep (10 species), and primates (15 species). In open grasslands look for the stocky nilgai, India's largest antelope, or elegantly horned blackbucks. The chital (spotted deer) is the most prolific deer in central India's high-profile tiger reserves.

India's primates range from the extremely rare hoolock gibbon and golden langur of the northeast to species that are so common as to be pests – most notably the stocky and aggressive rhesus macaque and the grey langur.

Project Tiger

When naturalist Jim Corbett first raised the alarm in the 1930s, no one believed that tigers would ever be threatened. It was believed there were 40,000 tigers in India. Then came Independence, which put guns into the hands of villagers who pushed into formerly off-limits hunting reserves seeking highly profitable tiger skins. When an official count was made in 1972, there were only 1800 tigers left, prompting Indira Gandhi to set up Project Tiger (National Tiger Conservation Authority; http://projecttiger.nic.in). It has since established 47 tiger reserves totalling over 68,676 sq km that protect not only this top predator but all animals sharing its habitat. Nevertheless, relentless poaching continued, causing tiger numbers to plummet from 3600 in 2002 to 1706 in 2011. Fortunately, the most recent tiger census results, from January 2015, show an encouraging rise in India's tiger population, to 2226.

Endangered Species

Wildlife is severely threatened by poaching and habitat loss. One report suggested India had more than 500 threatened species, including 53 species of mammals, 78 birds, 22 reptiles, 68 amphibians, 35 fish, 22 invertebrates and 247 plants.

All of India's wild cats face extinction from habitat loss and poaching for the lucrative trade in skins and body parts for Chinese medicine (a tiger carcass can fetch upwards of UK£32,000). Even highly protected rhinos are poached for the medicine trade – rhino horn is highly valued as an aphrodisiac in China and for making dagger handles in the Gulf.

Ivory poaching has reportedly been responsible for between 44% and 68% of all male elephant deaths in three Indian provinces; we implore you not to support this trade by buying ivory souvenirs.

Birds

With well over 1000 bird species, India is a birdwatcher's dream. Wherever critical habitat has been preserved in the midst of human activity, you might see phenomenal numbers

★ Parks & Reserves

Ranthambhore National Park, Rajasthan

Kaziranga National Park, Assam

Corbett Tiger Reserve, Uttarakhand

Bandhavgarh Tiger Reserve, Madhya Pradesh

Nagarhole National Park, Karnataka

Rhinoceros, Kaziranga National Park

of birds in one location. Winter can be a particularly good time, as wetlands throughout the country host northern migrants arriving for the lush subtropical warmth of the Indian peninsula. Throughout the year, wherever you're travelling, look for colourful kingfishers, barbets, sunbirds, parakeets and magpies, or the blue flash of an Indian roller.

Plants

India was once almost entirely covered in forest; now its forest cover is estimated to be around 22%. The country still boasts 49,219 plant species. Those on the southern peninsula show Malaysian ancestry, while desert plants in Rajasthan are more clearly allied with the Middle East, and the Himalayan conifer forests have European and Siberian origins.

Nearly all the lowland forests are types of tropical forest, with native sal forests forming the mainstay of the timber industry. Some tropical forests are true rainforest, staying green year-round, but most forests lose their canopies during the hot, dry months of April and May (often the best time to spot wildlife).

National Parks & Wildlife Sanctuaries

India has 166 national parks and 515 wildlife sanctuaries, adding up to around 5% of its territory. There are also 14 biosphere reserves, overlapping many of the national parks and sanctuaries, providing migration channels for wildlife and allowing scientists to monitor biodiversity.

Visiting a national park or sanctuary is an experience that can stay with you for a lifetime, especially if you come face-to-face with a wild elephant, rhino or tiger. Your visits also add momentum to efforts to protect India's natural environment. Wildlife reserves tend to be off the beaten track and infrastructure can be limited – book transport and accommodation in advance, and check opening times, permit requirements and entry fees before you visit.

Straddling the Future

India is grappling with a growing dilemma: how to modernise and expand economically without destroying what's left of its environment or adding to the global climate problem.

Prime Minister Modi has made it his personal mission to clean up the heavily polluted River Ganges, has launched the much-publicised Swachh Bharat campaign to reduce rubbish pollution, and supports large-scale solar-power generation. His government aims to increase renewable energy capacity to 175 gigawatts by around 2022. But it faces challenges when it comes to domestic coal mining (a major source of greenhouse gases). India is the world's third-largest producer of coal and production has risen in recent decades – but it is still not meeting the growing demand for electricity generation, making India increasingly reliant on imported coal.

Autorickshaws (p307), Mumbai

FILEDIMAGE/GETTY IMAGES ©

Survival Guide

DIRECTORY A–Z 290

Accommodation 290
Customs Regulations 291
Electricity 291
Food 291
Gay & Lesbian
Travellers 291
Health 291
Climate 292
Insurance 295

Internet Access 295
Legal Matters 296
Money 296
Opening Hours 298
Photography 298
Public Holidays 298
Safe Travel 298
Solo Travellers 300
Taxes & Refunds 300
Telephone 300
Time 301

Toilets 301
Travellers with
Disabilities 301
Visas 302
Weights & Measures 302
Women Travellers 302

TRANSPORT 305

Getting There & Away 305
Getting Around 305

Directory A–Z

Accommodation

Accommodation in India ranges from new-style hostels, with charging stations and soft pillows, to opulent palaces with private plunge pools, and from dodgy dives with bucket showers to guesthouses with superlative home cooking.

Prices are highest in large cities (eg Delhi, Mumbai), and lowest in rural areas. Costs are also seasonal – hotel prices can drop by 20% to 50% outside peak season.

Reservations

○ It's a good idea to book ahead, especially when travelling to more popular

---

Book Your Stay Online

For more accommodation reviews by Lonely Planet authors, check out http://hotels.lonely planet.com. You'll find independent reviews, as well as recommendations on the best places to stay. Best of all, you can book online.

---

destinations. Some hotels require a credit-card deposit at the time of booking.

○ Some places may want a deposit at check-in – ask for a receipt and be wary of any request to sign a blank impression of your credit card. If the hotel insists, pay cash.

○ Verify the check-out time when you check in.

Seasons

○ High season usually co-incides with the best weather for the area's sights and activities – normally March to May and September to November in the mountains, and around November to mid-February on the plains.

○ In areas popular with foreign tourists, there's an additional peak period over Christmas and New Year; make reservations well in advance.

○ At other times you may find significant discounts; if the hotel seems quiet, ask for one.

○ Some hotels in places like Goa close during the monsoon period, or in hill stations such as Manali during winter.

Budget & Midrange Hotels

○ Shared bathrooms (often with squat toilets) are usually only found at the cheapest lodgings.

○ If you're staying in budget places, bring your own sheet

---

or sleeping-bag liner, towel and soap.

○ Insect repellent, a torch (flashlight) and padlock are essential accessories in many budget hotels.

○ Sound pollution can be irksome (especially in urban hubs); pack earplugs and request a room that doesn't face a busy road.

Hostels

There is an ever-increasing array of excellent back-packer hostels across India, notably in Delhi, Varanasi, Goa and Kerala, all high quality, with air-con dorms, cafe/bar, lockers, and free wi-fi, which are hugely popular with travellers wanting to connect with like-minded folk.

They'll usually have mixed dorms, plus a female-only option. Impressive chains with branches dotted over India include **Stops** (www. gostops.com), **Backpacker Panda** (www.backpackerpanda. com), **Vedanta Wake Up!** (www.vedantawakeup.com), **Moustache** (http://www. moustachehostel.com) and **Zostel** (www.zostel.com).

Top-End & Heritage Hotels

India's top-end properties are stupendously fabulous, creating a cushioning bubble from the outside world, and ranging from wow-factor five-star chain hotels to historic palaces.

You can browse members of the Indian Heritage

Hotels Association on the tourist board website **Incredible India** (www.incredibleindia.org).

Customs Regulations

Technically you're supposed to declare Indian rupees in excess of ₹10,000, any amount of cash over US$5000, or total amount of currency over US$10,000 on arrival.

You're also prohibited from importing more than one laptop, 2L of alcohol, 100 cigarettes or equivalent, or gifts and souvenirs worth over ₹8000.

Electricity

Type D
230V/50Hz

Type C
230V/50Hz

Food

Price categories in this book reflect the cost of main dishes.

$ less than ₹150
$$ ₹150–300
$$$ more than ₹300

Gay & Lesbian Travellers

Homosexuality was made illegal in India in 2013, after having only been decriminalised since 2009. Trans rights have fared better: in 2014, there was a ruling that gave legal recognition of a third gender in India, a step towards increased acceptance of the large yet marginalised transgender (*hijra*) population.

LGBT visitors should be discreet in this conservative country. Public displays of affection are frowned upon for both homosexual and heterosexual couples.

Despite the ban, there are gay scenes (and Gay Pride marches) in a number of cities including Mumbai (Bombay), Delhi, Kolkata (Calcutta), Chennai (Madras) and Bengaluru (Bangalore), as well as a holiday gay scene in Goa.

Websites & Support Groups

Gay Bombay (www.gaybombay.org) Lists gay events as well as offering support and advice.

Indian Dost (www.indiandost.com/gay.php) News and information including contact groups in India.

Indja Pink (www.indjapink.co.in) India's first 'gay travel boutique' founded by a well-known Indian fashion designer.

Health

There is huge geographical variation in India, so in different areas, heat, cold and altitude can cause health problems. Hygiene is poor in most regions so food and water-borne illnesses are common. A number of insect-borne diseases are present, particularly in tropical areas. Medical care is basic in various areas (especially beyond the larger cities) so it's essential to be well prepared. Don't travel

Climate

Delhi

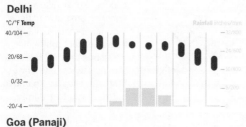

Goa (Panaji)

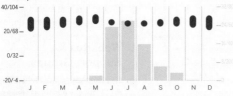

Manali

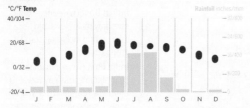

without health insurance (p295).

Fortunately, most travellers' illnesses can be prevented with some common-sense behaviour or treated with a well-stocked travellers' medical kit – however, never hesitate to consult a doctor while on the road, as self-diagnosis can be hazardous.

It's a good idea to consult your government's travel-health website before departure, if one is available:
Australia (www.smartraveller.gov.au)
Canada (www.travelhealth.gc.ca)
New Zealand (safetravel.govt.nz/health-and-travel)
UK (www.fco.gov.uk/en/travelling-and-living-overseas)
US (www.cdc.gov/travel)

Medical Care

Medical care is hugely variable in India. Some cities have clinics catering specifically to travellers and expatriates; these clinics are usually more expensive than local medical facilities, and offer a higher standard of care. Additionally, they know the local system, including reputable local hospitals and specialists. They may also liaise with insurance companies should you require evacuation. It is usually difficult to find reliable medical care in rural areas.

Self-treatment may be appropriate if your problem is minor (eg traveller's diarrhoea), you are carrying the relevant medication, and you cannot attend a recommended clinic. If you suspect a serious disease, especially malaria, travel to the nearest quality facility.

Before buying medication over the counter, check the use-by date, and ensure the packet is sealed and properly stored (eg not exposed to sunshine).

Drinking Water

○ Never drink tap water.

○ Bottled water is generally safe – check the seal is intact at purchase.

○ Avoid ice unless you know it has been made hygienically.

○ Boiling water is usually the most efficient method of purifying it.

Infectious Diseases

Malaria

This is a serious and potentially deadly disease. Before you travel, seek expert advice according to your itinerary (rural areas are especially risky) and on medication and side effects.

Malaria is caused by a parasite transmitted by the bite of an infected mosquito. The most important symptom of malaria is fever, but general symptoms, such as headache, diarrhoea, cough or chills, may also occur. Diagnosis can only be properly made by taking a blood sample.

Two strategies should be combined to prevent malaria: mosquito avoidance and antimalarial medications. Most people who catch malaria are taking inadequate or no antimalarial medication.

Travellers are advised to prevent mosquito bites by taking these steps:

○ Use a DEET-based insect repellent on exposed skin. Wash this off at night – as long as you are sleeping under a mosquito net. Natural repellents such as citronella can be effective, but must be applied more frequently than products containing DEET.

○ Choose accommodation with proper screens and fans (if not air-conditioned).

○ Wear long sleeves and trousers in light colours.

○ Use mosquito coils.

Other Diseases

Dengue Fever This mosquito-borne disease is becomingly increasingly problematic, especially in the cities. As there is no vaccine available it can only be prevented by avoiding mosquito bites at all times. Symptoms include high fever, severe headache and body ache and sometimes a rash and diarrhoea. Treatment is rest and paracetamol – do not take aspirin or ibuprofen as it increases the likelihood of haemorrhaging. Make sure you see a doctor to be diagnosed and monitored.

Hepatitis A This food- and water-borne virus infects the liver, causing jaundice (yellow skin and eyes), nausea and lethargy. There is no specific treatment for hepatitis A, you just need to allow time for the liver to heal. All travellers to India should be vaccinated against hepatitis A.

Hepatitis B This sexually transmitted disease is spread by body fluids and can be prevented by vaccination. The long-term consequences can include liver cancer and cirrhosis.

HIV Spread via contaminated body fluids. Avoid unsafe sex,

Vaccinations

The only vaccine required by international regulations is **yellow fever**. Proof of vaccination will only be required if you have visited a country in the yellow-fever zone within the six days prior to entering India.

The World Health Organization (WHO) recommends the following vaccinations for travellers going to India (as well as being up to date with measles, mumps and rubella vaccinations):

Adult diphtheria & tetanus Single booster recommended if none in the previous 10 years.

Hepatitis A Provides almost 100% protection for up to a year; a booster after 12 months provides at least another 20 years' protection.

Hepatitis B Now considered routine for most travellers. Given as three shots over six months. A rapid schedule is also available, as is a combined vaccination with hepatitis A. In 95% of people lifetime protection results.

Polio Only one booster is required as an adult for lifetime protection. Inactivated polio vaccine is safe during pregnancy.

Typhoid Recommended for all travellers to India, even those only visiting urban areas. The vaccine offers around 70% protection, lasts for two to three years and comes as a single shot. Tablets are also available.

Varicella If you haven't had chickenpox, discuss this vaccination with your doctor.

Immunisations recommended for long-term travellers (more than one month) or those at special risk include rabies (three injections in all; a booster after one year will then provide 10 years' protection). Seek further advice from your doctor.

unsterile needles (including in medical facilities) and procedures such as tattoos. The growth rate of HIV in India is one of the highest in the world.

Rabies This fatal disease is spread by the bite or possibly even the lick of an infected animal – most commonly a dog or monkey. You should seek medical advice immediately after any animal bite and commence postexposure treatment. If an animal bites you, gently wash the wound with soap and water, and apply iodine-based antiseptic. If you are not vaccinated you will need to receive rabies immunoglobulin as soon as possible, and this is very difficult to obtain in much of India.

Typhoid Serious bacterial infection spread via food and water. It gives a high and slowly progressive fever and headache, and may be accompanied by a dry cough and stomach pain. It is diagnosed by blood tests and treated with antibiotics. Vaccination is not 100% effective, so you must still be careful with what you eat and drink.

Travellers' Diarrhoea

This is by far the most common problem affecting travellers in India – between 30% and 70% of people will suffer from it within two weeks of starting their trip. It's usually caused by a bacteria, and thus responds promptly to treatment with antibiotics.

Travellers' diarrhoea is defined as the passage of more than three watery bowel actions within 24 hours, plus at least one other symptom, such as fever, cramps, nausea, vomiting or feeling generally unwell.

Treatment consists of staying well hydrated; rehydration solutions like Gastrolyte are the best for this. Antibiotics such as ciprofloxacin or azithromycin should kill the bacteria quickly. Seek medical attention quickly if you do not respond to an appropriate antibiotic.

Loperamide is just a 'stopper' and doesn't get to the cause of the problem. It can be helpful, though (eg if you have to go on a long bus ride). Don't take loperamide if you have a fever or blood in your stools.

Giardiasis Giardia is a parasite that is relatively common in travellers. Symptoms include nausea, bloating, excess gas, fatigue and intermittent diarrhoea. The parasite will eventually go away if left untreated but this can take months; the best advice is to seek medical treatment. The treatment of choice is tinidazole, with metronidazole being a second-line option.

Environmental Hazards

Food

Dining out brings with it the possibility of contracting diarrhoea. Ways to help avoid food-related illness:

- Eat only freshly cooked food.

- Avoid shellfish and buffets.

- Peel fruit.

- Eat in busy restaurants with a high turnover of customers.

Heat

Many parts of India, especially down south, are hot and humid throughout the year. For most visitors it takes around two weeks to comfortably adapt to the hot climate. Swelling of the feet and ankles is common, as are muscle cramps caused by excessive sweating. Prevent these by

Government Travel Advice

The following government websites offer travel advice and information on current hot spots.

Australian Department of Foreign Affairs (www.smarttraveller.gov.au)

British Foreign Office (www.gov.uk/fco)

Canadian Department of Foreign Affairs (www.voyage.gc.ca)

German Foreign Office (www.auswaertiges-amt.de)

Netherlands Ministry of Foreign Affairs (www.government.nl)

Swiss Department of Foreign Affairs (www.eda.admin.ch)

US State Department (http://travel.state.gov)

DIRECTORY A–Z SURVIVAL GUIDE **295**

avoiding dehydration and excessive activity in the heat. Drinking rehydration solution or eating salty food helps. Treat cramps by resting, rehydrating with double-strength rehydration solution and gently stretching.

Dehydration is the main contributor to heat exhaustion. Recovery is usually rapid and it is common to feel weak for some days afterwards. Symptoms include the following:

o feeling weak

o headache

o irritability

o nausea or vomiting

o sweaty skin

o a fast, weak pulse

o normal or slightly elevated body temperature.

Treatment:

o get out of the heat

o fan the sufferer

o apply cool, wet cloths to the skin

o lay the sufferer flat with their legs raised

o rehydrate with water containing one-quarter teaspoon of salt per litre.

Heat stroke is a serious medical emergency. Symptoms:

o weakness

o nausea

o a hot dry body

o temperature of over 41°C

o dizziness

o confusion

o loss of coordination

o seizures

o eventual collapse.

Treatment:

o get out of the heat

o fan the sufferer

o apply cool, wet cloths to the skin or ice to the body, especially to the groin and armpits.

Insurance

o Comprehensive travel insurance to cover theft, loss and medical problems (as well as air evacuation) is strongly recommended.

o Some policies exclude potentially dangerous activities such as scuba diving, skiing, motorcycling, paragliding and even trekking: read the fine print.

o Some trekking agents may only accept customers who have cover for emergency helicopter evacuation.

o If you plan to hire a motorcycle in India, make sure the rental policy includes at least third-party insurance.

o Check in advance whether your insurance policy will pay doctors and hospitals directly or reimburse you later (keep all documentation for your claim).

o It's crucial to get a police report in India if you've had

anything stolen; insurance companies may refuse to reimburse you without one.

o Worldwide travel insurance is available at www.lonelyplanet.com/bookings. You can buy, extend and claim online anytime – even if you're already on the road.

Internet Access

Wi-fi/3G/4G access is widely available; wi-fi is usually free but some places charge. Many restaurants and cafes offer wi-fi, including Cafe Coffee Day branches.

o The simplest way to connect to the internet, when wi-fi is unavailable, is to use your smartphone as a personal wi-fi hot spot (use a local SIM to avoid roaming charges).

o Alternatively, companies that offer prepaid wireless 3G/4G modem sticks (dongles) include Reliance, Airtel, Tata Docomo and Vodafone. To connect you have to submit your proof of identity and address in India; activation can take up to 24 hours. At Vodafone, for example, the dongle costs ₹1500 plus ₹549 for the SIM. A 20GB recharge costs around ₹1999. Portable wi-fi is also available via a pocket-size modem: the device costs ₹2399 plus ₹549 for the SIM with the same recharge fees.

Prohibited Exports

To protect India's cultural heritage, the export of certain antiques is prohibited, especially those which are verifiably more than 100 years old. Reputable antique dealers know the laws and can make arrangements for an export-clearance certificate for old items that are OK to export. Detailed information on prohibited items can be found on the Archaeological Survey of India (ASI) website (http://asi.nic.in).

The Indian Wildlife Protection Act bans any form of wildlife trade. Don't buy any product that endangers threatened species and habitats – doing so can result in heavy fines and even imprisonment. This includes ivory, shahtoosh shawls (made from the down of chirus or rare Tibetan antelopes) and anything made from the fur, skin, horns or shell of any endangered species. Products made from certain rare plants are also banned.

○ Make sure your destinations are covered by your service provider.

Legal Matters

If you're in a sticky legal situation, contact your embassy immediately. However, be aware that all your embassy may be able to do is monitor your treatment in custody and arrange a lawyer. In the Indian justice system, the burden of proof can often be on the accused and stints in prison before trial are not unheard of.

Drugs

Possession of any illegal drug is regarded as a criminal offence, which will result in a custodial sentence. This may be up to 10 years for possession, even for personal use, or up to 20 years

if it's deemed the purpose was for sale or distribution. There's also usually a hefty fine on top.

Police

You should always carry your passport; police are entitled to ask you for identification at any time.

If you're arrested for an alleged offence and asked for a bribe, be aware that it is illegal to pay a bribe in India. Many people deal with an on-the-spot fine by just paying it to avoid trumped-up charges.

Smoking

Smoking in public places is illegal but this is rarely enforced; if caught you'll be fined ₹200, which could rise to ₹1000 if proposed changes go ahead. People can smoke inside their homes and in most open spaces such as streets (heed any signs stating otherwise).

The status of e-cigarettes is in flux, but there are currently bans in Karnataka, and sale bans in Maharashtra and Punjab.

Money

There are ATMs in most towns; carry cash as backup.

ATMs

○ Visa, MasterCard, Cirrus, and Maestro are the most commonly accepted cards.

○ ATMs at Axis Bank, Citibank, HDFC, HSBC, ICICI and State Bank of India recognise foreign cards. Other banks may accept major cards (Visa, Mastercard etc).

○ The limit you may withdraw in one transaction can be as low as ₹2000, up to a maximum of usually ₹10,000. The higher the amount you withdraw, the less charges you will incur. Citibank ATMs are often the best for withdrawing a large amount of cash in one transaction.

○ Notify your bank that you'll be using your card in India to avoid having it blocked; take along your bank's phone number in case.

Bargaining

Bargaining is a way of life in many contexts in India, including at markets and most shops. As always, keep things in perspective: haggle hard but not without a sense of humour. There are also plenty of more upmarket shops and government emporiums where haggling is inappropriate, as prices are fixed. You'll also usually have to agree to a price before hiring a taxi or auto or, for longer trips, a car and driver.

Cash

○ Major currencies such as US dollars, pounds sterling and euros are easy to change throughout India.

○ Some banks also accept other currencies such as Australian and Canadian dollars and Swiss francs.

○ Private money-changers deal with a wider range of currencies.

○ When travelling off the beaten track, always carry an adequate stock of cash (including rupees).

○ It can be tough getting change, so a stock of smaller currency (₹10, ₹20 and ₹50 notes) is invaluable.

○ You can change leftover rupees into foreign currency most easily at the airport. You may have to present encashment certificates or credit-card/ATM receipts, and show your passport and airline ticket.

Credit Cards

○ Credit cards are accepted at a growing number of shops, upmarket restaurants, and midrange and top-end hotels, and they can

usually be used to pay for flights and train tickets.

○ Cash advances on major credit cards are possible at some banks.

○ MasterCard and Visa are the most widely accepted cards.

Currency

The Indian rupee (₹) is divided into 100 paise, but only 50 paise coins are legal tender and these are rarely seen. Coins come in denominations of ₹1, ₹2, ₹5 and ₹10 (the 1s and 2s look almost identical); notes come in ₹5, ₹10, ₹20, ₹50, ₹100, ₹500 and ₹2000.

On 8 November 2016 the Indian government made a shock announcement that the existing ₹500 and ₹1000 banknotes (86% of the currency in circulation) were to be withdrawn, a controversial measure to address the problems of black money, forgery and tax evasion. The notes have been replaced by a new, grey ₹500 bill, with the Red Fort on one side and Mahatma Gandhi on the other, and a pink ₹2000 note.

Money-changers

Private money-changers are usually open for longer hours than banks and are found almost everywhere (many also double as internet cafes or travel agents). Hotels may also change money, but their rates are usually not as competitive.

Tipping

○ A service fee is often added to your bill at restaurants and hotels, in which case tipping is optional. Elsewhere, a tip is appreciated.

○ Hotel bellboys and train/airport porters appreciate anything around ₹50; hotel staff should be given similar gratuities for services above and beyond the call of duty.

○ It's not mandatory to tip taxi or rickshaw drivers, but it's good to tip drivers who are honest about the fare.

○ If you hire a car with driver, a tip is recommended for good service.

Exchange Rates

Australia	A$1	₹51
Canada	C$1	₹51
Euro zone	€1	₹73
Japan	¥100	₹61
New Zealand	NZ$1	₹48
UK	UK£1	₹85
US	US$1	₹69

For current exchange rates see www.xe.com

Opening Hours

Banks (nationalised) 10am to 2pm or 4pm Monday to Friday, to noon, 1pm or 4pm Saturday; closed second and fourth Saturday of month.

Restaurants 8am to 10pm, or lunch noon to 3pm, dinner 7pm to 10pm or 11pm.

Bars & Clubs Noon to 12.30am.

Shops 10am to 7pm or 8pm, some closed Sunday.

Markets 10am to 7pm in major cities, usually with one closed day; rural markets may be once weekly, from early morning to lunchtime.

Post Offices 9.30am to 5pm Monday to Saturday.

Photography

Memory cards for digital cameras are available in most large cities and towns. However, quality is variable – some don't carry the advertised amount of data. Expect to pay upwards of ₹700 for a 32GB card.

○ India is touchy about anyone taking photographs of military installations – this can include train stations, bridges, airports, military sites and sensitive border regions.

○ Many places of worship – such as monasteries, temples and mosques – prohibit photography. Taking photos inside a shrine, at a funeral, at a religious ceremony or of people publicly bathing (including rivers) can be offensive – ask first.

○ Exercise sensitivity when taking photos of people, especially women, who may find it offensive – obtain permission in advance.

○ It is not uncommon for people in touristy areas to ask for a posing fee in return for being photographed. Exercise your discretion in these situations. Ask first to avoid misunderstandings later.

Public Holidays

There are three official national public holidays – Republic and Independence Days and Gandhi's birthday (Gandhi Jayanti) – plus a lot of other holidays celebrated nationally or locally, many of them marking important days in various religions and falling on variable dates. The most important are the 'gazetted holidays' (listed) which are observed by central-government offices throughout India. On these days most businesses (offices, shops etc), banks and tourist sites close, but transport is usually unaffected. It's wise to make transport and hotel reservations well in advance if you intend visiting during major festivals.

Republic Day 26 January
Holi February/March
Ram Navami March/April
Mahavir Jayanti March/April
Good Friday March/April
Dr BL Ambedkar's Birthday 14 April
Mahavir Jayanti March/April
Buddha Purnima May
Eid al-Fitr May/June
Independence Day 15 August
Janmastami August/September
Eid al-Adha July/August
Dussehra September/October
Gandhi Jayanti 2 October
Muharram August/September
Diwali October/November
Guru Nanak Jayanti November
Eid-Milad-un-Nabi November/December
Christmas Day 25 December

Major Religious Festivals

Holi (Hindu) February/March
Easter (Christian) March/April
Mahavir Jayanti (Jain) March/April
Buddha Purnima May
Eid al-Fitr (Muslim) May/June
Dussehra (Hindu) October
Diwali (Hindu) October/November
Nanak Jayanti (Sikh) November
Christmas (Christian) 25 December

Safe Travel

Travellers to India's major cities may fall prey to opportunistic crime, but many problems can be avoided with a bit of common sense and appropriate caution. Reports of sexual assaults have increased in recent years, so women should take care to avoid potentially risky situations (p302).

Have a look at the India branch of Lonely Planet's Thorn Tree forum (www.lonelyplanet.com/thorntree), where travellers often post warnings about problems they've encountered on the road. Always check your government's travel advisory warnings.

Keeping Safe

○ A good travel-insurance policy is essential.

○ Email copies of your passport identity page, visa and airline tickets to yourself, and keep copies on you.

○ Keep your money and passport in a concealed money belt or a secure place under your shirt.

○ Store at least US$100 separately from your main stash.

○ Don't publicly display large wads of cash.

Scams

Credit-Card Con

Some private (as opposed to government-run) souvenir shops have been known to surreptitiously run off extra copies of the credit-card imprint slip and use them for phoney transactions later. Ask the trader to process the transaction in front of you. Memorising the CVV/CVC2 number and scratching it off the card is also a good idea, to avoid misuse. In some restaurants, waiters

will ask you for your PIN with the intention of taking your credit card to the machine – never give your PIN to anyone, and ask to use the machine in person.

Druggings

Be extremely wary of accepting food or drink from strangers, even if you feel you're being rude. Women should be particularly circumspect.

Occasionally, tourists (especially those travelling solo) have been drugged and robbed or apparently attacked. A spiked drink is the most commonly used method for sending them off to sleep – chocolates, chai from a co-conspiring vendor, 'homemade' Indian food and even bottled water are also known to be used.

Touts & Commission Agents

○ Cabbies and autorickshaw drivers will often try to coerce you to stay at a hotel of their choice, to collect a commission (included within your room tariff) afterwards.

○ Wherever possible, prearrange hotel bookings (if only for the first night), and request a hotel pick-up. You'll often hear stories about hotels of your choice being 'full' or 'closed' – check things out yourself.

○ Avoid friendly people and 'officials' in train and bus stations who offer unsolicited help, then guide you to a commission-paying travel agent. Look confident, and if anyone asks if this is your first trip to India, say you've been here several times.

Transport Scams

○ Upon arriving at train stations and airports, if you haven't prearranged a pick-up, call an Uber or go to the radio cab, prepaid taxi or airport shuttle bus counters. Never choose a

Etiquette

Dress modestly Avoid offence by avoiding tight, sheer or skimpy clothes.

Shoes It's polite to remove shoes before entering homes and places of worship.

Photos Best to ask before snapping people, sacred sites or ceremonies.

Bad vibes Avoid pointing soles of feet towards people or deities, or touching anyone with your feet.

Hello Saying 'namaste' with hands together in a prayer gesture is a respectful Hindu greeting; for Muslims say 'salaam alaikum' ('peace be with you'; response: 'alaikum salaam').

Pure touch The right hand is for eating and shaking hands, the left is the 'toilet' hand.

loitering cabbie who offers you a cheap ride into town, especially at night.

● When buying a bus, train or plane ticket anywhere other than the registered office of the transport company, make sure you're getting the ticket class you paid for. Use official online booking facilities where possible.

● Train station touts (even in uniform or with 'official' badges) may tell you that your intended train is cancelled/flooded/broken down or that your ticket is invalid or that you must pay to have your e-ticket validated on the platform. Do not respond to any approaches at train stations.

Theft

● Keep luggage locked and chained on buses and trains. Remember that snatchings often occur when a train is pulling out of the station, as it's too late for you to give chase.

● Remember to lock your door at night; it is not unknown for thieves to take things from hotel rooms while occupants are sleeping.

Solo Travellers

Travelling solo in India may be great, because local people are often so friendly, helpful and interested. It's a great opportunity to make friends

and get a deeper understanding of local culture. If you're keen to hook up with fellow travellers, tourist hubs such as Delhi, Goa, Rajasthan, Kerala, Manali, McLeod Ganj, Agra and Varanasi are popular places to do so.

The most significant issue facing solo travellers is cost: single-room accommodation rates are sometimes not much lower than double rates, and some midrange and top-end places don't offer a single tariff at all. You'll save money if you find others to share taxis and autorickshaws, as well as when hiring a car for longer trips.

Safety

● Some less honourable souls (locals and travellers alike) view lone tourists as an easy target for theft and sexual assault.

● Single men wandering around isolated areas have been mugged, even during the day.

Taxes & Refunds

You'll find several different taxes added to your restaurant bill, though only if eating in an air-conditioned eatery. First is the service tax of 14%. The Krishi Kalyan Cess and Swachh Bharat Cess are also levied, at rates of 0.5%, to collect funds for development of the agriculture (krishi) industry and Clean India initiatives respectively.

Restaurants also charge VAT on the food bill; rates vary from state to state, but it's usually around 12.5%. VAT on alcohol is higher, for example, in Delhi it's 20%.

A luxury tax of not over 15% is added to hotel prices above around ₹1000, and a tax on spa services of 3%.

Many upmarket hotels also add an additional 'service tax' (usually around 10%).

Goa is currently the only place where tourists can reclaim VAT on luxury items bought in the region; make your claim, with supporting receipts, at the airport.

Telephone

STD/ISD/PCO call booths, found around the country, offer inexpensive local, interstate and international calls at lower prices than calls made from hotel rooms.

Mobile Phones

Roaming connections are excellent in urban areas, poor in the countryside. To avoid expensive roaming costs (often highest for incoming calls), get hooked up to the local mobile-phone network by applying for a local prepaid SIM card at a phone shop, local STD/ISD/PCO booth or grocery store; this involves some straightforward paperwork and sometimes a wait of up to 24 hours for activation. Mobiles bought in some countries may be locked to a particular network; you'll have to get them unlocked or buy a local phone (available from ₹2000) to use an Indian SIM card.

The leading service providers are Airtel, Vodafone, Reliance, Idea and BSNL. Coverage varies from region to region. It's best to buy your SIM from an official Airtel, Vodafone, etc, shop and check it has been properly activated before you leave the area where you bought it.

Indian mobile numbers usually have 10 digits, mostly beginning with 9 (but sometimes with 7 or 8). To make interstate calls to a mobile phone, add 0 before the 10-digit number.

Charges

○ Calls made within the state or city where you bought the SIM card may be around ₹0.10 a minute. You can call internationally for less than ₹10 a minute.

○ International outgoing SMS messages cost ₹5. Incoming calls and messages are free.

○ Unreliable signals and problems with international texting (messages or replies not coming through

or being delayed) are not uncommon.

○ A SIM card or ISD (international subscriber dialling) package is usually only valid for a particular region, and once you leave it, it may function but you'll pay roaming charges, however, these are not particularly steep (eg ₹1 per minute within India rather than ₹0.10). There are no roaming charges for internet data packs.

Time

Indian Standard Time (GMT/UTC plus 5½ hours).

Toilets

Public toilets are most easily found in major cities and tourist sites; the cleanest (usually with sit-down and squat choices) are often at modern restaurants, shopping complexes and cinemas.

Beyond urban centres, toilets are of the squat variety and locals may use the

'hand-and-water' technique, which involves carrying out ablutions with a small jug of water and the left hand. It's always a good idea to carry your own toilet paper and hand sanitiser, just in case.

Travellers with Disabilities

If you have a physical disability or are vision-impaired, the difficulties of travel in India can be exacerbated. If your mobility is considerably restricted, you may like to ease the stress by travelling with an able-bodied companion. One way that India makes it easier to travel with a disability is the access to employed assistance – you could hire an assistant, or a car and driver to get around, for example.

Accommodation
Wheelchair-friendly hotels are almost exclusively top-end. Make enquiries before travelling and book ground-floor rooms at hotels that lack adequate facilities.

Accessibility Some restaurants and offices have ramps but most tend to have at least one step. Staircases are often steep; lifts frequently stop at mezzanines between floors.

Footpaths Where pavements exist, they can be riddled with holes, littered with debris and crowded. If using crutches, bring along spare rubber caps.

Transport Hiring a car with driver will make moving around a lot easier; if you use a wheelchair, make sure the

Emergency & Important Numbers

To call India from another country, dial your international access code, India's country code (☏91), then the number (minus the initial '0'). For mobile numbers, the area code and initial zero are not required.

Country code	☏91
International access code	☏00
Emergency (Ambulance/Fire/Police)	☏112

car-hire company can provide an appropriate vehicle.

The following organisations may proffer further information:

Accessible Journeys (www.disabilitytravel.com)

Access-Able Travel Source (www.access-able.com)

Enable Holidays (www.enableholidays.com)

Global Access News (www.globalaccessnews.com)

Mobility International USA (www.miusa.org)

Download Lonely Planet's free Accessible Travel guide from http://lptravel.to/AccessibleTravel.

Visas

To enter India you need a valid passport and an onward/return ticket, and a visa. Your passport needs to be valid for at least six months beyond your intended stay in India, with at least two blank pages.

Everyone needs to apply for a visa before arriving in India except for citizens of Nepal, Bhutan and Maldives (Nepali citizens are, however, required to get a visa if they enter via China). Over 100 nationalities can obtain a 30-day e-Tourist visa/Visa on Arrival, applying online prior to arrival; this is valid from the day you arrive. For longer trips, you'll need to obtain a six-month tourist visa, which will be valid from

the date of issue, not the date of arrival in India.

Visas are available at Indian missions worldwide, though in many countries, applications are processed by a separate private company.

o Student and business visas have strict conditions (consult the Indian embassy for details).

o A standard 180-day tourist visa permits multiple entry for most nationalities.

o Five- and 10-year tourist visas are available to US citizens *only*, under a bilateral arrangement; however, you can still only stay in the country for up to 180 days continuously.

o An onward travel ticket is a requirement for some visas, but this isn't always enforced (check in advance).

o Check with the Indian embassy in your home country for any special conditions that may exist for your nationality.

Visa on Arrival (VOA)

Citizens from over 100 countries, from Albania to Zimbabwe, can apply for a 30-day e-Tourist visa online at http://indianvisaonline.gov.in, a minimum of four and a maximum of 30 days before they are due to travel.

The fee is US$60, and it's necessary to upload a photograph as well as a copy of your passport, have at least six months' validity in your passport, and at least two pages blank. The facility

is available at 16 airports, including Delhi, Mumbai, Bengaluru, Chennai, Kochi (Cochin), Goa, Hyderabad, Kolkata and Trivandrum airports, though you can exit through any airport. You should also have a return or onward ticket, though proof of this is not usually requested.

If your application is approved, you will receive an attachment to an email, which you'll need to print out and take with you to the airport. You'll then have the e-Tourist visa stamped into your passport at the airport, hence the term 'Visa on Arrival', though you need to apply for it beforehand. It is valid from the date of arrival.

Weights & Measures

Officially India is metric. Terms you're likely to hear are lakhs (one lakh is 100,000) and crores (one crore is 10 million).

Women Travellers

Reports of sexual assaults against women and girls are on the increase in India, despite tougher punishments being established following the notorious gang rape and murder of a local woman in 2012. There have been several instances of sexual attacks on tourists over the last few years, though the vast majority of visits are trouble free.

Clothing

Although in upper/middle-class Delhi, Mumbai and Chennai you'll see local women dressing as they might in New York or London, elsewhere women are dressed traditionally. For travellers, culturally appropriate clothing will help reduce undesirable attention.

● Steer clear of sleeveless tops, shorts, short skirts (ankle-length skirts are recommended) and anything else that's skimpy, see-through, tight-fitting, or reveals too much skin.

● Wearing Indian-style clothes is viewed favourably.

● Draping a dupatta (long scarf) over T-shirts is another good way to avoid stares – it's also handy if you visit a shrine that requires your head to be covered.

● Wearing a *salwar kameez* (traditional dresslike tunic and trousers) will help you blend in; a smart alternative is a kurta (long shirt) worn over jeans or trousers.

● Avoid going out in public wearing a choli (sari blouse) or a sari petticoat (which some foreign women mistake for a skirt); it's like being half-dressed.

● Except at pools, many Indian women wear long shorts and a T-shirt when swimming in public view; it's wise to wear a sarong from the beach to your hotel.

Health & Hygiene

● Sanitary pads are widely available but tampons are usually restricted to pharmacies in some big cities and tourist towns. Carry additional stock for travel off the beaten track.

Sexual Harassment

Many female travellers have reported sexual harassment while in India, most commonly lewd comments and groping.

● Women travellers have experienced provocative gestures, jeering, getting 'accidentally' bumped into on the street and being followed.

● Incidents are particularly common at exuberant (and crowded) public events such as the Holi festival.

● Women travelling with a male partner will receive less hassle; but you should still be careful to avoid crowds or lonely places, even during daylight hours.

Staying Safe

The following tips will help you avoid uncomfortable or dangerous situations during your journey.

● Always be aware of your surroundings. If it feels wrong, trust your instincts. Tread with care. Don't be scared, but don't be reckless either.

● Don't accept any drinks, even bottled water, from strangers. Don't drink or eat with local men that you don't know: there have been several cases where tourist guides or hotel employees have allegedly drugged foreign women by offering them a drink or food.

● Try always to have a plan of where you're going and what's next. If you haven't a clue, look as if you do.

● After a time of being in the country, you may start to feel safer and relax your guard. Don't stress, but maintain your vigilance.

● Keep conversations with unknown men short – getting involved in an inane conversation with someone you barely know can be misinterpreted.

● If you feel that a guy is encroaching on your space, he probably is. A firm request to keep away may well do the trick, especially if your tone is loud and curt enough to draw the attention of passers-by.

● Follow local women's cues and instead of shaking hands say *namaste* – the traditional, respectful Hindu greeting.

● Avoid wearing expensive-looking jewellery and carrying flashy accessories.

● Only go for massage or other treatments with female therapists.

● At hotels, keep your door locked, as staff could knock and walk in without waiting for your permission.

● Don't let anyone you don't know or have just met into your hotel room, even if they work for the tourist company you're travelling with and claim it's to discuss an aspect of your trip.

○ Avoid wandering alone in isolated areas, even during daylight. Steer clear of *gallis* (narrow lanes), deserted roads, beaches, ruins and forests.

○ In larger towns, smart-phone users can download a map so you can track where you are – this way it's easier to avoid getting lost and you can tell if a taxi/rickshaw is taking the wrong road.

○ Act confidently in public; to avoid looking lost (and thus more vulnerable) consult maps at your hotel (or at a restaurant) rather than on the street.

Transport

Women can usually queue-jump for buses and trains without consequence and on trains there are special ladies-only carriages. There are also women-only waiting rooms at some stations.

Taxi & Autorickshaw

○ Prearrange an airport pick-up from your hotel. This is essential if your flight is arriving after dark.

○ If travelling after dark, use a recommended, registered taxi service.

○ Never hail a taxi in the street or accept a lift from a stranger.

○ Avoid taking taxis alone late at night and never agree to have more than one man (the driver) in the car –

ignore claims that this is 'just my brother' etc.

○ Delhi and some other cities have licensed prepaid radio cab services such as Easycabs – they're more expensive than the regular prepaid taxis, but promote themselves as being safe, with drivers who have been vetted as part of their recruitment.

○ Uber and Ola Taxis are also useful, as the rates are fixed and you get the driver's license plate in advance so you can check it's definitely the right taxi and pass details on to someone else if you want to be on the safe side.

○ When taking rickshaws alone, call/text someone, or pretend to, to indicate someone knows where you are.

Bus & Train

○ Don't organise your travel in such a way that means you're hanging out at bus/train stations or arriving late at night, or even after dark.

○ Avoid empty rail carriages.

○ Solo women have reported less hassle by opting for the more expensive classes on trains.

○ If you're travelling overnight by train, the best option is the upper outer berth in 2AC; you're out of the way of wandering hands, but surrounded by plenty of other people and not locked in a four-person 1AC room (which might only have one other person in it).

○ On public transport, don't hesitate to return any errant limbs, put an item of luggage between you and others, be vocal (attracting public attention), or simply find a new spot.

Unwanted Attention

○ Be prepared to be stared at; it's something you'll simply have to live with, so don't allow it to get the better of you.

○ Increased use of smart-phones means more and more people taking surreptitious photos of you – again, try not to let it get to you.

○ Refrain from returning male stares; this will be considered encouragement.

○ Dark glasses, phones, books or electronic tablets are useful props for averting unwanted conversations.

○ Wearing a wedding ring and saying you're married, and due to meet your husband shortly, is another way to ward off unwanted interest.

Websites

Peruse personal experiences from fellow female travellers at www.journey woman.com and www. wanderlustandlipstick.com. Blogs such as Breathe, Dream, Go (breathedream go.com/) and Hippie in Heels (hippie-inheels.com/) are also full of tips.

Transport

Getting There & Away

Air

India is well served by international airlines. The six main gateways for international flights are the following:

Bengaluru (☎1800 4254425; www.bengaluruairport.com)

Chennai (☎044-22560551; Tirusulam)

Delhi (☎01243376000; www.newdelhiairport.in)

Hyderabad (☎040-66546370; http://hyderabad.aero; Shamshabad)

Kolkata (NSCBIA (CCU); ☎033-25118036)

Mumbai (☎022-66851010; www.csia.in)

International carriers also serve other destinations such as Goa, Kochi and Thiruvananthapuram (Trivandrum).

India's national carrier is **Air India** (☎1800-1801407; www.airindia.com), which operates international and domestic flights. Air travel in India has had a relatively decent safety record in recent years.

Land

Although most visitors fly into India, it is possible to travel overland between India and Bangladesh, Bhutan, Nepal, Pakistan and Myanmar. If you enter India by land, you must have a valid Indian visa in advance, as no visas are available at the border. Check routes, rules and regulations carefully before travelling. Lonely Planet's Thorntree forum (www.lonelyplanet.com/thorntree) is helpful.

Getting Around

Transport in India is frequent and inexpensive, though prone to overcrowding and delays. Trains, buses and shared jeeps run almost everywhere. To save time, consider domestic flights over long-distance buses and trains. Urban transport is cheap and frequent, and you'll never struggle to find a taxi or autorickshaw.

Air

Transporting vast numbers of passengers annually, India has a very competitive domestic airline industry. Major carriers include Air India, IndiGo, SpiceJet and Jet Airways.

Apart from airline sites, bookings can be made through portals such as **Cleartrip** (www.cleartrip.com), **Make My Trip** (www.makemytrip.com) and **Yatra** (www.yatra.com).

Security norms require you to produce your ticket and passport when entering an airport. Every item of cabin baggage needs a label, which must be stamped as part of the security check (collect tags at the check-in counter).

The recommended check-in time for domestic flights is two hours before departure – the deadline is 45 minutes. The usual economy-class baggage allowance is 20kg (10kg for smaller aircraft).

Bus

Buses go almost everywhere in India and are the only way to get around many mountainous areas. They tend to be the cheapest way to travel. Services are fast and frequent.

Roads in mountainous or curvy terrain can be perilous; buses are often driven with wilful abandon, and accidents are always a risk.

Avoid night buses unless there's no alternative: driving conditions are more hazardous and drivers may be inebriated or overtired.

Classes

State-owned and private bus companies both offer several types of buses, graded loosely as 'ordinary', 'semi-deluxe', 'deluxe' or 'super deluxe'. These are usually open to interpretation, and the exact grade of luxury offered in a particular class varies.

Ordinary buses tend to be ageing rattletraps while

Climate Change & Travel

Every form of transport that relies on carbon-based fuel generates CO_2, the main cause of human-induced climate change. Modern travel is dependent on aeroplanes, which might use less fuel per kilometre per person than most cars but travel much greater distances. The altitude at which aircraft emit gases (including CO_2) and particles also contributes to their climate change impact. Many websites offer 'carbon calculators' that allow people to estimate the carbon emissions generated by their journey and, for those who wish to do so, to offset the impact of the greenhouse gases emitted with contributions to portfolios of climate-friendly initiatives throughout the world. Lonely Planet offsets the carbon footprint of all staff and author travel.

the deluxe grades range from less decrepit versions of ordinary buses to flashy Volvo buses with air-con and reclining seating.

Travel agencies in many tourist towns offer relatively expensive private two-by-two buses, which tend to leave and terminate at conveniently central stops.

On any bus, try to sit up-front to minimise the bumpy effect of potholes. Never sit directly above the wheels.

Luggage

Luggage is stored in compartments underneath the bus (sometimes for a small fee) or carried on the roof.

Arrive at least an hour before departure time – some buses cover roof-stored bags with a canvas sheet, making last-minute additions inconvenient/impossible.

If your bags go on the roof, make sure they're securely locked, and tied to the metal baggage rack.

Theft is a (minor) risk: watch your bags at snack and toilet stops.

Reservations

Most deluxe buses can be booked in advance at the bus station, travel agencies, and online at the portals **Cleartrip** (www.cleartrip.com), **Makemytrip** (www.makemytrip.com), and **Redbus** (www.redbus.in).

Reservations are rarely possible on 'ordinary' buses; travellers can be left behind in the mad rush for a seat. To secure a seat, send a travelling companion ahead to claim some space, or pass a book or article of clothing through an open window to bag an empty seat.

Many bus stations have a separate women's queue, but women also have an unspoken right to elbow their way to the front of any bus queue.

Car

Few people bother with self-drive car hire – not only because of the hair-raising driving conditions, but also because hiring a car with driver is potentially affordable in India, particularly if several people share the cost.

Hiring a Car & Driver

Most towns have taxi stands or car-hire companies where you can arrange short or long tours.

Not all hire cars are licensed to travel beyond their home state. Those that are will pay extra state taxes, which are added to the hire charge.

Ask for a driver who speaks some English and knows the region you intend visiting. Try to see the car and meet the driver before paying anything.

A wide range of cars now ply as taxis. From a proletarian Tata Indica hatchback to a comfy Toyota Innova SUV, there's a model to suit every pocket.

Hire charges for multiday trips cover the driver's meals and accommodation, and drivers should make their own sleeping and eating arrangements.

It's essential to set the ground rules from day one; politely but firmly let the driver know that you're boss to avoid difficulties later.

Costs

Car-and-driver-hire costs depend on the distance and the terrain.

One-way trips usually cost the same as return ones (to cover the petrol and driver charges for getting back).

Some taxi unions set a maximum time limit or a maximum distance for day trips – if you go over, you'll have to pay extra. Prices also vary according to the make and model of the taxi.

To avoid misunderstandings, get *in writing* what you've been promised (quotes should include petrol, sightseeing stops, all your chosen destinations, and meals and accommodation for the driver). If a driver asks you for money for petrol en route because he is short of cash, get receipts for reimbursement later. If you're travelling by the kilometre, check the odometer reading before you set out to avoid confusion later.

For sightseeing day trips around a single city, expect to pay upwards of ₹1400/1800 for a non-aircon/air-con car with an eight-hour, 80km limit. For multiday trips, operators usually peg a 250km minimum running distance per day and charge around ₹8/10 per km (non-aircon/air-con) for anything over this.

A tip is customary at the end of your journey; at least ₹150 to ₹200 per day is fair.

Local Transport

For any transport without a fixed fare, agree on the price *before* you start your journey and make sure that it covers your luggage

and every passenger. Even where meters exist, drivers may refuse to use them, demanding an elevated 'fixed' fare; bargain hard. Fares usually increase at night (by up to 100%) and some drivers charge a few rupees extra for luggage.

Carry plenty of small bills for taxi and rickshaw fares, as drivers rarely have change.

Apps such as Uber and Ola Cabs have transformed local transport: if you have a smartphone you can call a taxi or autorickshaw and the fare is electronically calculated.

Autorickshaw

Similar to the tuk-tuks of Southeast Asia, the Indian autorickshaw is a three-wheeled motorised contraption with a tin or canvas roof and sides, usually with room for two passengers (although you'll often see many more squeezed in) and limited luggage.

They are also referred to as autos, scooters and riks.

You can call autos via the Ola Taxi and Auto app (www.olacabs.com), which electronically calculates your fare when you finish the journey – no more haggling! Flagfall is around ₹25, then it's ₹8 to ₹14 per km.

Travelling by auto is great fun but, thanks to the open windows, can be noisy and hot (or severely cold!).

Cycle-Rickshaw

A cycle-rickshaw is a pedal cycle with two rear wheels, supporting a bench seat for

passengers. Fares must be agreed in advance – speak to locals to get an idea of a fair price for the distance you intend to travel.

Metro & Suburban Train

Metro systems have transformed urban transport in the biggest cities and are expanding. Delhi's metro opened in 2002, and increases its reach every year. Bengaluru's metro opened in 2011, Mumbai's in 2014. Kochi Metro opened in 2017. Mumbai and some other cities also have useful suburban trains leaving from ordinary train stations.

Taxi

To avoid fare-setting shenanigans, use prepaid taxis where possible. Apps such as Uber and Ola, or radio cabs, are the most efficient option in larger cities.

Prepaid Taxis

Major Indian airports and train stations have prepaid-taxi and radio-cab booths. Here, you can book a taxi, even long distance, for a fixed price (which will include baggage) and thus avoid commission scams. Hold onto your receipt until you reach your destination, as proof of payment.

Radio cabs cost marginally more than prepaid taxis, but are air-conditioned and fitted with electronic, receipt-generating fare meters, and GPS units so that the company can monitor the vehicle's movement around town. These

Railway Razzle Dazzle

You can live like a maharaja on one of India's luxury train tours, with accommodation on board, tours, admission fees and meals included in the ticket price.

Palace on Wheels (www.palaceonwheels.net) Luxury tours of Rajasthan, departing from Delhi. Trains run on fixed dates, September to April; the fare per person for seven nights starts at US$6500/4890/4325 in a single/double/triple cabin. Try to book 10 months in advance.

Royal Rajasthan on Wheels (www.royalrajasthanonwheels.co.in) Lavish one-week trips from October to March, starting and finishing in Delhi. The fare per person per night starts from US$875/625 for single/twin occupancy in deluxe suites.

Deccan Odyssey (www.deccan-odyssey-india.com) Seven nights covering the main tourist spots of Maharashtra and Goa. Fares per person start at US$5810/4190 for single/double occupancy. There are also several other shorter luxurious trips on offer.

Golden Chariot (www.goldenchariottrain.com) Seven-night tours seeing the south in sumptuous style from October to March, starting in Bengaluru (Bangalore). Fares per person start at single/double US$5530/4130 (Indian tourists ₹182,000/154,000).

minimise chances of errant driving or unreasonable demands for extra cash by the driver afterwards.

Smaller airports and stations may have prepaid autorickshaw booths instead.

Motorcycle

Long-distance motorcycle touring is hugely popular in India. However, it can be quite an undertaking; there are some popular motorcycle tours for those who don't want the rigmarole of going it alone. Popular starting points are Delhi and Manali; popular destinations include Rajasthan, South India, Himachal Pradesh and Ladakh.

Hire

The classic way to motorcycle around India is on a Royal Enfield, built to both vintage and modern specs. Fully manual, these are easy to repair (parts can be found almost everywhere in India). On the other hand, Enfields are often less reliable than many of the newer, Japanese-designed bikes.

Plenty of places rent out motorcycles for local trips and longer tours. Technically you're required to have a valid international drivers' permit in addition to your domestic licence. In tourist areas, some places may rent out a motorcycle without asking for a driving permit/licence, but you won't be covered by insurance in the event of an accident, and may also face a fine.

You'll need to leave a large cash deposit (ensure you get a receipt that stipulates the refundable amount) or your passport/air ticket. We strongly advise not leaving these documents, in particular your passport, which you need for hotel check-ins and if stopped by the police.

For three weeks' hire, a 500cc Enfield costs from ₹25,000 to ₹28,000; a 350cc costs ₹18,000 to ₹22,000. The price should include accessories, spare parts, tolls required for the journey and an invaluable free maintenance course. Reputable companies will include third-party cover in their insurance policies; those that don't probably aren't trustworthy.

Anu Auto Works (Royal Moto Touring; ☑9816163378; www.royalmototouring.com; Vashisht Rd; ⊘office 9am-9pm or later, approx Jun-Sep) Manali-based; rents Enfields and takes tours over high Himalayan passes to Ladakh and Spiti from June to September.

Kerala Bike Tours (0484-2356652, 9388476817; www.keralabiketours.com; Kirushu-paly Rd, Ravipuram) Organises motorcycle tours around Kerala and the Western Ghats and hires out touring-quality Enfield Bullets (from US$155 per week) with unlimited mileage, full insurance and free recovery/maintenance options.

Lalli Motorbike Exports (011-28750869; www.lallisingh.com; 1740-A/55 Hari Singh Nalwa St, Abdul Aziz Rd; 10am-7pm Tue-Sun; MKarol Bagh) This Delhi-based outfit sells and rents out Enfields and parts.

Rajasthan Auto Centre (0141-2568074, 9829188064; www.royalenfieldsalim.com; Sanganeri Gate, Sanjay Bazaar; 10am-8pm Mon-Sat, to 2pm Sun) Recommended for rentals in Jaipur.

Organised Tours

Dozens of companies offer organised motorcycle tours around India with a support vehicle, mechanic and guide. Here are a few well-established companies:

Blazing Trails (05603-666788; www.blazingtrailstours.com)

H-C Travel (www.hctravel.com)

Himalayan Roadrunners (www.ridehigh.com)

Indian Motorcycle Adventure (www.indianmotorcycleadventures.com)

Lalli Singh Tours (www.lallisingh.com)

Moto Discovery (www.motodiscovery.com)

Royal Expeditions (011-26238545; http://royalexpeditions.com)

World on Wheels (www.worldonwheels.tours/)

Road Conditions

Given the varied road conditions, India can be challenging for novice riders. Hazards range from cows and chickens to broken-down trucks, unruly traffic, pedestrians on the road, and ubiquitous pot-holes and unmarked speed humps.

Try not to cover too much territory in one day and never ride in the dark – many vehicles drive without lights, and dynamo-powered motorcycle headlamps are useless at low revs while negotiating around potholes.

Train

Travelling by train is a quintessential Indian experience. Trains offer a smoother ride than buses and are especially recommended for long journeys that include overnight travel. India's rail network is one of the largest and busiest in the world and Indian Railways is the largest utility employer on earth, with roughly 1.5 million workers. There are almost 7000 stations scattered across the country.

The best way of sourcing updated train information is from websites such as **Indian Railways** (http://enquiry.indianrail.gov.in) and the excellent **India Rail Info** (http://indiarailinfo.com), with added offline browsing support, as well as the user-friendly **Erail** (http://erail.in).

Booking Tickets

You can book through a travel agency or hotel (for a commission), or in person at the train station. Big stations often have English-speaking staff who can help with reservations. At smaller stations, the stationmaster and deputy usually speak English.

You can also book online, and this is possible from outside India as well as once you're in India, though it has its share of glitches: travel-

Express Train Fares in Rupees

Distance (km)	1AC	2AC	3AC	1st Class	Chair Car (CC)	2nd (II)
100	1047	613	428	262	205	48
300	1047	613	561	558	378	103
500	1794	1058	733	843	577	151
1000	2940	1708	1352	1371	931	258

lers have reported problems with registering themselves on some portals and using credit cards.

Bookings open up to 120 days before departure for long-distance trains and you must make a reservation for chair-car, executive chair-car, sleeper, 1AC, 2AC and 3AC classes. No reservations are required for general (2nd class) compartments; you have to grab seats here the moment the train pulls in.

Trains are always busy so it's wise to book as far in advance as possible, especially for overnight journeys.

Reserved tickets show your seat/berth and carriage number. Carriage numbers are written on the side of the train (station staff and porters can point you in the right direction). A list of names and berths is posted on the side of each reserved carriage.

Online Booking

Start by visiting http://erail. in – the search engine will bring up a list of all trains running between your chosen stations, with their numbers, times and information on classes and fares.

Step two is to register for an account with **IRCTC** (www.irctc.co.in), the government-run ticket booking service. This is required even if you plan to use a private ticket agency. Registration is a complex process, involving passwords, emails, scans of your passport and texts to your mobile phone.

You'll usually need an Indian mobile number, though a possible workaround is to enter a random number then use email to communicate. The ever-helpful **Man in Seat 61** (www.seat61.com/ India.htm) has a detailed guide to all the steps.

Once registered, you can use a credit card to book travel on specific trains, either directly with IRCTC, or with private agencies. You'll be issued with an e-ticket, which you must print out ready to present alongside your passport and booking reference once you board the train.

The following websites are useful for online bookings, all accepting Mastercard and Visa.

Cleartrip (www.cleartrip.com) A reliable private agency and the easiest way to book.

IRCTC (www.irctc.co.in) The e-ticketing division of Indian Railways.

Make My Trip (www.makemy trip.com) Reputable private agency.

Yatra (www.yatra.com) Books flights and trains.

At the Station

Get a reservation slip from the information window, fill in the name of the departure station, destination station, the class you want to travel and the name and number of the train. Join the long queue for the ticket window where your ticket will be printed. Women should take advantage of the separate women's queue – if there

isn't one, go to the front of the regular queue.

Tourist Reservation Bureau

Larger cities and major tourist centres have an International Tourist Bureau, which sells tourist quota seats on certain classes of train, and allows you to book tickets in relative peace.

Tourist Quota

A special (albeit small) tourist quota is set aside for foreign tourists travelling between popular stations. These seats can only be booked at dedicated reservation offices in major cities, and you need to show your passport and visa as ID.

Classes

Express and mail trains form the mainstay of Indian rail travel. Not all classes are available on every train, but most long-distance services have general (2nd-class) compartments, with unreserved seating, and more comfortable reserved compartments, usually with the option of sleeper berths for overnight journeys. Sleeper trains offer the chance to travel huge distances for not much more than the price of a midrange hotel room. More expensive sleeper categories provide bedding. In all classes, a padlock and a length of chain are useful for securing your luggage to baggage racks.

Shatabdi express trains are same-day services with seating only.

Air-Conditioned 1st Class (1AC) The most expensive class, with two- or four-berth compartments with locking doors and meals included.

Air-Conditioned 2-Tier (2AC) Two-tier berths arranged in groups of four and two in an open-plan carriage. Bunks convert to seats by day and there are curtains, offering some privacy.

Air-Conditioned 3-Tier (3AC) Three-tier berths arranged in groups of six in an open-plan carriage with no curtains; popular with Indian families.

AC Executive Chair (ECC) Comfortable, reclining chairs and plenty of space; usually on Shatabdi express trains.

AC Chair (CC) Similar to the Executive Chair carriage but with less-fancy seating.

Sleeper Class (sl) Open-plan carriages with three-tier bunks and no AC; the open windows afford great views.

Unreserved/reserved 2nd Class (II/SS or 2S) Wooden or plastic seats and a lot of people – but cheap!

Costs

Fares are calculated by distance and class of travel; Rajdhani express and Shatabdi express trains are slightly more expensive, but the price includes meals. Most air-conditioned carriages have a catering service (meals are brought to your seat). Male/female seniors (those over 60/58) get 40/50% off all fares in all classes on all types of train. Children below six travel free, those aged between six and 12 are charged half price, up to 300km.

Language

Hindi

Hindi has about 180 million speakers in India, and it has official status along with English and 21 other languages.

If you read our pronunciation guides as if they were English, you'll be understood. The length of vowels is important (eg 'a' and 'aa'), and 'ng' after a vowel indicates nasalisation (ie the vowel is pronounced 'through the nose'). The stressed syllables are marked with italics. The abbreviations 'm' and 'f' indicate the options for male and female speakers respectively.

Basics

Hello./Goodbye.
नमस्ते ।   na·ma·*ste*

Yes.
जी हाँ ।   jee haang

No.
जी नहीं ।   jee na·*heeng*

Excuse me.
सुनिये ।   su·ni·*ye*

Sorry.
माफ़ कीजिये ।   maaf *kee*·ji·ye

Please ...
कृपया ...   kri·pa·*yaa* ...

Thank you.
थैंक्यू ।   *thayn*·kyoo

How are you?
आप कैसे/कैसी   aap *kay*·se/*kay*·see
हैं?   hayng (m/f)

Fine. And you?
मैं ठीक हूँ ।   mayng teek hoong
आप सुनाइये ।   aap su·*naa*·i·ye

Do you speak English?
क्या आपको अंग्रेज़ी   kyaa aap ko an·*gre*·zee
आती है?   *aa*·tee hay

How much is this?
कितने का है?   *kit*·ne kaa hay

I don't understand.
मैं नहीं समझा/   mayng na·*heeng* sam·jaa/
समझी ।   *sam*·jee (m/f)

Accommodation

Do you have a single/double room?
क्या सिंगल/डबल   kyaa *sin*·gal/da·*bal*
कमरा है?   *kam*·raa hay

How much is it (per night/per person)?
(एक रात/हर व्यक्ति)   (ek raat/har *vyak*·ti)
के लिय कितने   ke li·*ye kit*·ne
पैसे लगते हैं?   *pay*·se *lag*·te hayng

Eating & Drinking

I'd like ..., please.
मुझे ... दीजिये ।   mu·*je* ... *dee*·ji·ye

That was delicious.
बहुत मज़ेदार हुआ ।   ba·*hut* ma·ze·*daar* hu·*aa*

Please bring the menu/bill.
मेन्यू/बिल लाइये ।   *men*·yoo/bil *laa*·i·ye

I don't eat ...
मैं ... नहीं   mayng ... na·*heeng*
खाता/खाती ।   *kaa*·taa/*kaa*·tee (m/f)

fish	मछली	*mach*·lee
meat	गोश्त	gosht
poultry	मुर्गी	*mur*·gee

Emergencies

I'm ill.
मैं बीमार हूँ ।   mayng *bee*·maar hoong

Help!
मदद कीजिये!   ma·*dad kee*·ji·ye

Call the doctor/police!
डॉक्टर/पुलिस   *daak*·tar/pu·*lis*
को बुलाओ!   ko bu·*laa*·o

Directions

Where's a/the ...?
... कहाँ है?   ... ka·*haang* hay

bank
बैंक   baynk

market
बाज़ार   *baa*·zaar

post office
डाक ख़ाना   daak *kaa*·naa

restaurant
रेस्टोरेंट   *res*·to·rent

toilet
टॉइलेट   *taa*·i·let

tourist office
पर्यटन ऑफ़िस   *par*·ya·tan *aa*·fis

Tamil

Tamil is the official language in the state of Tamil Nadu and one of the major languages of South India, with about 62 million speakers. Note that in our pronunciation guides, the symbol 'aw' is pronounced as in 'law' while 'ow' is pronounced as in 'how'.

Basics

Hello.
வணக்கம்.   va·*nak*·kam
Goodbye.
போய் வருகிறேன்.   *po*·i va·*ru*·ki·reyn
Yes./No.
ஆமாம்./இல்லை.   *aa*·maam/*il*·lai
Excuse me.
தயவு செய்து.   ta·ya·*vu* sei·*du*
Sorry.
மன்னிக்கவும.   *man*·nik·ka·vum
Please ...
தயவு செய்து ...   ta·ya·*vu* chey·*tu* ...
Thank you.
நன்றி.   *nan*·dri
How are you?
நீங்கள் நலமா?   *neeng*·kal na·*la*·maa
Fine, thanks. And you?
நலம், நன்றி.   na·*lam nan*·dri
நீங்கள்?   *neeng*·kal
Do you speak English?
நீங்கள் ஆங்கிலம்   *neeng*·kal *aang*·ki·lam
பேசுவீர்களா?   *pey*·chu·*veer*·ka·la
How much is this?
இது என்ன விலை?   i·*tu en*·na vi·*lai*
I don't understand.
எனக்கு   e·*nak*·ku
விளங்கவில்லை.   vi·*lang*·ka·vil·*lai*

Accommodation

Do you have a single/double room?
உங்களிடம் ஓர்   *ung*·ka·li·tam awr
தன/இரட்டை   ta·*ni*/i·*rat*·tai
அறை உள்ளதா?   a·*rai* ul·la·taa
How much is it per night/person?
ஓர் இரவுக்கு/   awr i·ra·*vuk*·ku/
ஒருவருக்கு   o·ru·va·*ruk*·ku
என்னவிலை?   *en*·na·vi·*lai*

Eating & Drinking

I'd like the ..., please.
எனக்கு தயவு   e·*nak*·ku ta·ya·*vu*
செய்து ...   chey·*tu* ...
கொடுங்கள்.   ko·*tung*·kal
   bill   வீலைச்சீட்டு   vi·*laich*·cheet·tu
   menu   உணவுப்–   u·na·*vup*·
     பட்டியல   pat·ti·yal

I'm allergic to ...
எனக்கு ... உணவு   e·*nak*·ku ... u·na·*vu*
சேராது.   *chey*·raa·tu
   dairy   பால்   paal
     products   சார்ந்த   *chaarn*·ta
   meat   இறைச்சி   i·*raich*·chi
     stock   வகை   va·*kai*
   nuts   பருப்பு வகை   pa·*rup*·pu va·*kai*
   seafood   கடல்   ka·*tal*
     சார்ந்த   *chaarn*·ta

Emergencies

Help!
உதவு!   u·ta·*vi*
Call a doctor!
ஐ அழைக்கவும்   i a·*zai*·ka·vum
ஒரு மருத்துவர்!   o·*ru* ma·*rut*·tu·var
Call the police!
ஐ அழைக்கவும்   i a·*zai*·ka·vum
போலீஸ!   pow·*lees*

Directions

Where's a/the ...?
... எங்கே   ... *eng*·key
இருக்கிறது?   i·*ruk*·ki·ra·tu
   bank
   வங்கி   *vang*·ki
   market
   சந்தை   *chan*·tai
   post office
   தபால் நிலையம்   ta·*paal* ni·*lai*·yam
   restaurant
   உணவகம   u·na·va·*kam*
   toilet
   கழிவறை   ka·*zi*·va·rai
   tourist office
   சுற்றுப்பயண   chut·*rup*·pa·ya·na
   அலுவலகம்   a·lu·va·la·*kam*

To enhance your trip with a phrasebook, visit **lonelyplanet.com**.

Behind the Scenes

Acknowledgements

Climate map data adapted from Peel MC, Finlayson BL & McMahon TA (2007) 'Updated World Map of the Köppen-Geiger Climate Classification', Hydrology and Earth System Sciences, 11, 163344.

Illustrations on pp40–1 and pp74–5 by Javier Zarracina, and illustrations on pp78–9 and pp202–3 by Michael Weldon.

This Book

This 1st edition of Lonely Planet's *Best of India* guidebook was curated by John Noble, and researched and written by John Noble along with Michael Benanav, Abigail Blasi, Lindsay Brown, Paul Harding, Bradley Mayhew, Kevin Raub, Sarina Singh and Iain Stewart.
This guidebook was produced by the following:

Destination Editor Joe Bindloss

Product Editors Kate Kiely, Catherine Naghten

Cartographers Lonely Planet Cartography

Book Designer Clara Monitto

Assisting Editors Carolyn Boicos, Katie Connolly, Bruce Evans, Helen Koehne, Victoria Smith, Saralinda Turner, Amanda Williamson

Assisting Book Designer Virginia Moreno

Cover Researcher Naomi Parker

Thanks to Sasha Drew, Shona Gray, Indra Kilfoyle, Kate Mathews, Martine Power, Kathryn Rowan, Tony Wheeler

Send Us Your Feedback

We love to hear from travellers – your comments keep us on our toes and help make our books better. Our well-travelled team reads every word on what you loved or loathed about this book. Although we cannot reply individually to postal submissions, we always guarantee that your feedback goes straight to the appropriate authors, in time for the next edition. Each person who sends us information is thanked in the next edition, the most useful submissions are rewarded with a selection of digital PDF chapters.

Visit lonelyplanet.com/contact to submit your updates and suggestions or to ask for help. Our award-winning website also features inspirational travel stories, news and discussions.

Note: We may edit, reproduce and incorporate your comments in Lonely Planet products such as guidebooks, websites and digital products, so let us know if you don't want your comments reproduced or your name acknowledged. For a copy of our privacy policy visit lonelyplanet.com/privacy.

Index

A

accessible travel 301-2
accommodation 290-1
  language 312-13
activities 18, 20, 250-3, *see also individual activities*
Agra 65-85, **67**
  accommodation 67
  food 84
  itineraries 66
  planning 66-7
  sights 84
  tourist information 85
  travel to/from 67, 85
  travel within 85
Agra Fort 80-3
AIDS 293-4
air travel 305
airports 17, 305
Ajanta Caves 15, 141-3, 144-7, **143**
  accommodation 143
  itineraries 142
  planning 142-3
  travel to/from 143
Akbar, Emperor 76-7, 269
Alappuzha, *see* Alleppey
Alleppey 190-2
Alleppey Lighthouse 191
Amber Fort 104-5
animals 286-7
Anjuna 174-5
Anjuna flea market 174
archaeological sites
  Bibi-qa-Maqbara 154
  Fatehpur Sikri 76-9
  Hampi 204-5
  Hazrat Nizam-ud-din Dargah 47

Humayun's Tomb 46
Jantar Mantar 110
Mehrauli Archaeological Park 50
Qutb Minar 44-5
architecture 18, 285
art galleries, *see* museums & galleries
arts 283-5
Ashoka, Emperor 266
Asiatic lion 287
ATMs 296
Aurangabad 154-7
Aurangzeb 269-70
autorickshaws 307
ayurveda 96, 111, 182-3

B

backwater boat trips 180-1
Bahai House of Worship 50
bargaining 296-7
Basilica of Bom Jesus 162
bazaars, *see* markets
beaches
  Anjuna 174
  Goa 164-7
  Kerala 184-5
  Kovalam 189
  Palolem 172
Benares Hindu University 235
Bharat Kala Bhavan 235
Bengaluru 206-9, **207**
Bhuleshwar Market 123
Bhutia Busty Gompa 221-2
Bibi-qa-Maqbara 154
birds 287-8
Bollywood 126-7, 284
books 25
border conflicts 263
Buddha, the 267
Buddhist temples
  Ajanta Caves 144-7
  Aurangabad Caves 154-5
  Bhutia Busty Gompa 221-2

Ellora Caves 148-52
Kalachakra Temple 247
Observatory Hill 223
Tsuglagkhang 247
budgeting 17, 291
bus travel 305-6
business hours 298
Butterfly Beach 172

C

cable cars 220
camel safaris 92-5
car travel 306-7
carbon offsets 306
caste system 276
cathedrals, *see* churches & cathedrals
caves
  Ajanta Caves 142-3, 144-7
  Aurangabad Caves 154-5
  Ellora Caves 142-3, 148-53
cell phones 16, 300-1
Central Museum (Jaipur) 110
Chandni Chowk 42-3
chapati 281
Chawri Bazaar 43
Chhatrapati Shivaji Maharaj Vastu Sangrahalaya 130
Chhatrapati Shivaji Terminus 130
children, travel with 32-3
Chinese fishing nets 193
Chor Bazaar 123
churches & cathedrals
  Basilica of Bom Jesus 162
  Church of Our Lady of the Immaculate Conception 170
  Church of St Cajetan 163
  Church of St Francis of Assisi 163
  Sé Cathedral 163
cinema 284
City Palace 106-7
climate 16, 22-4, 292
climate change 306

costs 17, 291
Crafts Museum 47
Crawford Market 122-3
credit cards 297
cricket 277
currency 297
customs 275-6
customs regulations 291, 296
cycle-rickshaws 307

D

Dalai Lama 246, 247, 248, 263
dance 284
Darjeeling 11, 211-25, **213**, **221**
  accommodation 213
  climate 224
  drinking & nightlife 224
  food 223-4
  itineraries 212
  planning 212-13
  shopping 223
  sights 220-3
  tourist information 224
  travel seasons 224
  travel to/from 213, 225
  travel within 225
Darjeeling Himalayan
  Railway 223
Daryaganj Sunday Book
  Market 43
Daulatabad Fort 155
dehydration 295
Delhi 10, 35-63, **36**, **48**, **53**, **63**
  accommodation 37, 63
  bazaars 42-3
  drinking & nightlife 56-8
  food 52-6
  itineraries 36
  planning 36-7
  safety 58
  shopping 51-2
  sights 46-50

tourist information 59
tours 50-1
  travel to/from 37, 59-61
  travel within 61-2
dengue fever 293
Desert Cultural Centre &
  Museum 96
Devaraja Market 201
dhal 281
diarrhoea 294
disabilities, travellers with 301-2
Diwani-i-Am Art gallery 107
Dr Bhau Daji Lad Mumbai City
  Museum 137
dress 277
drinking 21
  language 312-13

E

Eid al-Fitr 24
electricity 291
Elephanta Island 136
elephants 286
Ellora Caves 15, 141-3,
  148-53, **143**
  accommodation 143
  itineraries 142
  planning 142-3
  travel to/from 143
emergencies 301
  language 312-13
entertainment 21
environmental hazards 294-5
etiquette 299
events, see festivals & events
exchange rates 297
exports, prohibited 296

F

family travel 32-3
Fatehpur Sikri 76-9
festivals & events 22-4, 298

films 25
fishing 253
food 19, 21, 280-2, 291, see
  also individual foods
  language 312-13
  seafood 190
  street food 125
forts
  Agra Fort 80-3
  Amber Fort 104-5
  Daulatabad Fort 155
  Jaisalmer Fort 90-1
  Nahargarh 110
  Red Fort 38-41

G

Gandhi, Indira 274
Gandhi, Mahatma 47, 272-3
Gandhi Smriti 47
Ganges River 240
Gateway of India 130
gay travellers 291
gems 113
geography 286
ghats 230-3
  Assi Ghat 231
  Dashashwamedh Ghat 232
  Hanuman Ghat 231
  Harishchandra Ghat 231
  Kedar Ghat 231
  Mahalaxmi Dhobi Ghat 137
  Man Mandir Ghat 232
  Manikarnika Ghat 232-3
  Munshi Ghat 231
  Pandhey Ghat 232
  Raj Ghat 230
  Scindhia Ghat 233
  Trilochan Ghat 233
giardiasis 294
Goa 8, 159-75, **161**
  accommodation 161, 175
  beaches 164-7

churches 162-3
itineraries 160
planning 160-1
travel to/from 161
gods 278-9
Gurdwara Bangla Sahib 49

H

Hadimba Temple 258
Hampi 204-5
Hamta Pass 251
Happy Valley Tea Estate 220
Hauz Khas Village 55
havelis 88, *see also* historic
    buildings
Hazrat Nizam-ud-din
    Dargah 47
health 291-5
    children 33
heat stroke 295
hepatitis A 293
hepatitis B 293
high tea 56
highlights 4-15
hijras 276
hiking, *see* trekking
Himachal Pradesh 14, 243-59,
    245
    accommodation 245
    itineraries 244
    planning 244-5
    travel to/from 245
Himalayan Mountaineering
    Institute 220
Himalayan Tibet Museum 222
Hindi language 313
Hindu temples
    Ellora Caves 148-50, 152
    Hadimba Temple 258
    Kailasa Temple 151
    Mahalaxmi Temple 137
    Observatory Hill 223

Sri Chamundeswari
    Temple 201
Vishwanath Temple 234-5
Hinduism 278-9
historic buildings
    Akbar's Mausoleum 84
    Chhatrapati Shivaji
        Terminus 130
    Hawa Mahal 110
    Humayun's Tomb 46
    Iswari Minar Swarga Sal 110
    Nathmal-ki-Haveli 96
    Patwa-ki-Haveli 96
    Royal Gaitor 110
    Salim Singh-ki-Haveli 96
history 264-74
    Aryan civilisation 265-6
    British rule 270-1
    European influence 270
    Guptas, the 266-7
    Hindus 267
    independence 272-3
    Maurya empire 266
    Mughal empire 269-70
    Muslims 267-8, 269-70
    Partition 273
    Rajputs 269
    War of Independence 271-2
HIV 293-4
Holi 22
holidays 298
homosexuality 276, 291
Hosapete 205
houseboats 180-1
Humayun's Tomb 46

I

Indo-Portuguese Museum 193
insurance 295
internet access 295-6
internet resources, *see*
    websites

itineraries 26-31, **2**, **26**, **27**,
    28, **30**, *see also individual
    locations*

J

Jain temples 91, 148-50,
    152-3
Jainism 267
Jaipur 7, 101-16, **103**, **111**
    accommodation 103, 115
    activities 110-11
    drinking & nightlife 114-15
    food 113-14
    itineraries 102
    planning 102-3
    shopping 111-12
    sights 110
    tourist information 115
    travel to/from 103, 115
    travel within 115
    walking tour 108-9, **108-9**
Jaisalmer 13, 87-99, **89**, **97**
    accommodation 89
    activities 96
    food 98-9
    itineraries 88
    planning 88-9
    shopping 97-8
    sights 96
    travel to/from 89, 99
    travel within 99
Jaisalmer Fort 90-1
Jantar Mantar 110
Jayachamarajendra Art
    Gallery 201
Jew Town 193
jewellery 59, *see also*
    gems

K

Kailasa Temple 151
Kalachakra Temple 247

Karnataka 15, 197-209, **199**
  accommodation 199
  itineraries 198
  planning 198-9
  travel to/from 199
Kashmir 263
Kathakali 186-7
Kerala 6, 177-95, **179**
  accommodation 179
  beaches 184-5
  itineraries 178
  planning 178-9
  travel to/from 179
Kochi 192-5
Kovalam 189-90
Krishnarajendra
  Market 206

L

language 16, 312-13
language, Persian 273
legal issues 296
leopards 287
lesbian travellers 291
Library of Tibetan Works &
  Archives 248
literature 285
Losel Doll Museum 257

M

Mahal, Mumtaz 39, 70, 72
Mahalaxmi Dhobi Ghat 137
Mahalaxmi Temple 137
Mahavir 267
Makaibari tea estate 219
malaria 292-3
Manali 250-3, 257-9
Mangaldas Market 123
markets 42-3, 122-3
  Anjuna flea market 174
  Bhuleshwar Market 123
  Chandni Chowk 42-3

Chawri Bazaar 43
Chor Bazaar 123
Crawford Market 122-3
Daryaganj Sunday Book
  Market 43
Devaraja Market 201
Krishnarajendra Market 206
Mangaldas Market 123
Spice Market (Delhi) 43
Zaveri Bazaar 123
marriage 275-6
Mattancherry 193
Mattancherry Palace 193
McLeod Ganj 246-9, 254-7,
  255
Mehrauli Archaeological
  Park 50
Men-Tsee-Khang 249
metro trains 307
mobile phones 16, 300-1
Modi, Narendra 262, 274, 288
money 16, 296-8
mosques
  Jama Masjid (Delhi) 46
  Jama Masjid (Fatehpur
    Sikri) 77
  Quwwat-ul-Islam Masjid 45
motorcycle travel 308-9
mountain biking 251
Mumbai 12, 119-39, **121,
  131, 134**
  accommodation 121
  drinking & nightlife 136-8
  food 124-5, 132-6
  itineraries 120
  orientation 133
  planning 120-1
  shopping 132
  sights 130
  tourist information 138
  travel to/from 121, 138-9
  travel within 139
  walking tour 128-9, **128-9**

museums & galleries
  Bharat Kala Bhavan 235
  Central Museum
    (Jaipur) 110
  Chhatrapati Shivaji Maharaj
    Vastu Sangrahalaya 130
  Crafts Museum 47
  Desert Cultural Centre &
    Museum 96
  Diwan-i-Am Art Gallery 107
  Dr Bhau Daji Lad Mumbai
    City Museum 137
  Himalayan Mountaineering
    Institute 220
  Himalayan Tibet
    Museum 222
  Indo-Portuguese
    Museum 193
  Jayachamarajendra Art
    Gallery 201
  Library of Tibetan Works &
    Archives 248
  Losel Doll Museum 257
  Mattancherry Palace 193
  Men-Tsee-Khang
    Museum 249
  Museum of History &
    Heritage 188
  Museum on India's Struggle
    for Freedom 39
  Napier Museum 188
  National Gallery of Modern
    Art (Bengaluru) 206
  National Museum
    (Delhi) 49
  National Rail Museum 50
  Shrimat Chatrapati Shivaji
    Museum 155
  Taj Museum 72
  Thar Heritage Museum 96
  Tibet Museum 247
music 25, 283-4
Mysuru 200-1, 209
Mysuru Palace 200-3

N

Nahargarh 110
Napier Museum 188
National Gallery of Modern Art (Bengaluru) 206
National Museum (Delhi) 49
national parks 288
 Ranthambhore National Park 116-17
 Singalila National Park 214-17
National Rail Museum 50
Nehru, Jawaharlal 273, 274
nightlife 21
Norbulingka Institute 257

O

Observatory Hill 223
opening hours 298

P

painting 284-5
palaces
 City Palace 106-7
 Fatehpur Sikri 76-9
 Jaganmohan Palace 201
 Jaisalmer Fort Palace 90-1
 Mattancherry Palace 193
 Mysuru Palace 200-3
Palolem 172-4
Panaji 170-1
paragliding 253
Pardesi Synagogue 193
parks & gardens
 Lloyd Botanical Gardens 220
 Lodi Gardens 49
 Mehrauli Archaeological Park 50
 Mehtab Bagh 84
Persian language 273
photography 298
Pink City 108-9, 110

planning
 budgeting 17, 291
 calendar of events 22-4
 climate 16, 22-4
 itineraries 26-31, **2**, **26**, **27**, **28**, **30**
 travel seasons 16, 290
 travel with children 32-3
plants 288
politics 262-3
polo 277
population 263

Q

Qutb Minar 44-5
Qutb-ud-din Aibak 44

R

rabies 294
rafting 252
Rajputs 269
Ramadan 23
Rangit Valley Ropeway 220
Ranthambhore National Park 116-17
Red Fort 38-41
reincarnation 279
religion 263, 278-9
rhinos 287
rice 281
river trips 240
rock climbing 252-3
roti 281

S

safety 298-300
 swimming 167
 women travellers 303-4
scams 299-300
Sé Cathedral 163
Shah Jahan 38-9, 70, 72, 82-3, 269

Shahpur Jat 59
shopping 20
Shrimat Chatrapati Shivaji Museum 155
Sikh temples 49
silent discos 173
silk weaving 157
Singalila Ridge Trek 214-17
skiing 252
snow leopards 287
snowboarding 252
solo travelling 300
Spice Market (Delhi) 43
spices 280
spirituality 19
sport 277
Sri Chamundeswari Temple 201
street food 125, 282
sweets 282

T

Taj Mahal 4, 66, 68-75
Taj Mahal Palace (Mumbai) 130
Taj Museum 72
Tamil language 313
taxes 300
taxis 307-8
tea 218-19
tea estates 219
 Happy Valley Tea Estate 220
 Makaibara Tea Estate 219
telephone services 300-1
temples, see Buddhist temples, Hindu temples, Jain temples, Sikh temples
Thar Heritage Museum 96
theft 300
Thiruvananthapuram 188-9
Tibet Museum 247
Tibetan Children's Village 249
Tibetan culture 246-9, 257

Tibetan Institute of Performing Arts 249
Tibetan Refugee Self-Help Centre 220-1
Tiger Hill 222-3
tigers 116-17, 287
time 16, 301
tipping 297
toilets 301
tours
  camel safaris 92-5
  Kerala backwater boat trips 180-1
  motorbike tours 309
touts 58, 99, 233
toy train 223
train travel 308, 309-11
transvestites 276
travel advisories 294
travel seasons 16, 290
travel to/from India 17, 305
travel within India 17, 305-11
trekking
  Hamta Pass Trek 251
  Manali treks 250-1
  Singalila Ridge Trek 214-17
  Triund Hike 254
Trivandrum 188-9
Tsuglagkhang 247
typhoid 294

V

vaccinations 293
Varanasi 8, 227-41, **229**, **237**
  accommodation 229
  drinking & nightlife 239-40
  entertainment 239-40
  food 236-9
  itineraries 228
  planning 228-9
  scams 235
  shopping 235, 236
  sights 234-5
  tourist information 240
  tours 235-6
  travel to/from 229, 240-1
  travel within 241
visas 16, 302

Vishwanath Temple 234-5
Vizhinjam Lighthouse 189-90

W

water 292
weather 16, 22-4, 292
websites 17
  gay & lesbian travellers 291
  women travellers 304
weights & measures 302
women in India 276-7
women travellers 302-5

Y

yoga 168-9, 174, 209

Z

Zaveri Bazaar 123
zoos
  Padmaja Naidu Himalayan Zoological Park 220
  Zoological Gardens (Trivandrum) 188

Symbols & Map Key

Look for these symbols to quickly identify listings:

- ◉ Sights
- ✪ Activities
- ⊜ Courses
- ⊙ Tours
- ✪ Festivals & Events
- ✪ Eating
- ⊖ Drinking
- ✪ Entertainment
- ⊕ Shopping
- ⊕ Information & Transport

These symbols and abbreviations give vital information for each listing:

🌿 Sustainable or green recommendation

FREE No payment required

- ☎ Telephone number
- ☉ Opening hours
- Ⓟ Parking
- ⊖ Nonsmoking
- ❄ Air-conditioning
- @ Internet access
- ⬁ Wi-fi access
- ⬥ Swimming pool
- ⊡ Bus
- ⬥ Ferry
- ⬥ Tram
- ⬥ Train
- ⬥ English-language menu
- ⬥ Vegetarian selection
- ⬥ Family-friendly

Find your best experiences with these Great For... icons.

 Art & Culture
 Beaches
 Budget
 Cafe/Coffee
 Cycling
 Detour
Drinking
 Entertainment
Events
Family Travel
Food & Drink

 History
 Local Life
 Nature & Wildlife
 Photo Op
 Scenery
 Shopping
  Short Trip
 Sport
Walking
Winter Travel

Sights
- ⊛ Beach
- ⊛ Bird Sanctuary
- ⊛ Buddhist
- ⊛ Castle/Palace
- ⊕ Christian
- ⊕ Confucian
- ⊛ Hindu
- ⊛ Islamic
- ⊛ Jain
- ⊛ Jewish
- ⊕ Monument
- ⊛ Museum/Gallery/ Historic Building
- ⊛ Ruin
- ⊛ Shinto
- ⊛ Sikh
- ⊛ Taoist
- ⊛ Winery/Vineyard
- ⊛ Zoo/Wildlife Sanctuary
- ⊙ Other Sight

Points of Interest
- ⊛ Bodysurfing
- ⊛ Camping
- ⊜ Cafe
- ⊛ Canoeing/Kayaking
- ● Course/Tour
- ⊛ Diving
- ⊛ Drinking & Nightlife
- ✪ Eating
- ⊛ Entertainment
- ⊛ Sento Hot Baths/ Onsen
- ⊛ Shopping
- ⊛ Skiing
- ⊛ Sleeping
- ⊛ Snorkelling
- ⊛ Surfing
- ⊛ Swimming/Pool
- ⊛ Walking
- ⊛ Windsurfing
- ⊛ Other Activity

Information
- ⊛ Bank
- ⊛ Embassy/Consulate
- ⊕ Hospital/Medical
- @ Internet
- ⊛ Police
- ⊛ Post Office
- ⊛ Telephone
- ⊕ Toilet
- ⊕ Tourist Information
- ● Other Information

Geographic
- ⊛ Beach
- ⊷ Gate
- ⊕ Hut/Shelter
- ⊕ Lighthouse
- ⊛ Lookout
- ▲ Mountain/Volcano
- ⊛ Oasis
- ⊕ Park
-)(Pass
- ⊛ Picnic Area
- ⊛ Waterfall

Transport
- ⊛ Airport
- Ⓑ BART station
- ⊗ Border crossing
- ⊛ Boston T station
- ⊡ Bus
- ⌗⊕⌗ Cable car/Funicular
- ⊛ Cycling
- ⊖ Ferry
- Ⓜ Metro/MRT station
- ⊡ Monorail
- Ⓟ Parking
- ⊛ Petrol station
- ⊛ Subway/S-Bahn/ Skytrain station
- ⊛ Taxi
- ⌗⊕⌗ Train station/Railway
- ⌗⌗⌗ Tram
- ⊜ Tube Station
- Ⓤ Underground/ U-Bahn station
- ● Other Transport

Lindsay Brown

Lindsay started travelling as a young bushwalker exploring the Blue Mountains west of Sydney. Then as a marine biologist he dived the coastal and island waters of southeastern Australia. He continued travelling whenever he could while employed at Lonely Planet as an editor and publishing manager. Since becoming a freelance writer and photographer, he has coauthored more than 30 Lonely Planet guides to Australia, Bhutan, India, Nepal, Pakistan and Papua New Guinea.

Paul Harding

As a writer and photographer, Paul has been travelling the globe for the best part of two decades, with an interest in remote and offbeat places and cultures. He's an author and contributor to more than 50 Lonely Planet guides to countries and regions as diverse as India, Iceland, Belize, Vanuatu, Iran, Indonesia, New Zealand, Finland and – his home patch – Australia.

Bradley Mayhew

Bradley has been writing guidebooks for 20 years now. He started travelling while studying Chinese at Oxford University, and has since focused his expertise on China, Tibet, the Himalaya and Central Asia. He is the coauthor of Lonely Planet guides *Tibet, Nepal, Trekking in the Nepal Himalaya, Bhutan, Central Asia* and many others. Bradley has also fronted two TV series for Arte and SWR, one retracing the route of Marco Polo via Turkey, Iran, Afghanistan, Central Asia and China, and the other trekking Europe's 10 most scenic long-distance trails.

Kevin Raub

Kevin grew up in Atlanta and started his career as a music journalist in New York, working for *Men's Journal* and *Rolling Stone* magazines. Being a pursuer of hops himself, he was all too happy to put Kingfisher in his rearview drinking mirror and immerse himself in Mumbai's exploding craft beer scene during research for this guide. Follow him on Twitter and Instagram (@RaubOnTheRoad). To learn more about Kevin, check out www.lonely planet.com/members/kraub.

Sarina Singh

After finishing a business degree in her hometown of Melbourne, Sarina went to India to pursue a corporate traineeship before working as a journalist. After five years she returned to Australia and completed postgraduate journalism qualifications before authoring Lonely Planet's first edition of *Rajasthan*. Apart from numerous Lonely Planet books, she has written for a raft of other publications and has been a scriptwriter and expert commentator. Sarina is also the author of *Polo in India* as well as *India: Essential Encounters*. Her award-nominated documentary premiered at the prestigious Melbourne International Film Festival before screening internationally.

Iain Stewart

Iain trained as a journalist and worked as a reporter and restaurant critic in London in the 1990s. He started writing guidebooks in 1997 and has penned more than 60 titles for destinations as diverse as Ibiza and Cambodia. For Lonely Planet, Iain's worked on books including *Mexico, Indonesia, Croatia, Vietnam, India, Sri Lanka* and *Central America*. Other passions include tennis, scuba and freediving. He'll consider working anywhere there's a palm tree or two and a beach of a generally sandy persuasion. Home is Brighton, UK, within firing range of the city's south-facing horizon. He tweets at @iaintravel.

Our Story

A beat-up old car, a few dollars in the pocket and a sense of adventure. In 1972 that's all Tony and Maureen Wheeler needed for the trip of a lifetime – across Europe and Asia overland to Australia. It took several months, and at the end – broke but inspired – they sat at their kitchen table writing and stapling together their first travel guide, *Across Asia on the Cheap*. Within a week they'd sold 1500 copies. Lonely Planet was born.

Today, Lonely Planet has offices in Franklin, London, Melbourne, Oakland, Dublin, Beijing and Delhi, with more than 600 staff and writers. We share Tony's belief that 'a great guidebook should do three things: inform, educate and amuse'.

Our Writers

John Noble

John has been travelling since his teens and doing so as a Lonely Planet writer since the 1980s. The number of Lonely Planet titles he's written or cowritten is well into three figures, covering a somewhat random selection of countries scattered across the globe, predominantly ones where Spanish, Russian or English are spoken (usually alongside numerous local languages). He still gets as excited as ever about heading out on the road to unfamiliar experiences, people and destinations, especially remote, off-the-beaten-track ones. Above all, he loves mountains, from the English Lake District to the Himalaya. See his pics on Instagram: @johnnoble11.

Michael Benanav

When Michael was young, his father handed him a biography of Lawrence of Arabia, along with adventure novels like *Around the World in 80 Days,* which sparked something in him. Today he is a veteran traveller, writer and photographer, who has authored three nonfiction books (set on three different continents) and writes and shoots for major publications. He also founded Traditional Cultures Project, which documents indigenous cultures around the world. To see some of his work, visit www.michaelbenanav.com.

Abigail Blasi

A freelance travel writer, Abigail has lived and worked in London, Rome, Hong Kong and Copenhagen. Lonely Planet has sent her to India, Egypt, Tunisia, Mauritania, Mali, Italy, Portugal, Malta and around Britain. She writes regularly for newspapers and magazines, such as the *Independent*, the *Telegraph* and *Lonely Planet Traveller*. She has three children and they often come along for the ride. Follow her on Twitter and Instagram: @abiwhere

More Writers

STAY IN TOUCH LONELYPLANET.COM/CONTACT

AUSTRALIA The Malt Store, Level 3, 551 Swanston St, Carlton, Victoria 3053
📞 03 8379 8000,
fax 03 8379 8111

IRELAND Unit E, Digital Court. The Digital Hub, Rainsford St, Dublin 8, Ireland

USA 124 Linden Street, Oakland, CA 94607
📞 510 250 6400,
toll free 800 275 8555,
fax 510 893 8572

UK 240 Blackfriars Road, London SE1 8NW
📞 020 3771 5100,
fax 020 3771 5101

 twitter.com/ lonelyplanet   facebook.com/ lonelyplanet   instagram.com/ lonelyplanet   youtube.com/ lonelyplanet   lonelyplanet.com/ newsletter